Creating Sacred Communities

Leading Practitioners Share Lessons Learned

Dr. Ron Wolfson
Rabbi Brett Kopin

Foreword by **Rabbi Angela Warnick Buchdahl**
Afterword by **Rabbi Sara Himeles**

Creating Sacred Communities
Leading Practitioners Share Lessons Learned

2022 Quality Paperback Edition, First Printing
© 2022 by Ron Wolfson and Brett Kopin
Foreword © 2022 by Angela Warnick Buchdahl
Afterword © 2022 by Sara Himeles

All rights reserved. No part of this book may be reproduced or reprinted in any form or by any means, electronic or mechanical, including photocopying, recording, or by any information storage and retrieval system, without permission in writing from The Kripke Institute.

For information regarding permission to reprint material from this book, please send your request in writing to The Kripke Institute, at the address / email address below.

The Kripke Institute
Center for Relational Judaism
5110 Densmore Avenue
Encino, CA 91436
ronwolfson1234@gmail.com

ISBN 978-0-578-32827-0

First Edition

Printed in the United States of America

Praise for Creating Sacred Communities

"Ron Wolfson has been teaching how to create sacred communities for years with our students in the Ziegler School of Rabbinic Studies. Now we can all learn from him, his students Rabbi Brett Kopin and Rabbi Sara Himeles, and his Master Class Contributors. *Creating Sacred Communities* is a gift for each of us, for the people we serve, and for the Jewish tradition we love!"
 —**Rabbi Bradley Shavit Artson**, vice president and dean, *Ziegler School of Rabbinic Studies, American Jewish University*

"'If only I could take this class!,' you might say if you read the syllabus. Now you have access to an important and most valuable 'master class in the art of crafting a sacred community.' The ingredients are all present. Ron Wolfson, predictably inspirational, draws out from the honored rabbinic and synagogue leaders invited to his class the delicious elements that create the kind of connections and relationships vital to congregational life. You have a front row seat and will feel warmly welcomed as if you are right there in these innovative and captivating sessions."
 —**Rabbi Elaine Zecher**, senior rabbi, *Temple Israel*, Boston

"This extraordinary publication effectively builds upon the insights offered in Ron's seminal work *Relational Judaism*. Overflowing with the candid and creative insights of some of this nation's leading clergy, educators, and community organizers, the reader is introduced to the principles and practices essential to strengthening and reinventing synagogue and communal life. Unlike most writings, one is exposed directly to both the thinking and the personal experiences of each of the fourteen participants who were interviewed for this volume. Their words come alive on these pages, and the authors conclude each interview with a set of thoughtful and challenging questions. This becomes a must read for our congregational and organizational leaders!"
 —**Steven Windmueller**, professor emeritus of Jewish Communal Studies, *Hebrew Union College-Jewish Institute of Religion*, Los Angeles

"Ron Wolfson has been one of the pioneers in the synagogue transformation field for three decades. With *Creating Sacred Communities*, he and his student Brett Kopin invite us into his classroom at the Ziegler School of Rabbinic Studies to eavesdrop on presentations from some outstanding leaders who share their secret sauce for creating compelling spiritual communities. It is well worth 'listening in' through this new book."
—**Rabbi Sid Schwarz**, director, *Clergy Leadership Incubator (CLI)*; author of *Finding a Spiritual Home: How a New Generation of Jews Can Transform the American Synagogue*

"Here is Ron Wolfson's master class on the art of building relational community, taught by our generation's master artists. This book invites you into the conversation about creating and becoming engaged and connected in communities of study, worship, and action. Grab a cup of coffee and join in!"
—**Rabbi Jacob Blumenthal**, CEO, *United Synagogue of Conservative Judaism and the Rabbinical Assembly*

"In *Creating Sacred Communities*, Ron Wolfson, the master of Relational Judaism, provides an extended conversation with some of the most inspired architects of synagogue transformation. These innovators literally teach the seminar on reinventing Jewish life by sharing their blueprints for new models of religious community. This is one class that won't put you to sleep but rather will wake you up to what sacred communities of tomorrow could be."
—**Rabbi Rick Jacobs**, president, *Union for Reform Judaism*

"In our era, Jewish spiritual leaders must build the communities they will serve by developing and catalyzing meaningful and values-driven relationships. Ron Wolfson has defined and leads the field of Relational Judaism. What a blessing to be able to enter his master class, learning from him and other leading experts as they teach rabbis the art and science of this holy task!"
—**Rabbi Shira Koch Epstein**, executive director, *Center for Rabbinic Innovation*

"*Creating Sacred Communities* provides tremendous insights into some of the most exciting work done in Jewish communities nationwide and how North American Jews might learn from the work of others. Based on a course at American Jewish University taught during the pandemic via Zoom, thereby allowing a much greater range of speakers than would have been possible if in-person, the voices range from leaders of long-standing synagogues to those who have created new communities from scratch to insights from Pastor Rick Warren. The book should be of great value to rabbis of all denominations, lay leaders of synagogues, and all concerned with invigorating twenty-first century Jewish practice."
   —**Dr. Jeffrey Herbst**, president, *American Jewish University*

"This book captures the dynamism, fun, curiosity, and practical tools that one learns in Dr. Wolfson's senior seminar at AJU (I would know, I took it!). Like the class, this book is full of gems not just from Ron, but also from leaders in the field. Like the class, it was over too quickly!"
   —**Rabbi Lizzi Heydemann**, *Mishkan Chicago*

"A gift: a peek into the most successful stories of Jewish communal life today. The book's conversational style allows us to dive right in and listen to a great conversation. From Chabad to Reform temples to start-up synagogues, Wolfson opens up the world of creative Jewish leaders and their world view. If you want to get a deep sense of what is animating the Jewish world today, and a feeling of deep optimism for the future, *read this book!*"
   —**Rabbi Elie Kaunfer**, CEO, *Hadar Institute,* author of *Empowered Judaism: What Independent Minyanim Can Teach Us about Building Vibrant Jewish Communities*

"'Decrying about the death of synagogues is going to be the death of synagogues,' Ron Wolfson writes. Read this book to be inspired by the *life* of synagogues and other sacred communities, as you get to listen in on some of the most skilled practitioners in the field. The passion and best practices that can be found in these pages will help us meet new challenges with good humor and with hope."
   —**Rabbi Lisa Grushcow**, senior rabbi, *Temple Emanu-El-Beth Sholom,* Montreal

For Stuart and Antoinette Matlins,
creators of sacred communities,
cherished counselors, beloved friends. —RW

For Marvell Ginsburg, z"l,
educator and visionary, who spent her life teaching others
how to build sacred Jewish communities.
Bubby, this one's for you! —BK

איך הָאב דיר ליב

Contents

FOREWORD	Rabbi Angela Warnick Buchdahl	xi
INTRODUCTION	Dr. Ron Wolfson & Rabbi Brett Kopin	xi
SYLLABUS		xxvii

CHAPTER 1	**Welcome!** Dr. Ron Wolfson	1
CHAPTER 2	**Welcoming Ambience** Dr. Ron Wolfson	15
CHAPTER 3	**Welcoming Worship** Rabbi Josh Warshawsky	39
CHAPTER 4	**Welcoming Membership** Rabbi Jonathan Bernhard	55
CHAPTER 5	**Building Organizations through Relationships** Janice Kamenir-Reznik	65
CHAPTER 6	**Relational Engagement Campaigns** Rabbi Nicole Auerbach Rabbi Lydia Medwin	81
CHAPTER 7	**The Purpose-Driven Congregation** Pastor Rick Warren	93
CHAPTER 8	**Emerging Spiritual Communities** Rabbi Sharon Brous Melissa Balaban	113
CHAPTER 9	**Rethinking Synagogue** Rabbi Ed Feinstein	127
CHAPTER 10	**Chabad** Rabbi Motti Seligson	141
CHAPTER 11	**Crafting Culture in Schools and Synagogues** Dr. Bruce Powell	151

CHAPTER 12	**A Synagogue President's View** Norman Levine, Esq.	165
CHAPTER 13	**Engaging the Next Generation** Rabbi Mike Uram	181
CHAPTER 14	**The Relational Rabbi** Rabbi Dan Moskovitz	199
AFTERWORD	Rabbi Sara Himeles	213
ACKNOWLEDGMENTS		215

ABOUT THE AUTHORS
    Dr. Ron Wolfson
    Rabbi Brett Kopin
		219

A WORD ABOUT THE KRIPKE INSTITUTE		221

Foreword

Rabbi Angela Warnick Buchdahl

Rabbi Angela Warnick Buchdahl serves as the senior rabbi of Central Synagogue in New York City and is the first woman to lead Central's Reform congregation in its 180-year history. Rabbi Buchdahl first joined Central Synagogue as senior cantor in 2006. In 2014, she was chosen by the congregation to be senior rabbi. Born in Korea to a Jewish American father and a Korean Buddhist mother, Rabbi Buchdahl is the first Asian American to be ordained as a cantor or rabbi in North America. She and her husband, Jacob Buchdahl, have three children.

RON: Angela, thank you for welcoming our invitation to reflect on how you create sacred communities. Brett and I will jump in with questions. When you think about what it takes to create a sacred community like Central Synagogue, what are the principles behind your work?

ANGELA: You need an organizing principle for a sacred community—a sense of purpose and mission that's clearly defined, that should be the impetus for belonging, for entry, and for leadership. As you know, our tradition can be interpreted in many ways. But I think at its core, it's about being agents for healing and repairing our communities and our larger world. We have thrown our arms open as a sacred community to those who want to join us in that mission. The power of our community is that it's constantly innovating off of an ancient root system.

RON: So how do you actually do the work?

ANGELA: The biggest reason that people join or want to be a part of our community is not what's on our website, not a mission statement we've written—it's what they observe, primarily through the vehicle of our worship service on a Friday night and on our High Holy Days. But it's also the way that we walk in the world, our social justice work that we have been doing such as criminal justice reform, what they hear preached on the bimah [pulpit], who they see in leadership roles, who we are featuring within our community, and whose stories we are lifting up. That to me is what people respond to. Rather than a mission statement, it's about _embodying the mission_, and I think that comes out in different ways.

RON: So you've identified a number of offers, if you will, to the community that you're engaged with. One is worship. One is social justice. I assume one is learning.

ANGELA: Yes, absolutely—education. My vision for where we are at Central, our directional strategy, is that we have to both grow bigger and smaller at the same time. People are responding to this manifestation of a lived Jewish life through the powerful combination of worship, social justice, and learning. We are working to meet the demand of people's interest in being connected to Central. That is a wonderful problem, but it's also a challenge for us. We think about how we put out this message in a bigger, wider way and reach more people.

We have our first-ever virtual membership now called "The Neighborhood." We have an enormous livestream community that really sees itself as part of Central. The Neighborhood is our attempt to enable people to feel connected to Central virtually, so that they can become our "neighbors." This was the first year we piloted it. We limited enrollment to no more than four hundred households because we really wanted to see how it would work and how it would affect our current members, and we want to be mindful of its impact on other communities.

We like to maintain what we call "an attitude of abundance," which means that we never say, "We've created this for us and we're not sharing it." It's that "more is more." If you can use our small groups curriculum, if you want to use a musical arrangement of a worship piece that we've put together, we will share it with you. Our feeling is this only adds more to the Jewish world and doesn't take away anything. So this is part of that sense of "getting bigger." But the "getting smaller" piece is also deeply important, and it must be simultaneous. We are operating on many different levels. We have hundreds of members in small core learning groups. There are people who create community around worship or around social justice work. There are many ways that we are creating smaller core communities within our large congregation.

We now use Salesforce as our database system, which is actually creating intimacy because now we can track things like relationships in a different way. We can reach out in a more efficient and targeted way. We can actually help assign clergy touches and keep track of them. Pastoral care is done in a much more systematic and recorded way. These are things that in some way sound very mechanical but are actually the nuts and bolts of creating a community where you are not anonymous. It's about thinking on all those levels—about how you actually build in a sense of intimacy and being known. That to me is the special sauce of any community. We live in a very big city where it would be easy to be anonymous, but actually, the magic of New York is when you live here, you actually feel like you're really part of a community and a neighborhood and a zip code. People feel connected in those ways. We are doing that on a microcosmic level, I guess, or maybe a macro level, for a synagogue. We're doing that at Central—it's a very large synagogue that contains a lot of little zip codes and neighborhoods.

RON: That to me is the definition of a relational community. You've put relationships at the core of what you do. While some might say, "Oh, look at these fabulous worship experiences that you offer," that's really just sort of the opening cover of the book, right?

ANGELA: That's how we get them in the door. That's how we embody our mission statement in a sense, but that's actually only the gateway.

RON: So I'd like to pick up on that. The very first chapter of this book is about Relational Judaism. But the second chapter is about welcoming worship. You're a cantor *and* a rabbi. So how do you shape welcoming worship in the twenty-first century for people who may or may not have access to the traditional forms of Jewish worship?

ANGELA: Well, I'm definitely biased. Music is one of the greatest ways that you can create a sense of inclusivity and welcome. But not all music is the same. I actually think that a large part of what we do is having multiple voices, and I mean that in a lot of different ways. We are lucky that we have different voices among the clergy, so you can hear people of different ages and different perspectives. We also feature eclectic musical selections, some of which makes you feel a sense of Jewish memory, and some of which speaks in your vernacular, that kind of immediately goes to your heart because it immediately feels familiar, and some which makes you feel like you're a part of a global Jewish community. We are trying to actually create multiple entry points, because we recognize that most people carry multiple identities, and we can speak to many of them. So people both feel this love of the tribal Jewish old-school sound and also want to feel like a cosmopolitan, a citizen of the world. The music reflects all of that. Sometimes you want to hear it in Hebrew, and although you might not even understand what it means, it's reaching something deep. Sometimes we'll sing something in English because it just hits right when you pray for healing in your native tongue. The way we think about worship overall is that we have multiple gateways; we're speaking to multiple needs and the multiple identities that people are bringing into the space when they come to us. You know, a surprising number of non-Jews tell us that they watch our services virtually. Some of them come in person; some of them are married or connected to a Jew. Even though they are not Jewish, they find some sort of spiritual valence that is universal and powerful and authentic.

We believe in genuine embodied prayer. It's this sense that it's not just what you say, it's what you do. Among our clergy, we're actually praying on the bimah when we're up there. When I was a cantor, there were times when people would say, "You can't just change that melody—we love it so much." And I would say, "Sure, but that melody was written eight years ago, and you know, what you think of as traditional was once brand-new." If the melody has gotten very stale, I'm not going to be able to convey it in a way that feels prayerful. There has to be true prayer. It makes me very sad to sometimes hear colleagues say that they have to go somewhere else to pray, not in their own synagogue, because they're not praying. I can't imagine that there can be an experience for others if there is not even one for those who are praying. Worship has to be an authentic experience for the clergy and the congregation.

The relationships between our clergy are also really authentic and genuine. We work on that off the bimah, so that when we're on the bimah, the sense of collegiality, warmth, affection, and admiration that we have for each other is truly genuine. I recently had a conversation with a congregant who's very introverted, but very precisely aware. She said, "You know, I noticed the way you always either give a thumbs-up or a smile or sometimes a pat on the back to one of your colleagues right after they give their sermon." These are very subtle cues, but they're not scripted. We're cheering each other on—we are there with each other and for each other. I can't tell you how many people talk about that as being a part of what the experience is, even though that is not worship, per se. It's what Larry Hoffman would call "the spectacle around the game." That stuff is real. They want to feel like they actually view us as people who care about each other, and who care about them, and who are actually praying. This is a really key part of how you shape a worship experience.

BRETT: You said that the clergy actually work on building relationships with each other off the bimah. Can you speak a little more about what you do in order to create that camaraderie and that sense that you are all on the same team?

ANGELA: Aside from weekly clergy meetings we have together, every week we will workshop everyone's Friday night sermon on Tuesday. We're helping each other be our best. Before the High Holy Days, we always do three sermon roundtables when we share our themes with each other. People will say, "Have you thought about this text? Have you thought about this story?" We are sharing drafts with each other, editing each other's drafts, and really getting down in it with each other. We want each other to shine, and we want to help each other—we're really invested in each other's success. Another very important thing, which we have not been able to do during the pandemic, but we've done for the fifteen years before that: we go away on clergy retreats twice a year. We actually go to a hotel, and we often bring in a facilitator. We do team building. If there are issues of tension in the team, we've addressed them on clergy retreats and not let them just fester; we actually face them head-on and talk about them with each other. We are a big clergy team, and we definitely have had those tense moments between us. We also go on hikes together and play silly games. These are the kinds of things that really build a sense of trust and love and affection and communication for the rest of the year.

RON: That's beautiful. You know, this course, "Creating Sacred Communities," is about training, teaching, and preparing senior students who are about to go into the field as rabbis. So Angela, as a rabbi of a major synagogue, what would these new rabbis need to know to be successful crafters of sacred community? What's the role of the rabbi?

ANGELA: I'm not going to give a traditional answer here. I can't say enough about how important it is to have a genuine spiritual life as a rabbi in order to be a spiritual leader. It sounds so obvious and yet I don't think enough rabbis actually take the time, because it takes time and space to do this. It really was a turning point for me when I found the space to do it for myself—this is so deeply important. I have a daily meditation practice in the morning. I have a prayer practice where I say prayers before I go to bed every night, which is something I've done since I was a child. Exercise is also deeply important to my mental and spiritual health. I don't love the term "self-care," but I will say that when we talk about the burnout that you often see with rabbis, it's the sense that you are giving until you're emptied out. When we feel spiritually enriched, we have to give, because it's an overflowing as opposed to the sense that someone is sucking it out of you. I can't say I have balanced this exactly right, but I would say that I have really felt my ability to be a spiritual leader is massively enhanced when I actually devote a little more time to my own inner spiritual life.

The second thing, which is somewhat related, is that rabbis go into this because we want to serve and we need to be needed in some way. I think there is a danger when you get all that assurance and love and affection from your community. I think it's dangerous when a rabbi relies on that for their own stability, happiness, self-perception, and esteem. Cultivating relationships, both with colleagues and having deep friendships outside my community, has been very, very important for me. But if you need to be needed, and you need all of that love to come from the people that you also have to serve and hold, that is a recipe for rabbis feeling constantly underappreciated or not brave enough to say the hard things because they need the love. There are a lot of dangers in that. So I have a sacred brain trust of professional women who are some of my closest friends. They are not my congregants, and I could not do this job without them. I also have an incredibly supportive husband.

RON: While we're on that point, what do you feel is the rabbi's role in relationship with lay leaders?

ANGELA: I feel like I have the greatest lay leaders in the world. I'm so blessed, and probably spoiled. I do not think that the role of a lay leader is to be a "yes man" to the rabbi. I actually think that's incredibly dangerous and not what I'm looking for. I want someone who is equally invested in the larger mission, who is going to be my sparring partner in thinking through whether or not what we are doing is truly in service of the mission. I know that I probably dream up way too many things, and some of them are not realistic. If I tried to do all of them, we would fail. So I count on the partners that I'm surrounded by, my lay leaders and my executive director, to ask the right questions and to get us to actually think about what the right things are to pursue and prioritize. I know I am better because I have strong, capable, confident lay leaders who have expertise that I do not have in lots of other areas and who push us to be better. I really feel deeply close to all of the people who have worked with us, and we do not always agree on the things we should be doing. Maimonides had this level of friendship—a *chaver ma'alah*—which is essentially a friend of a higher purpose. It's the relationship that you have with someone for whom it's not just that you care about each other, but that you need each other in order to fulfill the higher purpose that you both want to work toward. That's how I feel about my relationship with my lay leaders. I could not do what we do without them, and they really do feel like sacred partners in the work.

BRETT: When you look back on the career you've already had, what are some of the things that keep you excited and motivated for the future?

ANGELA: There are so many people who haven't yet been turned on to what Judaism can do for their lives. I feel this deep sense of mission to share with them that your life would be more grounded and meaningful, you would have less anxiety, you would be more connected, if you found not only Judaism, but a Jewish community. I feel so strongly about that, and I've seen how it can be transformative. I feel driven that we need to share this more widely and in a bigger way. We are seeing waning levels of engagement in religion all over North America. I know that joining a sacred community is actually the antidote to all the things that people are talking about: the levels of anxiety and depression and isolation and loneliness and even illness. I'm not saying that this is the only thing, but communal life is, to me, maybe the most powerful thing we can do for the things that are ailing our society most of all. When we are able to present it in a way that feels accessible, inclusive, rooted, intellectually rigorous, honest, and authentic, we can reach these people. We just need to put more of that out there. That's what drives me every day.

RON: This leads to my concluding question to you. Some people in the Jewish world are not so convinced that synagogues can do this—whether it's a large congregation like yours or an independent minyan. Yet, I'm hopeful, I'm optimistic. And I think that the wonderful people we have in this book, who are on the cutting edge of creating twenty-first-century sacred communities, will inspire many others with the principles and practices that have enabled them to find great success. Synagogues are not dying. What's your Emerald City view of the next ten years of sacred community life? What are all the people who are reading this book going to need to do to get there?

ANGELA: We need to be <u>restless</u> in our pursuit of this. There has to be a sense of an <u>entrepreneurial spirit</u>. Too often, especially in the Jewish world, but also in the larger world, innovation is seen as something that happens outside of any kind of traditional institution: it has to be a startup, it has to be a non-synagogue, it has to be something else. I absolutely believe that synagogues and some of our deeply rooted Jewish institutions are capable of doing this—if we cannot, we are sunk. But it's only possible when institutions see that their driving force has to be continued innovation and change and are willing to take some risks along the way. I do think that innovation and risk-taking is part of the culture at Central. I did not create that culture; I was very lucky to inherit that culture from Rabbi Peter Rubinstein, who really helped inculcate that feeling at Central and among the leadership. I really give our community credit for doing that—everything from trying new things every year at the High Holy Days to also taking risks with technology and other ideas long before anyone was looking at or thinking about that. There has to be a sense that there are problems to be solved and we're going to have to change the way we do business in order to solve them. They're not always going to work, but with that spirit of innovation, synagogues are absolutely poised to fulfill our mission. Yes, it can be hard to change, but you have to be willing to continue to rethink these things. We already have a built-in membership, and we have an infrastructure. We are lucky we have so many members who have deep roots and feel committed to this community and have a sense of Jewish memory attached to it. It's deep and makes them feel very, very invested. That can at times be a double-edged sword because people have a hard time with change, but we've helped people see that this is how this community is going to thrive.

RON: Beautiful, Angela. We were lucky to invite all of these really thoughtful people who've met with us over the last few months in the course. What do you hope readers of this book will take away?

ANGELA: You've compiled the spiritual practices of some of the greatest spiritual practitioners that we have in North America. They've shown that you can truly transform people's spiritual lives and lives of purpose and meaning by creating sacred communities. Clearly, there is not just a cookie-cutter way that this should be done in any one community. But I think taking the principles that have driven these spiritual leaders and then adapting them to your own personal community, by thinking about how you evolve and adapt—well, there could be no higher calling than the creation of sacred communities. Each of these chapters offer us tremendous wisdom and fruitful inspiration for creating them in our own communities.

RON: Angela, thank you so much.

ANGELA: Thank you for this book.

Introduction

Dr. Ron Wolfson

What does a newly minted rabbi need to know about leading a sacred community in the twenty-first century?

For nearly two decades, this is the question that has guided me in crafting the seminar "Creating Sacred Communities" for the senior rabbinical students at the Ziegler School of Rabbinic Studies of the American Jewish University in Los Angeles. By the time we gather, these bright women and men have been immersed in years of intensive study, learning Hebrew, Torah, Talmud, rabbinic literature, philosophy, history, homiletics, pastoral counseling, and management. We meet in the spring semester, just as the students in their final year of rabbinical school enter the placement process, interviewing with congregations and organizations looking to hire them for pulpits, Hillels, day schools, and chaplaincies. Within a few months of our learning together, they will be out in the field, charged with creating communities of meaning, purpose, belonging, and blessing.

They are eager to learn … and they have questions. Why aren't more people attracted to and engaged in these bedrock institutions of the Jewish people? Where are interesting experiments happening in synagogues and independent minyanim? How can we sharpen our leadership skills? Who are the frontline clergy and their lay partners effectively reimagining sacred communities?

In the spring of 2021, the seminar "Creating Sacred Communities," like all other Ziegler courses, was forced to meet weekly on Zoom due to the COVID-19 pandemic. As I prepared the syllabus outlining each session of the semester, I realized there was a silver lining to meeting online: I could invite the leading practitioners of the art of sacred community building to join us from wherever they lived—New York, Philadelphia,

Atlanta, Chicago, Vancouver, Lake Forest, and Los Angeles. Everyone I asked to teach eagerly accepted my invitation. Fortunately, I remembered to record each of the fourteen sessions. Our guests were so compelling, the conversations so engaging, the principles and best practices so exciting, by the middle of the semester during a debrief, I mused, "What we are learning would make a terrific book!"

Creating Sacred Communities is a peek behind the curtain of rabbinical school. To quote a favorite Broadway musical, readers of this book will be transported into "the room where it happened." We have transcribed the recordings, retaining the conversational tone of the sessions, revealing how these remarkable future colleagues share their knowledge and passion with these future rabbis. The result is a master class in the art of crafting a sacred community.

The seminar kicks off with an exploration of the current state of synagogue life and the challenges of transforming a congregation from a transactional/programmatic-driven community into one animated by the principles of what I have called Relational Judaism. We look at how to establish a welcoming ambience for all who enter our buildings, our sanctuaries, even our Zoom rooms.

We then turn to shaping an engaging worship experience with our first guest, Rabbi Josh Warshawsky, a talented prayer leader and composer of contemporary liturgical melodies.

Rabbi Jonathan Bernhard, the bold senior rabbi at Adat Ari El in Los Angeles, tells the story of how a congregation studied and then implemented a "sustainability" model of revenue generation.

Janice Kamenir-Reznik, a dynamic lay leader, reveals how her partnership with the legendary Rabbi Harold M. Schulweis, may his memory be a blessing, led to the creation of Jewish World Watch, a synagogue-based social justice initiative.

My coauthors of *The Relational Judaism Handbook*, Rabbi Nicole Auerbach of Central Synagogue in Manhattan and Rabbi Lydia Medwin of The Temple in Atlanta, two of the leading organizers of relational engagement campaigns, teach how congregations can grow bigger by getting smaller, connecting members into small groups.

At this point in the seminar, I suggest logging onto saddleback.com to watch any archived worship service led by the extraordinary, world-renowned pastor Rick Warren and read his seminal book, *The Purpose Driven Church*, which tells the tale of how he created Saddleback Church, the most famous of all evangelical megachurches in the world. Every year, I take my students to Saddleback, a mind-blowing experience. This year, my good friend Pastor Rick Zoomed in, offering thoughtful and challenging remarks to our seminar as he favored us with his brilliance.

Another amazing story of creating sacred community from scratch is told by the visionary rabbi Sharon Brous and her lay partner Melissa Balaban, the cofounders of IKAR, an independent minyan in Los Angeles. While many congregations struggle to maintain membership, IKAR has grown from a handful of people in a living room envisioning a community founded on the nexus of spirituality and social justice to nearly one thousand members. How does that happen?

The very next week, we learn how an innovative rabbi, Ed Feinstein, is rethinking synagogue life as he leads Valley Beth Shalom in Encino, California, into the future. Successfully transforming an existing mainstream congregation is a far more challenging task than creating one anew.

Chabad is unquestionably the most successful Jewish outreach organization in the world. The dynamic director of media relations for Chabad-Lubavitch, Rabbi Motti Seligson, shares the ideological principles motivating the thousands of Chabad *shluchim*/rabbis and families who create sacred communities across the globe.

Dr. Bruce Powell, my coauthor of *Raising A+ Human Beings: Crafting a Jewish School Culture of Academic Excellence and AP Kindness*, brings his expertise on culture creation as the leading Jewish day school educator in North America. The principles Bruce discusses are immediately applicable to any sacred community.

When Norman Levine became president of Valley Beth Shalom, he invited me to lunch to discuss Relational Judaism and his role as a lay leader in creating sacred community. His outstanding presidency demonstrates how the relationship between rabbi and president can result in a partnership that animates a relational culture throughout the congregation.

During his remarkable run as the Hillel rabbi at the University of Pennsylvania, Mike Uram developed an innovative relational strategy that engaged students who otherwise would never have entered the Hillel building. He shares the principles of how to reach and teach the next generation.

In a short five years, Rabbi Dan Moskovitz of Temple Sholom in Vancouver, Canada, increased the membership of his Reform congregation by 40 percent on the strength of his engagement strategies, a shining exemplar of what it takes to be a relational rabbi.

When I suggested the idea of shaping these conversations into a useful volume, Brett Kopin and Sara Himeles, two of my students with experience in writing, enthusiastically concurred. Brett and I edited each session and sent the transcripts to our guests for their review, and Sara agreed to write the afterword. Rabbi Angela Warnick Buchdahl, the extraordinary senior rabbi of Central Synagogue in Manhattan, graciously accepted my invitation to be interviewed for the foreword.

So, dear reader, if you've ever wondered what it is like to be in a rabbinical school class, read on. If you are a leader of a congregation, professional or lay, read on. If you are eager to explore how your sacred community can grow and thrive, use this book as a "community read" to get everyone on your team—your staff, your board, your committees, even your members—*literally* on the same page. Brett and I have provided suggested questions for creating your sacred community at the end of each chapter for your deliberations.

Welcome! Class is about to begin . . .

Rabbi Brett Kopin

In August of 2016, on the first day of the Ziegler School of Rabbinic Studies orientation, my cohort gathered at the home of our dean, Rabbi Bradley Shavit Artson. That day happened to be his and his wife Elana's anniversary. As a group, we bought them flowers and a card that we all signed. One of our classmates, a talented musician, brought her guitar along. After a full afternoon and evening discussing what our studies over the next five years would look like, we took time as a class to honor their anniversary through song and blessing. Within just a few moments, we created a warmth that set a tone which carried us through the next five years together. It was clear then, as it is now, that becoming rabbis was about so much more than just deep and devoted study. Rather, becoming rabbis meant becoming part of a tradition of <u>community builders</u>, <u>seeking out sacred moments of celebration alongside our learning and teaching</u>.

When the singing was over, our dean invited us to close our eyes and imagine that as we sat around the table, Miriam the Prophetess was joining us, her tambourine in hand. King David and Solomon as well. Soon, Abraham, Sarah, Isaac, Rebekah, Jacob, Rachel and Leah, Moses, Aaron, Deborah, Hillel and Shammai, Rashi, Rambam, the Baal Shem Tov, Regina Jonas, Heschel and Kaplan joined us, too. We were sitting around the table with our Ziegler professors and future colleagues, and also with our ancestors throughout Jewish history, taking on the mantle of leadership and absorbing the wisdom of the tradition to then reshape and share for our time.

I carried that image, and have felt the immense responsibility that comes with it, throughout rabbinical school. What a pleasure and joy it was to spend my last semester with some of the great spiritual and community building masters of our generation, whom we affectionately referred to as "Ron's friends." Our course, *Creating Sacred Communities,* reinforced what I already learned that first night of orientation. In order to be a master educator and leader, one must also be a master of relationships. It is through relationships, and relationships alone, that we create and maintain sacred communities. I feel blessed, along with my friend and colleague Rabbi Sara Himeles, and so many others, to have had the opportunity to sit at the table–or rather, the COVID-era "Zoom room"–with those I am now humbled to call colleagues, and whose many lessons I now implement again and again in my own classroom and rabbinate. I hope their wisdom, presented in these pages, influences you the way it influenced us.

American Jewish University
Syllabus

Class Number/Name: EDU 567, Spring 2021, Creating Sacred Communities

Instructor: Dr. Ron Wolfson
Zoom Room Number: https://zoom.us/j/2675229043

Class Meeting Days: Wednesday
Time: 1:00 P.M.–3:30 P.M.

Instructor Office Hours: By appointment
Phone: 818-231-1441
Email: rwolfson@aju.edu

Welcome to the seminar!

It is a special pleasure for me to be teaching a group of Ziegler School of Rabbinic Studies students. I myself once thought of becoming a rabbi—but my "calling" led me in a different direction . . . into Jewish education. A *rav* is many things; for me, a teacher most of all!

In my view, the "rabbi as teacher" takes on a variety of assignments, including the visioning of the congregation as a "community of learners," conceptualizing the educational programming of the synagogue, modeling outstanding pedagogy, and leading efforts to transform the synagogue from a twentieth-century paradigm to a twenty-first-century spiritual community.

The seminar itself will center on this question: how do we shape a sacred community? We will read widely in the developing literature in synagogue transformation. We will meet guest speakers who are working on the frontlines of the most exciting initiatives to reinvigorate synagogue life. And we will travel via Zoom to Orange County for a visit to one of the more famous megachurches, Saddleback Church.

As our semester project, I invite you to join me in researching a cutting-edge issue in synagogue life that I have called Relational Judaism. Briefly put, I believe that congregations must move from synagogues of programming to synagogues of relationships. For your written assignment, I will ask each of you to research best practices and best principles of Relational Judaism and to keep a reflective practice journal detailing your reactions to our class conversations and readings.

The seminar will be just that: a seminar. I expect everyone to have read the assigned material in advance of our meetings and be prepared to engage in a lively dialogue about the topics at hand.

The specific educational objectives of the seminar are listed below. Students will:

1. Acquire techniques for creating a sense of community in the classroom
2. Analyze how group dynamics work within the classroom setting
3. Learn how enculturation functions as the primary vehicle for religious education
4. Identify the challenges facing Jewish religious school and day school education
5. Learn specific strategies for creating an "ambience of welcome" in congregations
6. Develop an understanding of "synagogue transformation" and "Relational Judaism"
7. Learn how to be a "courageous spiritual leader"
8. Articulate a personal educational "theory in action"
9. Learn the role of the rabbi as "educational leader"
10. Consider your personal rabbinate as you confront the challenges of synagogue transformation

Required Reading

Eliezrie, David. *The Secrets of Chabad.* Tobey Press, 2015.

Powell, Bruce, and Wolfson, Ron. *Raising A+ Human Beings: Crafting a Jewish School Culture of Academic Excellence and AP Kindness.* Kripke Institute, 2021.

Warren, Rick. *The Purpose Driven Church.* Zondervan, 1995.

Wolfson, Ron. "Growing a Field of Dreams." In *First Fruit: A Whizin Anthology of Jewish Family Education.* Whizin Institute, 1998. (handout)

Wolfson, Ron. *Relational Judaism: Using the Power of Relationships to Transform the Jewish Community.* Jewish Lights, 2013.

Wolfson, Ron. *The Spirituality of Welcoming: How to Transform Your Congregation into a Sacred Community.* Jewish Lights, 2006.

Wolfson, Ron, Nicole Auerbach, and Lydia Medwin. *The Relational Judaism Handbook: How to Create a Relational Engagement Campaign to Deepen Relationships in Your Community.* Kripke Institute, 2018.

Recommended Reading

Fishkoff, Sue. *The Rebbe's Army: Inside the World of Chabad-Lubavitch.* Schocken Books, 2005.

Gladen, Steve. *Small Groups with Purpose.* Baker Books, 2013.

Halevi, Baruch, and Ellen Frankel. *Revolution of Spirit.* Jewish Lights, 2013.

Hoffman, Lawrence A. *Rethinking Synagogues.* Jewish Lights, 2006.

Kaunfer, Elie. *Empowered Judaism: What Independent Minyanim Can Teach Us about Building Vibrant Jewish Communities.* Jewish Lights, 2010.

Olitzky, Kerry, and Avi Olitzky. *New Membership and Financial Alternatives for the American Synagogue.* Jewish Lights, 2015.

Schwarz, Sid. *Finding Your Spiritual Home: How a New Generation of Jews Can Transform the American Synagogue.* Jewish Lights, 2003.

Uram, Mike. *Next Generation Judaism: How College Students and Hillel Can Help Reinvent Jewish Organizations*. Jewish Lights, 2016.

Wolfson, Ron. *Passover: The Family Guide to Spiritual Celebration*. 2nd ed. Jewish Lights, 2003.

Wolfson, Ron. *Shabbat: The Family Guide for Preparing for and Celebrating the Sabbath*. 2nd ed. Jewish Lights, 2002.

Schedule

JANUARY 20	**Welcome!**
JANUARY 27	**How to Transform a Congregation into a Sacred Community I**
	Reading: *The Spirituality of Welcoming*, Part One
	Welcoming Ambience
FEBRUARY 3	**How to Transform a Congregation into a Sacred Community II**
	Reading: *The Spirituality of Welcoming*, Part Two
	Welcoming Worship
	Guest: Rabbi Josh Warshawsky
FEBRUARY 10	**How to Transform a Congregation into a Sacred Community III**
	Reading: *The Spirituality of Welcoming*, Part Three
	Welcoming Membership
	Guest: Rabbi Jonathan Bernhard
FEBRUARY 17	**Building Organizations through Relationships**
	Guest: Janice Kaminer-Reznik
FEBRUARY 24	**Relational Engagement Campaigns**
	Reading: *Relational Judaism Handbook*, Wolfson, Auerbach, and Medwin
	Guests: Rabbi Nicole Auerbach and Rabbi Lydia Medwin
FEBRUARY 28	**Saddleback Church Service online**
MARCH 3	**The Purpose-Driven Congregation**
	Guests: Pastor Rick Warren, Pastor David Chrzan, and Pastor Steve Gladen
MARCH 10	**Emerging Spiritual Communities**
	Guests: Rabbi Sharon Brous and Melissa Balaban

MARCH 17	**Rethinking Synagogue Life**
	Guest: Rabbi Ed Feinstein
MARCH 24	**Case Study in Relational Judaism: Chabad**
	Guest: Rabbi Motti Seligson
	Reading: *The Secret of Chabad*, Eliezrie
	The Rebbe's Army, Fishkoff
APRIL 7	**Crafting Culture in Schools and Synagogues**
	Guest: Dr. Bruce Powell
APRIL 14	**A Synagogue President's View**
	Guest: Norm Levine, Past President, Valley Beth Shalom
APRIL 21	**Engaging the Next Generation**
	Guest: Rabbi Mike Uram
APRIL 28	**The Relational Rabbi**
	Guest: Rabbi Dan Moskovitz
MAY 5	*Siyum*

CHAPTER 1

Welcome!

Dr. Ron Wolfson

RON: Welcome Sara and Brett! I so enjoyed our pre-seminar one-on-one conversations.

SARA: Is that something you do before every class you teach?

RON: Yes, it is. It's my practice to reach out to my students, just to say "hi," to welcome them to class, to hear a bit of their stories, to learn something about them. It's the beginning of a relationship.

BRETT: I appreciated it.

SARA: I did, too!

RON: Great. So, we'll be talking a lot about relationship building—it is the core of what I've called Relational Judaism. I've been working on synagogue transformation since I was a high school student in United Synagogue Youth back in my hometown of Omaha, Nebraska. I was the regional president of EMTZA USY. We kids loved being together at conventions, conclaves . . . but we thought the services were boring. Our *ruach* [spirit] sessions were fantastic—lots of singing and cheering. But davening was not at all moving. Here's a question for you:

When have you ever been emotional in a religious service?

SARA: I have been moved during the Yizkor memorial service.

RON: Can you think of a time, Brett, when you were in tears or laughing during a service?

BRETT: What you reminded me of was Intersem last year, our annual gathering with seminarians from other religious groups. During the

Protestant service, they do testimonials. They had two different people get up and tell a story about a miracle that happened to them. This guy gets up, he's Hispanic, and he is talking about the experience of going into undocumented Hispanic communities, teaching them about what an angel is. He says there is another word for angel—"messenger." He tells these people that when they came across the border, they were angels, bringing a new gospel into America. As he said this, he started crying. And it was so moving, I mean, I have shivers just talking about it, it was that powerful. Then the next person who got up was from South Korea. And she said that she's actually an undocumented immigrant, who has been trying for fifteen years to get documentation. She's terrified of being deported every day. She says nobody knows there's a South Korean population in the same boat as the Hispanic population. So, not only is her status as an American constantly in question, she's also invisible in terms of the entire discussion. She was crying too. I'm like, wow, this is the most moving service I've seen in a very, very long time. They were both talking about how God was with them on their entire journey. This was real stuff right, what they were doing.

RON: That's right. They understand the power of testimony. Or, if you don't like the word "testimony," it's the power of *story*. It's so interesting, because here we are telling stories every week during the Torah reading, but we do it in such a traditional way that it kind of misses its emotional power. We do it intellectually. As rabbis and teachers, we decipher it intellectually, but where's the emotion of it? That's what I love about Amichai Lau-Lavie and his work with "Storahtelling." Do you know Storahtelling?

SARA: Yeah.

RON: My nephew Alex actually worked with Amichai for a number of years doing Storahtelling. The first time I experienced it was at the very first Synagogue 2000 conference in 1995. Larry Hoffman, a professor of liturgy and ritual at Hebrew Union College, and I decided to partner on a synagogue transformation initiative. The first thing we did was invite sixteen congregations to send teams of clergy and lay leaders to Camp Ramah in Ojai, California, for a three-day conference. The idea was to show them what was possible to do in synagogue worship and welcoming. We invited Amichai to come, and he did a model Storahtelling experience, translating the Torah reading into a dramatically moving experience that blew everybody away. It was just unbelievable. Amichai, a brilliant guy, has now been ordained at JTS [Jewish Theological Seminary] and created "Lab/Shul," one of the Jewish Emergent Network independent minyanim we'll learn about from Rabbi Sharon Brous and Melissa Balaban in a few weeks. Whether testimony or storytelling or drama, there are ways to make services come alive, even for those with few liturgical access skills.

Okay, let's think about what we're going to do in our class together. You know, I sent you three books, *The Spirituality of Welcoming*, *Relational Judaism*, and *The Relational Judaism Handbook*.

SARA: Thanks so much!

BRETT: Thank you!

RON: You're very welcome! The books represent a progression of my thinking and the work we've been doing in synagogue transformation since that senior year in high school as president of the USY region. I traveled to every chapter from Winnipeg to St. Louis, from Denver to Iowa City, spending fifteen weekends on the road visiting different Conservative synagogues in the Midwest. That was the start of my career interest in experiencing hundreds of synagogues of all flavors, all over the world. Until the COVID-19 pandemic hit in March 2020, I had spent the past fifteen years as a one-hundred-thousand-mile flyer on American Airlines. Were you guys in a youth group in high school?

SARA: I grew up in the Reform movement.

RON: NFTY, right?

SARA: Yes, I grew up in NFTY. We had regional conventions. I was the president of my youth group at my temple.

RON: What about you, Brett?

BRETT: I was more into high school clubs, so that was where I spent most of my time. I had two older siblings who weren't into it. If I could do it again, I think I'd be more interested.

RON: Well, besides my family, it was USY that sparked my interest in Judaism. I was going to become a rabbi; I was on the list for three years at JTS.

BRETT: Oh, wow. Why didn't you go through with it?

RON: During the height of the Vietnam War, the seminary was good enough to keep me on the list for three years. But then I got involved in teaching at a Conservative synagogue, Congregation B'nai Amoona, near the campus in St. Louis. It changed my life and I decided against the rabbinate in favor of getting a PhD in education. But I promised my mentor rabbi I would get a stronger foundation in Judaica. Everybody should have a mentor, especially rabbis. I hope you have one or two mentors. Do you have one, Sara?

SARA: Yes, there are many different people I turn to for advice.

BRETT: I definitely do.

RON: That's great. It's a good thing to have. Mine was this rabbi who recruited me into teaching. His name was Bernard Lipnick, may he rest in peace, the senior rabbi of B'nai Amoona, the big Conservative synagogue in St. Louis. When I started teaching, I had no idea what I was doing. My only model of a Hebrew school teacher was a guy named Mr. Friedman, not his real name, who just yelled at me all afternoon: "*Sheket, sheket, sheket!*" I've learned to translate every Hebrew word I use—good practice for rabbis—so, I sort of joke about "*Sheket.*" I'll ask a crowd if anyone knows what it means. Inevitably, someone says, "Quiet." I say, "Not the way he was saying it! It meant: 'Shut up.' And, I never once heard him say, '*Sheket b'vakasha*—Shut up, please.'" It's one of my favorite stories. I had Friedman for three years in a row and that's the only Hebrew word I learned. I was a good kid in public school, but bored in Hebrew school, so, honestly, I was pretty wild. "*Sheket, sheket, sheket!*" That's all I heard in his class. Another true story: I went for my first Bar Mitzvah lesson. The tutor was also a lovely man from the Old Country. He pinched my cheek and asked, "Sonny, what's your name in Hebrew?" I said, "*Sheket!*" I thought my Hebrew name was *Sheket ben Avraham* for the longest time.

BRETT (laughing): That's hilarious!

RON: The funniest thing is that it took twenty years for my synagogue in Omaha to invite me back to give a lecture. They couldn't believe I had become a Jewish educator! It was a Friday night. My mother, bless her soul, ensured the sanctuary was packed. I give the lecture. It went fine. Then, I asked if there were any questions. From the front row, I see a hand. I look down from the bimah ... it's Mr. Friedman. He doesn't have a question. He stands up, turns to face the congregation, and says, "Ronnie Wolfson was the best student I ever had in Hebrew school!" It was so funny—revisionist history.

Since my only teaching experience was Mr. Friedman, I knew Jewish education had to change. But I didn't know how to do it. Along comes Rabbi Lipnick, who had been one of the founders of Camp Ramah in Wisconsin, the first Camp Ramah. He asked a simple, but profound question: "Why are we doing the same Hebrew school model, especially with kids post–Bar and Bat Mitzvah?" They've emerged from childhood into adolescence, but we treat them the same way—same old, same old Hebrew school. You can probably remember that experience of transitioning to teenage years; you are reborn as a different human being. Even at this very successful synagogue, 95 percent of the kids were dropping out of Hebrew school after their Bar or Bat Mitzvah because they gave them the same Hebrew school experience they had as children. So, Lipnick asked another profound question: "Why don't we do camp during the year?" It's a great question. We know camp is so successful, right? You know why? Because we're creating full-time sacred communities. His idea was to have monthly retreats with eighth graders, fourteen-year-olds, and he needed a camp counselor youth group type person, and he knew me. The program called for two meetings a week between the monthly Shabbatonim in a classroom to prepare for the upcoming weekend. There was no curriculum. I knew absolutely nothing about teaching. Lipnick just threw me in the classroom and told me to invent the program. So, I did.

That was the first time I thought about the importance of building community and culture in the classroom. The very first thing I did with those eighth graders, instead of meeting them in the classroom, I hung out in the lobby when they came in. I greeted them by name, because I had memorized their names before our first class. We hung out in the lobby until everybody gathered. None of the other teachers did this, so already I was doing something unique in their experience of Hebrew school. By the way, that's our first lesson in creating a welcoming culture as a rabbi: *greet your people before you get up to teach them.* I taught this lesson on a scholar weekend at Rabbi Wes Gardenswartz's congregation in Newton, Massachusetts, and Wes, who used to walk into services from a green room off the bimah, changed his practice by standing at the front door of the sanctuary to greet his people as they come in.

I walked those fifteen kids toward our classroom and then stopped and said, "Come on, we're going to do something crazy. Follow me!" We walked into the sanctuary, where I had set up a record player on the bimah. I played two songs: "Revolution" by the Beatles, and "Tradition" from the Broadway play *Fiddler on the Roof*. I gave them song sheets with the lyrics and said, "Let's talk about the differences between revolution and tradition. This class is going to be revolutionary. We're going to these weekend retreats, and we're going to learn together in a different kind of way in religious school." The kids were mesmerized. Long story short: by the end of that year, the parents were shocked that the kids loved coming to Hebrew school all of a sudden and wondered why. So, I asked the kids why they liked coming. One of them said, "Well, we're learning to live together on the weekends." I added the word "Jewishly." This became our purpose: "We're learning to live together Jewishly." We built relationships with each other through the weekend and class experiences we shared. And if you think about a synagogue or a spiritual community, that's really what its purpose is: *learning to live together Jewishly.*

This is my main thesis for our seminar: "It's all about relationships." Unfortunately, the twentieth-century model of synagogue really lost that notion of relationship being at the center of our work. Instead, many synagogues used programming as the engagement strategy. You know, let's have a whole calendar of programs for different age groups, different stages of life. There's nothing wrong with programs; people come to the programs and enjoy the programs. But often they leave, not ever connecting to what I would say are *three tiers of engagement* we should think about in crafting a sacred community: a *kehilla kedosha.*

One tier we're pretty good at: *linking people to Jewish living and Jewish texts and Jewish knowledge and Jewish wisdom.* That is the tier I don't focus on, because everybody else focuses on it. The second tier is *how we create relationships between the clergy, the staff, and the leadership of the sacred community and the members and the new people we're trying to reach.* How do you create that relationship? We'll talk a lot about that, especially how rabbis spend their time creating and deepening relationships with the people you are serving. That's going to be a big question for the semester. But the third tier is the weakest and yet perhaps the most important challenge: *how do you connect the members with each other, so that each person has a deep connection to the community, so that each person has a group of people who care about you and are going to be there with you and for you in good times and bad?*

This used to happen. Still does in smaller communities. But certainly, in the midsize and larger synagogue communities, that social fabric of relationship is not being attended to. Like, what do you think was the most common way synagogues would connect people to each other in that twentieth-century model?

SARA: Shabbat services?

RON: Yes, there is socialization that can happen during Shabbat services, but it happens by accident. It's not socially engineered. A synagogue doesn't do that much during services to connect people together. Right? So, people will sit with the friends they *already* have. That's nice. That's important. But what if you're new? What if you don't know anyone? What happens in a worship service to connect the people who are in the room? And the answer is: virtually nothing!

BRETT: What about the *Oneg* [after-service reception]? That seems to be the most social moment.

SARA: But, even in the Oneg, a newcomer could see people talking to their friends, paying little attention to a newcomer.

RON: Or think of a guest of the Bar Mitzvah. If I had one dollar for every time someone said to me, "Oh, I visited a synagogue and no one said hello," I'd be a very rich man. One of the things we want to talk about is *what are the strategies to build relationships?* We'll hear from many of our guests about strategies of engagement, but I want us to think about the *principles* underlying the strategies. In creating sacred communities, it's the principles that are crucial; the strategies will change depending on which community you are shaping. Sara, you told me you're not likely to be serving in a congregational setting. Maybe a Hillel or a social justice organization, right? Well, the principles still apply. So, when we get into the *Relational Judaism* book and *The Relational Judaism Handbook*, we'll see how we can change the model from *programmatic* to *relational*.

The other thing we'll read about in *Relational Judaism* is the paradigm shift from *transactional* to *relational*. There are large synagogues in Los Angeles where each year one hundred new members join and one hundred members leave. There's a revolving door. So, they don't grow.

BRETT: Why is there a revolving door?

RON: Some of the attrition happens because people move. Some die. But a lot of it happens because, for the member, the transaction is over. I paid you dues to get a rabbi on call, seats for the High Holy Days, a Bar or Bat Mitzvah for my kid, and then . . . I don't need you anymore. It's sort of like a gym membership. I sign up for a gym, I engage with it for a few months, and then, I drop out. Why? Because *I'm not using it anymore*! And, I haven't made any friends. And there are a lot of other organizations competing for my time and resources. But what does it say about a congregation that has members in it while their kids are growing up for what, ten, twelve, fifteen years, and then when the youngest kid becomes a Bar/Bat Mitzvah, it's not just the kid who disappears, it's the entire family that goes bye-bye? It says that the experience has centered on the kids, not the adults. It says that the synagogue has failed to connect on those three tiers—the person is not engaged Jewishly, the person doesn't know the clergy, and the person doesn't know anyone in the synagogue. So, why stick around?

BRETT: You know, Ron, I'm the recruitment person for Ziegler. I've always seen my job as building real relationships with prospective students. That's the entire job.

RON: That's my job as a teacher, and it's going to be your job as rabbis. That's why we'll be starting each class session with a "check-in." We taught this principle to our Synagogue 2000 teams: start every meeting with a personal check-in, an opportunity to bring your whole self, your whole life to the work of creating sacred community. During check-in, amazing things can happen. One of my favorite S2K stories is when one of the team's leaders called me to say during their third or fourth meeting, when people realized it was a safe place to bring your whole self, one of the people said, "My father was just diagnosed with terminal cancer," and everything stopped. At that point, a really wonderful rabbi simply said, "We need to pray." They stopped the check-in and began singing Debbie Friedman's "Mi Shebeirach," the prayer for healing. Everybody was in tears. And everybody understood: *we've created a sacred space.* That's back to my point about emotionality. We encouraged the rabbis to bring their whole personal selves to the table. Talk to people about your life. You, too, are a human being with emotions, with struggles, with triumphs. And it makes it all very real.

You know, Sara and Brett, even though we are early in our relationship building, I see the two of you have a beautiful relationship that's been built over a long time now. I'm the new guy. I hope I can get to the point where I can be with you in the same way. It will be my goal to do that.

It's about crafting a culture of what my colleague Bruce Powell calls "the embrace of welcoming." There's nothing more important. I'm the first one to say that content is critical. Learn all the skills—the Hebrew language, the text knowledge, the homiletics, the rituals, the pastoral counseling—so you are prepared to do the job of a rabbi. But if you don't have these other skills—the interpersonal skills, the community organizing skills—it will be much more difficult to lead a sacred community. In the synagogue world, your challenge is how to craft a community of people who are so engaged with each other and with the leaders of the community that they wouldn't think of quitting after thirteen years. If they do quit after being in your congregation that long, then they are not connected to you and not connected to each other. That's an indictment. You could do some serious *cheshbon ha-nefesh* [soul-searching] over that one!

Let's talk about our seminar together. I've invited a spectacular group of guests who are on the frontlines of creating sacred communities. Each one will spend an hour or so with us, and then we will debrief afterwards. Then, I have two assignments for you. The first is I'd like you to keep a journal to write your reflections and to document your takeaways from each guest. Yes, I would like to read it, but it's not for me. It's for you. My students in the past have told me that by doing this, they look back at it a few years into their rabbinate and say, "Oh, yeah, those are important things that we talked about that I don't want to lose."

The second assignment is to invite you to think with me about a Big Idea I'm developing for gathering the community once we come out of this pandemic, God willing. Everyone I've spoken to, including rabbis of major synagogues across the country, loves the idea of a communal "homecoming." This came to me when I saw the Netflix series *Queer Eye*, season two, episode one. The five men travel from Philadelphia to the Town of Gay in Georgia to do a makeover of an African American woman named Tammye. They ask her what she wants renovated in her home, and she asks them to finish the new community social hall in the church where she is a very active volunteer. The big reveal at the end of the week will be at the annual church "homecoming," a kind of annual reunion of current members and, crucially, of former members who are invited to "just come on home." There's a potluck lunch, some singing, a little ritual, and lots of fellowship. When I saw this, I turned to my wife Susie and said, "When the pandemic is over, this is exactly what we should do in our Jewish communities."

I've looked at the calendar. Rosh Hashanah is very early this coming year [2021], September 6. Today is January 20. Even with the vaccine rollout, I'm not convinced we'll be back in our buildings in huge numbers by the High Holy Days. But maybe Hanukkah? How perfect would that be? The themes of moving from darkness to the light, of rededicating our sacred spaces and community centers, of highlighting the importance of belonging to a sacred community of relationships . . . it's all there. So, in addition to our conversations with the guests, I would love for the two of you to be my in-house consultants as the idea evolves. Are you up for that?

SARA: Absolutely! That's exciting!

BRETT: I'm in! Are you thinking just about American Jewish communities?

RON: No, I think this could be worldwide, like the "Global Day of Jewish Learning." Each congregation, each JCC, would plan their own gatherings, and we would simply provide a platform to indicate on a world map who is doing something to celebrate.

SARA: When exactly would this happen?

RON: Originally, I thought, "What about the eighth night of Hanukkah, December 5?" It's a Sunday. But one of the rabbis said, "Ron, if we can gather on that Sunday by then, why not celebrate on Shabbat Hanukkah? I thought well, college homecomings are celebrated all weekend. So, now the idea is to call it "Hanukkah Homecoming Weekend."

BRETT: Love it!

RON: We'll need to think about helping local communities design their gatherings. Do you know the wonderful book *The Art of Gathering*, by Priya Parker? She makes the point that organizations should not think about their programs by category, but by purpose. What's the purpose of the gathering?

SARA: I'm beyond crazy excited. I think it'll be cool.

RON: I also think there's a real opportunity here to reinvent the synagogue. It won't just be rededicating a sanctuary. It can be a rededication of the relational community. We will not have seen each other in more than a year. I've been dreaming about how to encourage whatever program there is to build in this notion of relational moment. It's not just some big party. You've got to have name tags. You've got to encourage people to meet someone you don't know.

BRETT: Who's the organizer of Hanukkah Homecoming?

RON: I'm president of a nonprofit I founded in honor of the rabbi I grew up with, Myer Kripke, *zichrono livracha*, may he rest in peace. He invested with his friend Warren Buffett and became very wealthy. I set up the Kripke Institute to honor him and his late wife, Dorothy, a children's book author. I tell the story in my memoir, *The Best Boy in the United States of America*.

SARA: I love that title. I assume, Ron, that *you're* the best boy in the United States of America.

RON (LAUGHING): My *zaydie* called me that. Whenever we would come over to Bubbie and Zaydie's house, first stop was Bubbie's kitchen for her incredible mandel bread we called "Bubbie's Cookies." Then, I'd rush into the living room, where Zaydie sat in his big red velvet chair, his throne. He was the king of our family. Next to the chair was a side table with three things: a pack of Camels unfiltered cigarettes (he smoked four packs a day), a silver-plated Ronson cigarette lighter, and a glass of water with his teeth in it. I would jump into Zaydie's lap, he would cross his legs around me, give me this big wet, scratchy kiss, look me straight in the eye, and say in his thick Russian immigrant accent, "Ronnie, you are da best boy in da United States of America!" I'd say, "Zaydie, I know, I know, let me go, let me go." He wouldn't. He had me in a World Wide Wrestling Federation leg lock, and he wouldn't let me go until he said it again, "Ronnie, you're da best boy da United States of America!" "Please let me go, Zaydie!" Nope. Third time: "Ronnie, you're da best boy in da United States of America," and finally, he would open his legs and I would run off. Then, my brother Bobby would come around the corner, and Bobby would jump in Zaydie's lap, who put him in that leg lock, gave him a big wet, scratchy kiss, looked him in the eye, and said, "Bobby, *you're* da best boy in the United States of America!"

BRETT: Wow!

RON: And then my brother Dougie: "Dougie, *you're* da best boy in da United States of America . . . and my cousin Laurie: "Laurie, you're da best girl in da United States of America." He had nine grandchildren, Zaydie Louie Paperny, and he convinced each of us that for him, we were the best boys and best girls in the United States of America. And Brett and Sara, you two are the best students I've ever had in da United States of America!

BRETT (LAUGHING): I guess after that story we shouldn't get so excited that you said that.

RON: Ah, but that's the point. At this moment, you are for sure. If you approach your rabbinate thinking that every single one of the people you touch and you influence is the best human being they can be, if you inspire them to be that best human being, created as a *b'tzelem Elohim*, created in the image of God, then you will have brought a spirituality into their lives that they'll never forget.

Okay, it's been great to meet, even on Zoom. Please write some reflections. Next week, please read the opening chapter of *The Spirituality of Welcoming*, and we'll talk about welcoming ambience. The following week, our guest will be your colleague Josh Warshawsky to talk about welcoming worship, and then Jonathan Berhnard will join us to talk about welcoming membership. We're off and running ...

You guys good? Was this okay?

SARA: Yeah!

BRETT: Two and a half hours!

RON: Holy moly! Wow! It'll be a lot of fun, I promise you that. We'll learn a lot. And thank you for agreeing to help me on the Homecoming project. I couldn't be more excited.

SARA: Yeah. It's exciting!

BRETT: It's very exciting!

RON: All right, then. Thank you. Thanks. Have a great week!

Questions for Creating Your Sacred Community

1. Share a story of your experience in synagogue.

2. Is your synagogue or independent minyan transactional/programmatic or relational?

3. Does your community have a "revolving door" of membership? What is the retention rate/new member ratio?

4. Let's create a baseline: how would you characterize the engagement of your clergy with the members and the engagement of members with each other?

CHAPTER 2

Welcoming Ambience

Dr. Ron Wolfson

RON: I hope you were able to read the chapter on welcoming ambience in *The Spirituality of Welcoming*. Let's start with this question: Have you ever had the experience of being ignored when you walked into a synagogue as a guest?

BRETT: I think for me, I've always been used to it. So, it's never out of the ordinary. From the time I was a kid, I was brought up to believe that synagogues were sort of intimidating, stoic, scary places. You can't laugh during services. You walk in and everyone kind of stares at you. You know? I suppose that's to reflect the larger fear of God. I think that is what the synagogue was always going for.

SARA: I think I have had both the experiences of feeling welcomed and ignored in synagogues.

RON: So, what happened after this book came out? Everybody ran to do two things: let's put greeters at the door into the sanctuary, and let's have name tags for everyone. This was not my intention. "Welcoming" is much deeper than simply putting a couple of people at the front door of the sanctuary and wearing name tags. Synagogue leaders thought, "Okay, we've done it. Now, we're warm and welcoming." This is not at all what I argue in the book . . . and even more so in *Relational Judaism*. It just illustrates an issue that I've been pounding at my whole career. We had the same experience in our work in Jewish family education. Everybody thought, "Oh, family education. You put a group of kids and parents together in a room and that's 'family education.'" No! Family education was about empowering the parents to be the teachers of their own children by creating a creative Jewish home environment. Just being together in a classroom or a social hall in a synagogue? That's not family education. People still don't get it.

So, I'm glad that both of you picked up on the fact that there are no easy solutions, no easy ways to change the culture of an institution from "corporate" to "relational." A relational sacred community, building relationships, begins by seeing and knowing your members and guests. Think of how a synagogue finds out about the people who come into their world. Do you know what the major way is?

BRETT: You get a survey?

RON: That's right. It's called a demographic form. Like when you go to a new doctor's office, they give you a clipboard with five pages of a demographic form to fill out with all kinds of information about yourself, your birthday, and your health issues, the medicines you take and the insurance information. I have looked at dozens of new member forms that get sent to people when they join a synagogue. You know what it is? It's "give us your name . . . in Hebrew"! I bet a lot of people don't know their Hebrew name. You're asked for your address and your phone numbers . . . that's fine. And then you get to list *yahrzeits*. Half the people don't know what *yahrzeit* means [recalling the anniversary of a death]. And then, the coup de gras: "Here's a list of committees we'd like you to volunteer for—the social justice committee, the ritual committee, the education committee, the youth department committee." There is nothing in what I just described to you that would let you know really anything about this person—about their interests, their passions, their talents, what they can bring to building the community. Nothing.

Let me share with you the story I tell when I consult with congregations to illustrate this. Our daughter Havi went to the University of Michigan. After she graduated, she came back to Los Angeles to go to Hebrew Union College to get a master's in social work and Jewish communal service. And a girlfriend of hers says, "You know, Havi, now that you're back in LA, the only way to meet people is JDate."

RON: She didn't want to do it. Eventually, she got talked into it. So, she put up a JDate profile. She is a very attractive, very smart, really terrific kid. All of a sudden, she's getting all these invitations to go on JDates, mostly to Starbucks. Now she's a kid in a candy store; she's going on six JDates a night. She was living in an apartment near us in Encino, and she's very close to us, so she'd come over to report on the JDates, bouncing off the walls from all the caffeine. One night she comes home all excited and says, "Mom, Dad, I met him." Susie says, "What!?!" She says, "I met him. He's perfect on paper." I ask, "What means 'perfect on paper'?" She says, "He's tall. He's handsome. He's Jewish. In his JDate profile photo, he has his arm around his *bubbie.*" Then, wait for it, Havi says, "And he's a dentist!" Havi was not the only one excited. The dentist took one look at Havi and says, "Forget coffee. We're going out to dinner." At this point in the story, I always joke, "In the JDate world, this is known as an instant upgrade!"

So, they're dating for three months, for six months, for a year, a year and a half. He comes to our house for Shabbos, we meet his parents . . . it's looking really promising. Then suddenly, the university here changes its dental plan and I don't have a dentist. So, I say to the dentist at Shabbos dinner one night, "I need a new dentist." He's right on it. He says, "Come to me. I'll take care of you." I'm all over that. I go to him. He's very good. I come back home and I say to Susie, "He's good. You've got to go to him." She says, "No way. I don't want . . . his hands . . . in my . . . No, it's too personal. I can't do it, Ronnie." I say, "Listen, he could be our son-in-law. You must go." Finally, she agreed. I'll never forget what Susie said when she got into the car to go to the dentist's office: *"Good thing he's not a gynecologist!"* I think that's the funniest thing I ever heard. She goes for the appointment . . . and comes back with an even better story. I ask, "How did it go? She says, "Oh, he was fine. But you know the first thing that happens when you go to a new doctor or dentist, they give you a clipboard with a demographic form to fill out? Well, I got one in his office. I sat down and the first line on the form was 'Name.' I wrote in: 'Susan Wolfson.' And the second line on the form was 'Name I Prefer to Be Called.' *I wrote in: 'Mom.'"* Now, *that's* the funniest thing I ever heard! Susie gives me all my best lines. The real punch line was yet to come. Susie says, "He never noticed it. He never said a word. I don't think he even looked at the form."

BRETT: That's amazing!

RON: And I tell synagogue leaders, "It's the same thing with your membership forms, your demographic forms. People fill out these forms and nobody looks at them. You know virtually nothing about your people. Most of the people won't volunteer for a committee; they're too busy. And they know, if you do volunteer for a committee, you're going to be made the chairperson immediately. And it's a life sentence—you'll never get off the committee. So, people don't do it."

Here's the point. You've got to personally connect with the people. You've got to hear their stories, find out their passions and talents, figure out what they could bring to the community. This is how you begin to build relationships. Yes, the welcoming piece is important—the greeters, the name tags. But the real goal is to create relationships. So, what's your response to some of these ideas that I wrote about in the book?

BRETT: You make a lot of really practical suggestions that are very helpful. One of the things I appreciate is your point about signage, or the lack of signage, in synagogue buildings. I remember the first time I walked into one LA synagogue, I had no idea where I was going. I wandered into an independent minyan and Rabbi Dorff saw me walking around, and because he's Rabbi Dorff, he essentially took me by the hand up to the main sanctuary and then sat with me for the rest of the service. So, he was really modeling "welcoming." Honestly, that was one of the reasons why I chose Ziegler for rabbinical school—because he did that. It was such an act of *chesed* on his part; I really did feel welcome. When I was making my decision, I kept thinking about that experience with Rabbi Dorff. It really did leave a big impression on me.

RON: Great. You might remember the example about the Barnes and Noble bookstore. You used to ask a clerk if they had a certain book, they would look it up on a computer, and send you to the third floor, aisle six. Yeah, we've got the book somewhere; good luck finding it. Then, they listened to their customers and now they *take you* to the third floor, aisle six, find the book, and hand it to you—a completely different level of service.

I don't worry about the regulars, the people who show up at services all the time. I worry about the guests of the Bat Mitzvah, the shul shoppers, the spiritual seekers who come to a synagogue for the first time. They don't know which book to pick up. And rabbis are not calling pages every two minutes. So, they're completely lost. When you see somebody like that, hand them your siddur [prayer book] and point out where you are in the service. It's a fantastic gesture that people will never forget.

And what about people who are asked to have an honor and they probably thought they were meant to open the ark, but, no, they are asked to chant the blessings and they have absolutely no idea what to do. You feel terrible. You start shaking. There are two hundred people staring at you. Try to remember your own first-time experience of having an *aliyah*, maybe as a kid. Even then, it's nerve-wracking. It reminds me of another one of my favorite true stories. I was scholar-in-residence at a big Conservative shul on a Shabbos morning with a huge crowd there for a Bar Mitzvah. It's Torah reading time. There's a *gabbai*, a guy who is orchestrating the reading, and a *shammes*, a guy rounding up all the members of the family who will have honors. I'm sitting on the bimah; I haven't given my talk yet. I look down at the front row of the sanctuary where all the people about to come up on the bimah are sitting. They all look nervous. Every single one of them, especially Number Five.

Number Five is wearing a gorgeous hand-tailored suit. Later, I learned he's the most powerful attorney in town. He's holding a little card, looking at it like his life depended on it. You know what was on the card? The *b'rachot*, the blessings he's about to recite in front of this big crowd. This guy probably hadn't been in a synagogue since his own Bar Mitzvah, if he had one. This guy probably wouldn't know a Torah from a hora. This guy is used to being in control, used to knowing what's going on, but now, he is totally out of his element. The readings start, and soon he's sitting in the on-deck circle, on the side of the bimah. Number Four is up and he's next. I look over at him and he is *shvitzing* ... buckets of sweat. Now, the *gabbai* realizes that many of these family members are uncomfortable up there; they don't know what to do. So, he's whispering stage instructions under his breath to people as they come up: "Stand here, go there." And he thinks no one can hear him, but unlike most synagogues in North America, this one had a very, very good sound system. So, all of his whispers are being caught by the mics. Everybody could hear everything he said. It's now Number Five's turn, and I swear, this is exactly what happened. He walks up to the Torah reading table, the *gabbai* looks at him and whispers the following instruction: "Grab your *tallis* ... and kiss your *tzitzis*!" Well, this man turned white. All the blood rushed out of his face. I thought he was going to faint. He was so shocked, he turned to the *gabbai* and whispered back, thinking no one could hear, but of course with the good sound system, everyone heard what he said. He whispers back to the *gabbai*, "Kiss my *what?!!*"

BRETT (laughing)**:** You've gotta be kidding me!

RON: Absolutely not. It was the most embarrassing thing I think this man could ever have experienced. You think he'll be back in the synagogue anytime soon? There were probably greeters at that shul, maybe ushers. But, oh, my, God. We have so much work to do in creating a truly welcoming experience.

SARA: Can you say something more about the things we can do to be more welcoming?

RON: Well, let's go back to the name tag issue. Even that gets goofed up. There's an art to name tags. First names should be in huge letters, right? And your surname, if at all, should be in smaller letters.

SARA: Could we add something else about yourself?

RON: You're right, Sara. If you want the name tag to help foster relationship building, you might put down the city you were born in. When we meet with my coauthors of *The Relational Judaism Handbook*, they'll show us how they've developed a way to use sentence stems to stimulate discussion among strangers. Lydia Medwin has preprinted name tags with a prompt like "I'm here to celebrate . . ." or "I'm here remembering. . . ." So, I meet Sara and her name tag says "Sara" and underneath her name "I'm here to celebrate . . . my mother's birthday." It's something to talk about in what I call "relational moments." Turns out, there's even a proper place to wear a name tag—on the right of the body underneath the collar bone. Why? Because when you go to shake someone's hand—I hope we can do that again soon—your eye goes there. I once did a workshop with three hundred people in a room who had put on one of those sticky name tags. As soon as I made this point, the entire room exploded with ripping sounds—people were tearing their name tags off and moving them onto their right shoulder. It was hilarious.

Okay. What else did you learn from the chapter?

BRETT: I really like the idea that everyone has a responsibility to be a greeter. It's not just up to the greeter or the rabbi and the cantor. To really change the culture of a synagogue, you need to educate the entire community about this kind of community that everyone wants to create.

RON: Okay, great. Now, what's the biggest challenge of doing that? Let's say you're the rabbi in some organization, whether it's a synagogue or a Hillel or a JCC. Your biggest challenge as the leader is to *educate the people* to do this welcoming. There are people who say to me, "Ron, I'm an introvert. I can't do this. I can't go up to a stranger comfortably." Okay, hey, we'll find something else for you to do in the synagogue community. But most people can learn the skills and take a few minutes to meet someone new. If you walk into most synagogues, what will you encounter?

BRETT: Even the best places can be intimidating. One LA-based synagogue I attend does a lot of nice things to be welcoming, but still, as a guest, you walk in and you encounter the people who go there every single week. There are maybe one hundred people sitting in the bleachers in the back, all talking to each other. It kind of feels like high school recess, or something, you know. I'm not a regular, so when I go, it's like, "Can I sit with you guys?" Clearly, there's an in-group. Or the same thing at the Library Minyan. There's a group that's been there forever. They've written a book about their group. You know, it's very established. But my experience is that there are people there who are very friendly. If you're in line together at the *Kiddush*, they will talk to you. I think it's just the dynamic of being a major synagogue with so many people in it.

RON: Sara, what do you think is the biggest challenge you see?

SARA: I feel like everybody's coming to synagogue for their own reasons. Maybe they don't *always* feel like being super welcoming, because they've had a long week and are there to recharge.

RON: Good point. People do come to synagogue for different reasons. Some are there to remember a loved one, some are there for the Bar Mitzvah. Some are just off the street, maybe looking for a place to meditate. Some don't want to be overwhelmed with friendly people. One of things we learned at the megachurch was *not* to make new people stand up and tell everybody about yourself. A number of synagogues think that's going to be a welcoming thing, but it's not.

SARA: Yeah, that's even more intimidating!

RON: Yes. So, at the megachurch, they've learned to let people be anonymous, if they want to be anonymous. There's a thin line between having people available to welcome you and overwhelming people. It's not a one-size-fits-all kind of prescription.

BRETT: I was very struck in the chapter when you're describing Saddleback Church. On a given Sunday, they'll have ten thousand people—five thousand in the first shift and five thousand in the second shift. How do these places get so massive?

RON: It was Rick Warren's birthday yesterday, so I sent him a note. He's an evangelical and you know, with evangelicals their number one priority is to establish a relationship with you and then lead you to accepting "J.C." and getting into their system. The only thing even close to them in our world is Chabad. I like to say Chabad are the "evangelical" Jews. Rick started with seven people in his living room. One of the books that I highly recommend to you is his book *The Purpose Driven Church*. It's on the syllabus for us to read. Please read it before we visit Saddleback, even virtually; you'll learn a ton. He is the most influential person in the congregational world and knows more about how to build a sacred community than anyone. All you need to do when you read the book is replace "Christian" with "Jewish" and nearly everything is applicable. Actually, the way he started the church was when God called him from Texas to Orange County, California, to an area called Lake Forest. He and his wife Kay and this group of seven decided to start the church to reach out to what he called the "unchurched." He literally went door-to-door, knocked on the door, and said, "Hi, I'm Rick Warren. Do you guys go to church?" If they said, "Yes," he said, "God bless you," and left. If they said, "No," he asked, "Why not?" Now, what do you think he heard? Why do you think people didn't go to church? What were the problems, the obstacles of going to church?

BRETT: They don't follow religion. They're secular.

RON: Okay, religion doesn't speak to me. In fact, religion doesn't say anything to me about my real life. All I hear is a lot of Bible stuff. You're not talking to me in your sermons. He heard that a lot. Okay, what else?

SARA: You don't know anyone?

RON: Right. I don't know anybody there. I don't want to be a stranger. Great. What else?

BRETT: It's the weekend. I don't want to do anything on the weekend. I sleep in on Sunday morning.

RON: And . . . I don't want to get dressed up, either. You have to go in a suit and tie. What else? "All you want is my money." And "I don't trust you with my children." Too many stories of priests molesting kids. "I'm not going to leave my kids with you." And "It's totally unwelcoming. I walk in, I'm a stranger, nobody says hello."

Now what did Rick do? The answer to your question, Brett, is he designed his church to do the exact opposite of those complaints. I wish we could do the site visit in person; it's incredible. The campus is one hundred acres. When we founded Synagogue 2000 back in 1994, my partner Larry Hoffman and I drove to the church for the first time. There were five thousand people backed up in traffic getting onto this property. I said, "Larry, we're going to be late." But then, we saw a big sign: *"First-time visitors: please move into the right-hand lane."* It was a carpool lane for first-time visitors! Now, Rick had taught his regulars that that was important, so he instructed them to park in the far parking lot. We get up to the Worship Center and the first fifty spaces are painted green: *"For First-Time Visitors."* Then, we got out of the car and there's a greeter to direct you to the right building. As we walked the path to transition from the secular space to the sacred space, there were more greeters along the way. *"Good morning!" "Welcome! Welcome to Saddleback."* At the entrance of the Worship Center, there was a greeter handing you an outline of the sermon that morning. Then, another greeter to help you find a seat. And then the most important thing of all, to circle back to the original question. Every single time in the twenty-five years I've taken a group to Saddleback Church, a group of rabbinical students wearing their kippot sitting in a row, every single time, the people behind us or in front of us or on the side of us would say, *"Welcome to Saddleback! Wonderful to see you!"*

Where does that come from? How does that happen? I'll tell you how. Because Rick had trained his new people in their "new member induction program" that the number one priority is to be evangelists, to create a relationship with people who are unchurched. To do that, you don't start by telling them about Jesus or telling them about the Bible or telling them how they should live their lives. You start by asking them, "Hey, how are you doing? Tell me about you." Not, "Let me tell you about our church." That's the exact opposite of what most synagogues do. Synagogues ply you with brochures and all kinds of ads and all kinds of things that tell you about them ... when the real job is *not* to speak, it's to *listen*. To hear someone's story. I tell synagogue leaders, "The central prayer of Judaism is *Sh'ma Yisrael*, "*Listen*, people of Israel," not *Dabeir Yisrael*, "Let me tell you about our shul!"

Rick did all sorts of other things. He recruited Disney Imagineers to design a great Sunday school facility. He offered great childcare, giving beepers to parents back in the early days so if the kid needed a parent, they were instantly contacted. Most of all, he developed sermons about how to live your life. Tips for finances, tips for personal relationships, tips for just about every part of your real life, all designed to help people navigate the most important, most meaningful, most purposeful things about living. He would often say to me, *"Ron, you gotta say something on Sunday that people can use on Monday."* His messages have a ton of biblical texts; Rick Warren is a great text teacher. So are you. You've been trained well. You know how to bring in commentaries, you pepper your *divrei Torah* [sermons] with what the rabbis through the centuries thought about the parashah [weekly Torah reading]. But *the real job is to change lives.*

Rabbi Harold Schulweis, may his memory always be a blessing, was my rabbi. We moved to the Valley in 1977, and we live four blocks up the street from the synagogue where he became one of the leading pulpit rabbis of our time. He used to make the same point as Rick Warren. Rabbi Schulweis would say the two most important words for a rabbi's sermon were *al kein*, "therefore." Eddie Feinstein probably taught you this in Homiletics—never finish a sermon without the "therefore," now what are we going to do? Now, how is this learning going to change your life? That's Rick Warren's secret of success, and it was Harold Schulweis's secret of success. You always walked away from their messages thinking, "Wow! I just learned something that I can use in my real life *now*."

The other thing about Saddleback is that everyone is on the lookout to be truly welcoming as the first step in building a relationship. The biggest problem in teaching your people how to be welcoming is this: they fall into default when they walk in the building, especially the "regulars," whose default is to talk to their friends. It is the best part of a sacred community—to have a group of friends. In this course, we'll talk a lot about how to build those groups of friends.

I remind you of my classic story of how I got kicked out of a seat. In a synagogue. Have you ever been kicked out of a seat in a shul?

BRETT: I don't think so.

SARA: No.

RON: Another true story of my adventures as a scholar-in-residence. I'm in Philadelphia, teaching in a huge Conservative synagogue. The rabbi emeritus was an old friend and on Friday night, he says, "Ron, you won't have to sit on the bimah tomorrow morning; you can sit with me." I loved that because I prefer to see the congregation from the pew, not the bimah. So I say, "Great. I'll look for you." Now when I'm a visitor, I'm a good soldier. The service began at nine o'clock; I'm there at ten minutes to nine. I sit down two rows from the back of the shul, on the aisle, so I can see the rabbi emeritus when he walks in and we can sit together. He's not there at nine o'clock. The service starts and we're fifteen minutes in when I feel this tap on my shoulder. I look up. It's a lovely elderly man. He says, "You know, I wouldn't tell you you're sitting in my seat," and he points to the empty seat right behind me in the last row. He says, "I would sit there. But, *if* I sat there, where would my friend who always sits there *sit*?" This was a sanctuary that sat 700 people, there were 685 empty seats, but this man needed that seat, his seat. And he needed to save the seat behind him for his friend who wasn't there yet. So, what do you think I did? I got out of there. Because I knew this man. I knew this was his *makom kavu'a*, his established place in the sanctuary. He had probably been sitting in that same seat for fifty years. I respect that. In fact, in many ways, he's right. If his friend is not sitting in his regular seat, what's he going to think? Maybe something happened to him. Maybe he's sick. I better check in on him. This is the best part of a sacred relationship in a community of sacred relationships. It really is. I knew all this. But

I'm thinking, if I were a guest of the Bar Mitzvah or a shul shopper and that happens to me, you're off my list. Done. There's nothing else that can happen that will bring me back to that place. I don't care how good the rabbi is. How good the music is. How good the davening is. I'm outta there!

BRETT: So, what did you do?

RON: I moved. I found another seat and eventually caught up with the rabbi emeritus. And you know what? The six people in the congregation who saw this happen went over to that man in the middle of services and berated him for what he did. You know why? *Because he kicked the scholar-in-residence out of his seat!* If I was some poor schlub off the street, no big deal.

When I tell this story to a group of synagogue leaders, I ask them the same question I will ask you: "What could that man have said to me that would have welcomed me to the shul . . . *and* gotten him his seat?"

BRETT: He could have just said, "Shabbat shalom, so happy you're here."

RON: Good, Brett! But I've asked dozens of synagogue leaders this question and not one of them gave that answer. I get, "Would you mind moving over?" I'm telling you, the regulars do not know how to handle such a situation. I shared this experience with the board of Valley Beth Shalom a few years ago, and one of the directors was a guy named Murray Geller. Murray and Rose Geller were two very active people at VBS. Murray hears me telling this story . . . and stops me. "Ron, I have to share this story with you. Everyone knows Rose and I always sit in the first two seats on the aisle in the fifth row of the sanctuary. We've been sitting there for forty-five years. And we're always among the first people at shul Shabbos morning. One week, we get there twenty minutes late. Sure enough, there's a couple sitting in our seats. So, we said, 'Shabbat shalom. Welcome to Valley Beth Shalom.' We knew they were strangers. And then we said, 'May we sit with you?' These people, the strangers, were so thrilled, they moved over two seats." So, I said to Murray, "That's incredible! You got your seats . . . and these people felt welcomed!" Murray says, "Right, right. Then it gets better, Ron. Because during the service, we started to schmooze, especially during the *hakafot*, the Torah parades. During the first *hakafah*, 'So where are you from?' 'We're visiting from Toronto.' 'Really? Oh, what brings you here? Are you here for the Bar Mitzvah this morning?' 'No, we just heard about Valley Beth Shalom and we thought, we're in Los Angeles, let's go to a synagogue.' During the second *hakafah*, we asked, 'Would you like to sit with us at the *Kiddush* lunch?' They loved that. So, we did. And from that first meeting, we've been friends with the Feldmans for twenty-five years. We've been to each other's kids' weddings. They're among our closest friends."

BRETT: Amazing!

RON: It gets better. Fast-forward a few years. I'm giving a workshop in Toronto. I tell this story. I ask the group, "Does anybody know the Feldmans?" From the back of the room come hands. "That's us!" I'm telling you, the people in that workshop will never forget that story, and neither will the board members at VBS. They'll know what to do next time it happens to them. It goes back to Sara's point: the "regulars" need to be taught to break out of their cliques for a few minutes every time they're in the shul. I learned this lesson at Disney University. The cast members of Disney are taught to spend five minutes during their shift to do something special for their guests. So, I tell synagogue leaders, "Spend five minutes at the *Oneg Shabbat*, go up to someone you don't know whether they're a member or not, it doesn't matter. Just walk up to someone you've never engaged with and say, 'Hey, good Shabbos, Shabbat shalom, I'm Ron. Let's chat for a few minutes.'" And you never know where it will go. But it will create the ambience of welcome that we're trying to get to.

Let's study the first eight lines of the parashah *Vayeira*. This text tells the whole story of welcoming. Let's spend ten minutes on this. I know you've learned it; the reason I want to do this is to teach you how I teach it, so you can teach it to your people. Okay, so who wants to read the first line?

BRETT:

וַיֵּרָ֤א אֵלָיו֙ יְהֹוָ֔ה בְּאֵלֹנֵ֖י מַמְרֵ֑א וְה֛וּא יֹשֵׁ֥ב פֶּֽתַח־הָאֹ֖הֶל כְּחֹ֥ם הַיּֽוֹם׃

The Lord appeared to him by the terebinths of Mamre; he was sitting at the entrance of the tent as the day grew hot.

RON: So, God appears to Abraham obviously here. Nobody knows what "terebinths" mean; you'll have to explain what that is. It's a bunch of trees, right? And Abraham's sitting at the entrance of his tent. The day grew hot. Great. Sara, do you want to read the next *pasuk* [sentence]?

SARA:

וַיִּשָּׂ֤א עֵינָיו֙ וַיַּ֔רְא וְהִנֵּה֙ שְׁלֹשָׁ֣ה אֲנָשִׁ֔ים נִצָּבִ֖ים עָלָ֑יו וַיַּ֗רְא וַיָּ֤רׇץ לִקְרָאתָם֙ מִפֶּ֣תַח הָאֹ֔הֶל וַיִּשְׁתַּ֖חוּ אָֽרְצָה׃

Looking up, he saw three men standing near him. As soon as he saw them, he ran from the entrance of the tent to greet them and, bowing to the ground,

וַיֹּאמַ֑ר אֲדֹנָ֗י אִם־נָ֨א מָצָ֤אתִי חֵן֙ בְּעֵינֶ֔יךָ אַל־נָ֥א תַעֲבֹ֖ר מֵעַ֥ל עַבְדֶּֽךָ׃

he said, "My lords, if it please you, do not go on past your servant."

RON: Okay, great. So now Abraham looks up. This is the very first important point. Strangers can't be seen unless I'm *seeing*, right? You've got to see these people, these strangers. You've got to be on the lookout for strangers. You've got to *look up*. If you don't look up, if you're only looking for your friends, you're not going to see the stranger. So, he looks up and he sees these "men" standing nearby. And then what does he do?

SARA: He says, "My lords, please, do not go on ..."

RON: Exactly! But wait, there's more! Look again at the text. What does he do when he sees them? What is the very first thing he does?

BRETT: He ran to greet them.

RON: Bingo. Right? He *ran* to greet them. Now, when I teach this text with a group—whether it's ten people, twelve people, or a hundred people—I break them up into *chavruta*, pairs. I invite them to meet someone in the room they do not know, introduce each other, and then read the text out loud. I'll say, "This room is going to be full of words of Torah. You're going to have ten minutes to read this text aloud and then to think with your partner about what the text teaches us about the art of welcoming, the spirituality of welcoming." The room explodes with energy; people love to study a text this way. Then, we debrief as a whole group. One of the things I ask is how many words in the text indicate "hurry." Here's the first: "he ran to greet them, *va-yaratz*." In *The Spirituality of Welcoming* book, I call this "a text in a hurry." Abraham looks up, he sees the strangers, and he runs to them. In fact, he greets them by bowing down, a sign of respect.

BRETT: He calls them *adonai*, "my lords."

RON: Yeah. He gives them honorifics. He treats them like "lords," but he has no idea who they are, right? They're just strangers. But he calls them "lords." Not "guest," not "interloper," not "stranger"—the kinds of things a lot of synagogue people will say about people they don't know who show up. And then, he offers an invitation: "Don't go past me. Stick around a while." Okay, Sara, do you want to read the next one?

SARA:

יֻקַּֽח־נָ֣א מְעַט־מַ֔יִם וְרַחֲצ֖וּ רַגְלֵיכֶ֑ם וְהִשָּׁעֲנ֖וּ תַּ֥חַת הָעֵֽץ׃

"Let a little water be brought; bathe your feet and recline under the tree."

RON: Okay, so what's that all about?

SARA: Get comfortable.

RON: Get comfortable. Exactly, right. Okay, Brett, take the next one.

BRETT:

וְאֶקְחָ֨ה פַת־לֶ֜חֶם וְסַעֲד֤וּ לִבְּכֶם֙ אַחַ֣ר תַּעֲבֹ֔רוּ כִּֽי־עַל־כֵּ֥ן עֲבַרְתֶּ֖ם עַֽל־עַבְדְּכֶ֑ם וַיֹּ֣אמְר֔וּ כֵּ֥ן תַּעֲשֶׂ֖ה כַּאֲשֶׁ֥ר דִּבַּֽרְתָּ׃

"And let me fetch a morsel of bread that you may refresh yourselves; then go on—seeing that you have come your servant's way." They replied, "Do as you have said."

RON: Okay, so what's happening?

BRETT: He's basically telling them the agenda of the afternoon.

RON: Yes, but what's the first thing he offers? First, sit down and bathe your feet, and then I'll get you some food to eat. And what's he going to get them?

BRETT: *Pat lechem*, "a morsel of bread."

RON: Right. That's important later on. "I'm going to give you a little piece of bread. Hey, you'll have a little bit to eat and then, you know, you'll go on." And they said, "Okay." Sara, you're up: "*Va-y'maheir . . .*"

SARA:

וַיְמַהֵר אַבְרָהָם הָאֹהֱלָה אֶל־שָׂרָה וַיֹּאמֶר מַהֲרִי שְׁלֹשׁ סְאִים קֶמַח סֹלֶת לוּשִׁי וַעֲשִׂי עֻגוֹת:

Abraham hastened into the tent to Sarah, and said, "Quick, three *seah*s of choice flour! Knead and make cakes!"

RON: Right. So, what's he do? How does he go into the tent? He *hurries* into the tent. And what's the first word he says to Sarah?

BRETT: "*Mahari.*"

RON: Yes! "Hurry up!" It's the same word. "Get the choice flour and make some cookies, some cakes." Okay, so now we've got the second and third example of the verb that indicates rushing, hurry. Okay, next.

BRETT: He delegated the responsibility.

RON: Yes. Well, we're gonna get to that in a second. All right. Sara, let's keep going . . .

SARA:

וְאֶל־הַבָּקָר רָץ אַבְרָהָם וַיִּקַּח בֶּן־בָּקָר רַךְ וָטוֹב וַיִּתֵּן אֶל־הַנַּעַר וַיְמַהֵר לַעֲשׂוֹת אֹתוֹ:

Then Abraham ran to the herd, took a calf, tender and choice, and gave it to a servant-boy, who hastened to prepare it.

RON: So, Abraham *ran*. Here we go again ... the Hebrew is *ratz*, "run." That's the fourth verb in the text indicating hurry. Right? And he gets what kind of calf?

SARA: Choice. Choice calf.

RON: He's getting USDA choice, man! He promised a morsel of bread, but he's serving prime rib. In the quality service literature, this is called "under promising and over delivering." He's getting them a prime rib! What does he do with it?

BRETT: He gives it to the lad.

RON: And he says what to him?

BRETT: "Hurry up!"

RON: There's the fifth verb: "hurry up ... go cook it." Now, he's got the servant boy involved. He's got Sarah involved ... he's got a team to welcome the strangers. It's not just him. Okay, Brett, bring us home ...

BRETT:

וַיִּקַּח חֶמְאָה וְחָלָב וּבֶן־הַבָּקָר אֲשֶׁר עָשָׂה וַיִּתֵּן לִפְנֵיהֶם וְהוּא־עֹמֵד עֲלֵיהֶם תַּחַת הָעֵץ וַיֹּאכֵלוּ:

He took curds and milk and the calf that had been prepared and set these before them; and he waited on them under the tree as they ate.

RON: What?! They're eating milk with meat?! The first thing people in a synagogue group will ask is, "Wait a minute, it's not kosher?!" So, you have to explain this as biblical, not Rabbinic.

BRETT: Right. Right!

RON: So, Abraham takes the food that has been prepared by the team, gives it to them, he waits on them ... under the tree as they ate. So, what's the meta message in this text?

SARA: We've got five verbs that indicate running, hurry.

RON: So, the meta message here is "You can't sit and wait for people to come to you. When you see strangers, you've got to get up and run to them." This is a very powerful, powerful message of hospitality. This is how you do hospitality—*hachnasat orchim*. This is how you do welcoming. And you tell your leaders who want to create sacred community, "Take these lessons and apply them to your own community." They'll think they're done with this . . . but wait! There's more! Then, you ask, "Does anybody know what's going on with Abraham? Before this incident? What's going on with Abraham?"

BRETT: He was just circumcised.

RON: I accept that answer. But let me emphasize that he was not *just* circumcised. He just circumcised *himself*! At the age of ninety-nine! At this point when I do this teaching, I turn to the group and I joke, "Can I talk to the men in the room for a minute? I'm ninety-nine years old, I just circumcised myself. I'm sitting in the entrance of my tent in the heat of the day, three strangers walk by, it's the day after this self-surgery, and I'm going to run to greet them??? I don't think so." Everyone laughs. And then I'll bring home the lesson: "I think this is intentional, to indicate that even in his illness, even though he is suffering from this surgery, he *runs* to greet strangers." And, then comes the final point, a transformative point. I ask it as a question: "Does Abraham have any idea who these three strangers are?" Absolutely not. He has no idea who they are until later in the parashah. He has no clue they are angels from God to tell him and Sarah they will finally have a child. And, you never know who's walking into your community! You don't know if they're Jewish, they're not Jewish; they're rich, they're poor; they're gay, they're straight. And, moreover, it shouldn't matter.

When you study the Rashi and other commentators on this text, you realize that this concept of hospitality is right at the top of the list of Jewish values. They wonder, "What was Abraham doing in the entrance of his tent in the heat of the day?" Rashi says Abraham was studying. Study is the way we hear God's voice. Another commentator says Abraham was praying. Praying is the way we talk to God. Either way, Abraham is in a relationship with God, three strangers walk by, and what does Abraham do? He says, "Excuse me, God. Gotta run to greet these guys!" He interrupts his praying, his studying, to welcome the stranger. You don't get a much more important directive than that to teach the synagogue "regulars" who only pay attention to the friends they already know, to encourage them to spend those few minutes creating an ambience of welcome in the congregation.

Now comes the most important value I can share with you that I've taught in my whole teaching career. Two words: *b'tzelem Elohim*. The most important words in the Torah. The idea that every human being is shaped in the image of God. People will say to me, "Ron, I don't believe in God." And I'll ask them to describe what they think God is. I'll often get a Sunday school version of God—an old man with a long white beard sitting on a throne in heaven. That's not my idea of God. My concept of God comes from two great teachers, Harold Schulweis and Martin Buber. Schulweis taught that God is a verb, not a noun. It's about "godliness." We are shaped "in the image of God" means that there's a spark of divinity in each one of us. So, don't look for God in the heavens. Look for God right here, in the "between." Between you and me. Between each other. That's Buber. Or, as Brad Artson puts it, "the God of relationship."

The key to understanding how to motivate people to do this welcoming work, to do the work of creating a sacred Jewish community, is to teach your people to engage each person as a human being made in the image of God, who has the spark of godliness in them. And our job as educators, as rabbis, is to ignite that spark, to get them to understand that they have God-given talents and passions and spiritual gifts to bring to the work of building a sacred community. Now, we're a world apart from "here's a list of committees to volunteer for."

BRETT: But, Ron, isn't it difficult to get these synagogue leaders to change?

RON: Yes, but it's not impossible. I often joke to a synagogue group, "You know the saying above the *aron kodesh*, the holy ark? In many synagogues, it says, *Da lifnei mi atah omeid*, "Know before whom you stand," meaning God. I think instead it should say, "But, we've always done it that way!" Larry Hoffman and I started Synagogue 2000 in 1994, and when the millennium came, we changed to "Synagogue 3000." We gained a thousand years!

We once had Ron Heifetz from Harvard come to one of our conferences to talk about the difference between adaptive and transformative change. It's not easy to do transformative change, unless you are starting a culture from scratch. Most rabbis are walking into an existing culture—much more challenging. But I'm here to tell you that with the right leadership, with the right approach, with the right organizational understanding of the organization, getting everybody on the same page, it's possible.

That's why in our project, we invited teams that had to include the senior rabbi, the cantor, the president of the synagogue, and some laypeople. This team of ten to fifteen people met regularly, once a month for three years, studying a graduate-level curriculum to think about how we do welcoming, how prayer and ritual works, and how to change the culture. We worked with more than a hundred congregations of all kinds in all parts of the country. I can't claim all of them changed. Honestly, some gave lip service to the idea, but once they realized what we were really trying to do, they stonewalled it at every turn. There's something in the work of institutional transformation called "readiness." A community must be ready to make changes. Sometimes it happens because of leadership—a rabbi is able to lay out a path that's worth investing in. Sometimes it's when people are in crisis. I often get calls from synagogues that are in crisis—"We've lost half of our membership" . . . and they wonder what went wrong. By that time, it's often too late to recover. This work of transformation, of welcoming, of what I've called Relational Judaism, has to begin at the very moment of engaging new people.

The twentieth-century model of engagement was programmatic and transactional. "Come to our programs . . . our big calendar of programs. We've got programs for everybody—families, kids, seniors." People would come to the programs and enjoy the programs, and then walk away never meeting anybody. And the relationship between the members and the synagogue is transactional. "I'm going to pay your dues, and you give me a rabbi on call, seats for the High Holy Days, a Bar Mitzvah for my kid, and as soon as I don't need you anymore, it's like the gym, I am done. I don't need you." And boy, if you don't think we've got a challenge now when I can go online and experience Central Synagogue or Park Avenue Synagogue or Romemu or Lab/Shul or IKAR for free? What's the value proposition for belonging to this local synagogue community? It has to be a sacred community. A community of relationships that will lead you to a path of meaning—what's it all about this life I'm leading?; <u>purpose</u>—what did God put me on earth to do with my talents and spiritual gifts?; <u>belonging</u>—a group of friends who will be there for me in good times and difficult times, like we're all experiencing with this pandemic; and a place to celebrate the many blessings in my life.

I hope we're going to meet Rick Warren. I've invited him to join us. Rick wrote the best-selling book in the English language next to the Bible. Can you imagine that? *The Purpose Driven Life*. He wrote it as a forty-day curriculum for churches. Every January, Rick launches a campaign to bring new people into the church through small-group study. The subtitle of his book for this campaign is so fabulous: *What on Earth Am I Here For?* Do you know what the first line in the book is? It's the complete opposite of American individualism. It's so shocking ... because he knows his audience—mostly Republican Orange County people who want nothing to do with church. The first line in *The Purpose Driven Life* is "It's not about you."

BRETT: Wow!

RON: Right, wow! And then in forty days of devotionals, you will explore every aspect of your life. You will discover your purpose. You know what your purpose is? It's the same as ours: to do the work God needs doing on earth. We do that in our church—that's his message. I once said to Rick I wanted to write a Jewish answer to his great question "What on earth am I here for?" So, I did. It's called *God's To-Do List: 101 Ways to*

Be an Angel and Do God's Work on Earth. It didn't sell as many copies as Rick's book, but of all my books, it is the most popular. Think of the difference between the invitation to join a sacred community to get your kid a Bar Mitzvah versus "You join our community, your life will be significantly transformed. You will find meaning, purpose, belonging, and blessing."

In this seminar, we'll meet some sacred community shapers who are unafraid to say this to the people they are hoping to engage. They are brave, courageous, and successful. So that's our challenge, Sara and Brett. This is the first step—welcoming. The next step is worship. And Josh Warshawsky will share with us what he's learned about how to engage people in prayer, particularly the people who are not regulars. My goal with you is to not think about the 20 percent of people who are already in the system, the people who already love synagogues. We've got to think about the 80 percent. How can we reach them? That's our task in this seminar. I love you. See you next week!

Questions for Creating Your Sacred Community

1. Have you ever felt unwelcomed in a synagogue?
2. What is your congregation currently doing to welcome the stranger?
3. How do you recruit volunteers?
4. Does your membership demographic form enable people to list their talents, hobbies, passions?
5. How do you learn about your members?

CHAPTER 3

Welcoming Worship

Rabbi Josh Warshawsky

Rabbi Josh Warshawsky is a pray-er, gatherer, music creator, and lifelong meaning seeker. He is a nationally touring Jewish musician, songleader, composer, and teacher of Torah. Josh seeks to build intentional praying communities, traveling to synagogues and Jewish communities across the country sharing his music and teachings on prayer. Josh was ordained as a rabbi in May 2019 by the Ziegler School of Rabbinic Studies in Los Angeles. He is on the faculty of Songleader Boot Camp and leads the Ramah Shabbaton and the Ramah Chavurah.

SARA: I want to say I'm noticing that we're all either artists or engaged in art, because I'm a writer, and Dr. Wolfson is a writer, Josh is a musician, and Brett is in writing and film. I'm sure we all have other interests as well, but I just feel like that's very unusual in rabbinical school that all four of us have those connections.

BRETT: I feel like that's the direction it needs to go; this is what people are looking for, right? They're looking for more avenues into Judaism. And there's so much more to create using what we have always had.

JOSH: And there's a way to take what we've always had and lift it up. What I do is I try to lift up the words of the siddur with new melodies to find new ways to understand them. So that's sort of what I'm thinking about all the time and trying to find ways to create spaces of worship that are really welcoming. And, Ron, you should know, I talk about Saddleback all the time. It was a really transformative experience for me that we showed up. We were immediately welcomed by the second pastor, who really wanted to talk to us. Ron introduced us to them and said, "Hey, you know, Josh is a musician." They said, "Oh, why don't we bring you backstage to come meet the worship band?" And I went backstage and met the band right before the service. And then we went in, but just the idea of opening up so that they weren't hiding back there, and even so the pastor was like, "You know what, we're going to bring you back, so we'll get you to meet them. We'll stay in touch." And the idea of just being open and opening up your spaces in a ton of different ways, I think is really powerful.

I was trying to think about moments in time when I had felt a worship space or a space was either really, really welcoming or really unwelcoming. I'm wondering if there's anything that really comes to mind right away, like a moment when you entered a prayer space or something like a prayer space and either felt immediately welcomed or felt immediately turned off?

SARA: Whenever I walk into CVS, they play the worst music, and it really makes me want to get out of there. But when I go to a service or store where there's good music, then I want to stay and I feel happy.

JOSH: So it's not like somebody coming up to you saying, "Hey, we're so glad you're here." But in some ways, the music and the intentionality draws you in, right? It makes you feel like you want to stay, like you feel at home. Awesome. Okay. And I love the idea that a lot of it is personal preference, right? You don't hang out in the CVS because you don't like the way that the music sounds. Any other memories?

BRETT: When I think about welcoming spaces, I think of a place like Nava Tehila in Jerusalem, where you walk in, and there's already a sacred atmosphere established because of all the music and people are up and dancing, and they're sitting in the round where the energy is so focused on the material. People are not watching the door for when people walk in, as opposed to some other spaces that do that model where I feel like every time I walk in the door, one hundred people are staring at me, and that's always a kind of shock to the system, feeling like now we need to be serious, walk to your seat, don't say hi to too many people, take your place. It's that "The service has already begun and you're late" feeling.

RON: I'll give you one that was a terrible turnoff. I actually happened to be visiting Omaha, my hometown, for Rosh Hashanah one year. I was in the overflow service in the social hall. And there were six doors into the social hall, and each door had a sign on it that said "Do Not Enter—Service in Progress." Yeah, that's a pretty clear messaging right there.

JOSH: I want to go back to what Brett said about sitting in the round. There are some really great things about a circle when everybody can see each other, and also the circle could be dangerous because some people are looking at the door and it could pull the energy away. So in being intentional in the way that you set up the space, the people of Nava Tehila plan on making sure that the energy is always focused in the center of the circle. They're never looking out at the sides. And the way that they've set up the room, even though it's in a circle, the center of the action is the part of the circle that's facing away from the door. There's a synagogue here in Los Angles that I think is an amazing space. They have their amazing setup where everybody's close by. But the ark is in the same direction as the door, right? So, when you're looking at the ark, and you're all sitting in the space, you can see everybody walking into the space. And I loved going there, and sometimes I would get there and the only open seats were the ones where I could see the door. And then every time I would look up, there were new people coming in. It was so nice to see everyone, which was always really wonderful because the social part is another really special part of the shul. But the place where I liked to sit was right when you walk in facing away from the door because I didn't want to be distracted. I want to make sure that I have my energy focused in the center of the space. But if you're setting up a space intentionally, you can make it so nobody's looking toward the door. And then you also don't get that awkwardness that Brett mentioned of being the one entering late who everyone stares at.

SARA: I love the idea that there's a way to set up the space.

JOSH: Yeah, I love that. I was also going to say a memory from my time in Israel when I was there for the year in rabbinical school. I would wander on Friday nights to various different *tisches* [tables] in Me'a She'arim. And those spaces are already unwelcoming to anyone who's not a man, so that sort of cuts off half the population already. But I was looking for a particular yeshiva called the Belz Yeshiva. They're very musical Hasidim, and their space looks basically like what the Third Temple would look like if it were to be rebuilt. It's just like this giant fortress and you walk in. It's very unclear how you get to the space where the *tisch* happens. But suddenly, I somehow found the back door to the basement, and then you walk all the way down the stairs and you're in this sort of dungeon. And then you open up a door suddenly, and you're in this giant Grand Hall underground that looks like it's a huge social hall with bleachers all around the space and giant tables in the middle. And everybody's sort of schmoozing and wandering around. And they're not looking to welcome anyone. No one said anything to me. And I felt totally out of place. I was totally underdressed, because I wasn't wearing the robe with the stripes. I was totally lost. And then at some point, the rebbe walks in, and everybody like makes a mad dash for the bleachers. But I didn't know the rules of the game. I didn't know that was what we were supposed to do. I was lost because I didn't know the etiquette, and I didn't have the right clothes. But then suddenly, everyone just started singing. And it was a melody that I didn't know and was very unfamiliar, and it was very complicated. But they sang it over and over again. And because of that—we were a thousand men in the room singing this very complicated tune and no one is singing any harmonies, everyone's just got the exact same part—you could sort of feel the energy of the melody hovering in the space, because there were just so many pieces. But I was caught up in it. I had been feeling so out of place and so lost, and then suddenly, it was like one of the most powerful prayer experiences that I've ever had, because I just got caught up in singing this melody. And I was trying to think: how did all these people learn this melody? Nobody taught it to them, right? They don't have music classes in their Hasidic yeshiva. They show up every Friday night from when they're little kids until they get to move a little bit closer in the bleachers. It was very clear that this section was the young boys and this was the Bar Mitzvah boys, and the closer you got to the rebbe, the more beards there were. They learned just by sitting in that space and then having it seep into their veins. I tried to think about how I could take that idea back to communities that share my value system, which is very hard because we can't tell people, "Hey, just come every week. And if you come, it's going to seep into you and you're going to love it, I promise." That just doesn't work for people anymore. And so, we have to find ways to prepare people and welcome them into the space before they arrive and before they even know that they want to come to the space, right? The more we can do that in preparation for the event before it happens, the more impactful the experience could be overall.

BRETT: As a rabbi who travels from congregation to congregation, you obviously don't have that consistent experience of seeping your melodies into the people's veins, because you're always moving. And I'm wondering, is that something that you feel is missing? Do you have some sort of way of filling that void for yourself? Because it's a really beautiful idea of having these melodies seep in, so how are you going about doing that?

JOSH: It's a great question. In my last year of rabbinical school, I asked Rabbi Artson if I could travel to different communities all over as my internship and he said, "Sure, as long as you have a rabbinic mentor here in Los Angeles." So, I started working with Rabbi Shawn Fields-Meyer, and she helped me come up with a language for talking about process-oriented versus product-oriented visits. The product was like, "Oh, you're Josh Warshawsky, come on in and just share your stuff." And the process ones were like, "How can we make sure that the melodies that you're bringing and the ideologies that you're sharing are going to stick with us when you're gone?" And sometimes those were the ones where I was going to a synagogue four times over the course of the year. But we can even find a way where if I was going once, we would prepare the community and share some of the melodies in a class I would do beforehand. I created all these videos so that these people could experience what that music was like. You know, I was trying to always find ways for the music to continue even though I wasn't going to be staying in these communities, so it continued to seep into people even beyond when I was gone.

I'm traveling all the time and almost everywhere I go, maybe they've heard one of my melodies or two, but most things are new. And there's a really powerful spark and elation in getting to share it, like it's new every single time, right? Because you get to see the spark on people's faces and how exciting it is when you open them up to this text in a totally different way. But on the other hand, it'd be nice to go deeper every time. If we're always staying on this level of opening people up and introducing it to people, when are we going to go to the next stage? The idea was to always have a place I wasn't traveling to every weekend, it was mostly like two or three weekends a month. So that one weekend a month, I would have a place that felt like my home community where I wasn't necessarily the one who was leading. But at least half of the synagogues that I've gone to this year are synagogues that I've been to before. I'm trying very intentionally to create relationships. You know, a lot of it has to do with what we talked about in Ron's class. I don't want to go somewhere and then leave and have the music not carry on and the relationships not carry on. Because what's going to make people want to come back and what's going to make the music really seep in and open people up is if we're able to continue the conversation. It's a slow process, but it's nice to be able to return and have another experience again with the same people.

RON: I want to underline the point about the accessibility of the melody. In your story, Josh, you said that the niggun was complicated. I think that melodies that are easily accessible—and we all know what they are: Top 40s, Broadway tunes—are hits right away. There are Josh Warshawsky melodies that the minute you hear it, you say, "Wow, that is a beautiful melody. That moves me, I want to learn that." And then you've got motivation, because it's easy to sing. It's fun to sing. It moves you. And what's interesting about this point you made that people don't come every week, the challenge that Josh and other songleaders and *hazzanim* [cantors] and rabbis and educators have is we don't get much of a shot at people to give them complicated melodies to learn right away. It's not gonna work if it flops. I can tell you a quick story about a synagogue that I can't tell you the name of. The cantor hired a band. He wrote his own melodies that were uber complicated, and he had three female singers singing with him. There was such a buzz in the community about this, and I was the scholar-in-residence that weekend. There were about five hundred people in the sanctuary, waiting for this big, powerful spiritual experience. Nobody could sing the music. The cantor's register was in the high tenor range. It was a disaster. All this energy that was in the room when they started *Kabbalat Shabbat* was dead by ten minutes in because no one could follow the music. No one could sing along with them. It turned into a terrible concert. This is really important stuff, what Josh is talking about.

JOSH: Yeah, absolutely. I think most of my melodies are on the more complicated end of the spectrum, but I would never start with one of those unless I felt like the community was really ready for something like that. It's all about what the intention behind it is and what's our intended goal. Sometimes the goal is to learn something great and feel really great afterwards because you've come out of this experience and you've learned something complicated.

I brought a couple different texts and things that I've been thinking about lately on how to craft space. This is one of my favorite texts from the Talmud on prayer from *Masechet B'rachot*. There are pages and pages and pages of conversation about when we're supposed to pray and why we're supposed to pray and what time we're supposed to pray and what we're supposed to be able to see at that time. And then somewhere in the middle, we get this really intense phrase from Rabbi Elazar. He says, "Anyone whose prayer is fixed, their prayer is not supplication." And so then there's this argument going on about what is fixed prayer.

So, we get three powerful examples about what fixed prayer could be. It says: Rabbi Yaakov bar Idi said that Rabbi Shaya said, "It means anyone for whom their prayer is like a burden on them." It's something that you don't want to do. If they're not feeling it, if it's a burden on them, then it's better not to do it than to have it be something that's a burden on you. Okay, opinion number two, the Rabbis say this refers to anyone who does not recite prayer in the language of supplication. What do we think that means, the language of supplication?

BRETT: Well, in this case it might mean *lashon kodesh*, Hebrew.

JOSH: Okay, so right, maybe it means we have to say it in Hebrew. The prayer's got to be said in Hebrew. If you don't say it in Hebrew, it doesn't work. Any other idea? What else could supplication be?

SARA: I think it's just like language of praise in general.

JOSH: Okay, right. We want it to feel like it has to be exclamatory. With that sort of language, I think that's another possibility that it has to be said with the right emotion. Concerning the language of prayers, how can we make sure that we understand what it is that we're saying? Because if you can't get into what the feel of the prayer is, maybe it's better to just wait until you're feeling it. Perhaps that's option number two. And then option number three, Rabbi and Rav Yosef both said it refers to anyone unable to introduce a novel element. I think that's the answer here. Every time you approach the prayer book, it's the same every single time, the words are always the same. They're right there, they've been the same for hundreds of years in the exact same order. We have to find one way that that moment can be novel and can be new and meaningful. Maybe that's a new melody. Maybe that's something new that you see in the text, maybe that's learning about a different way to understand one of the words, maybe that's even just you, right, you come into this text today, as opposed to coming to it yesterday, you have more experiences in your internal memory bank than you had yesterday. The way that you approach it, hopefully, it will be different today than it was yesterday, but only if we can set an intention for that to be the case.

For me, that's what I try to think about whenever I'm crafting worship. How can there be at least one moment in this experience that feels different from the way you've done it before? What's one new thing that we can do? And so that's sort of what guides me whenever I'm crafting a prayer experience. The idea is not to have tons of new things, right? If there's too much new, then it's also not going to be good for people because then it will feel like a burden or people won't be able to get into the language, right? *We want to be able to have a balance of what feels new and what feels like this is something that we can really jump into and be motivated by.* The way in which I do that usually is I think about a lot of different questions. These are the main questions that I like to think about in crafting space for work. This one I created for Camp Ramah. But also, the questions, I think, apply all the time.

The who: who are we gathering? And I think this goes for worship, but it also really goes for creating sacred space period. Who's coming into the space? Where are they coming from? What's their background? Do they have experience with this Hebrew? Do they have experience with these kinds of texts? What are we? Is it with the same group all the time? Can we delve deeper every time because we have the same ten students coming every week, or is it something that when there are new people, we have to incorporate that into it? Also, when's it happening? What time of day? Where are they coming from beforehand? If they were in day school, or they were in elementary school all day long, and now it's a Wednesday afternoon, and they have to come to Hebrew school, you're going to think about crafting that experience differently than if it's a Sunday morning. Where is it happening? What does the space look like? Are we inside? Are we outside? How's it set up? Why? What are our goals? Are we trying to accomplish the same goals every time? And then, what are we trying to say? What mediums are we using? We were talking about creative writing; we were talking about the technology and movies and music. What are we using? What is the medium that's getting this experience across?

I spent a lot of time preparing over the last couple of weeks for Songleader Boot Camp, which is this conference that Ron and I both taught at a bunch of times. We're doing it virtually right now, and my friend who's another amazing Jewish musician, Billy Jonas, came up with a whole document on thinking about the ways in which we set up a space using a bunch of different food metaphors. The more you can be intentional about setting up the space, the more welcoming the space can be for anybody who's going to walk into it. There are a whole bunch of different ways you could set up your space. If it's like a matzah, it's a square. If it's a bagel, you have concentric circles. A jelly doughnut is like everyone's smooshed together, like the jelly inside the donut. The hamantaschen is my personal favorite with mostly younger people, because the hamantaschen is basically you putting yourself in the corner of the room and put everybody right in front of you facing you in the corner of the room. Let's say you're in a giant social hall and there's a lot of programs and things happening. Now the attention is just directed toward you in the corner, with no distractions around. And you could change any space to do something like that. I walk into a sanctuary and sometimes I'm not going to be leading from the bimah because that's not the best space to create an engaging experience. Maybe I'll take three steps off the bimah, or maybe I'll be in the third row because no one sits in the first three rows anyway. If I stand in the third row, I'm right next to the first row of people. Where am I going to be, and where are people going to be so that this experience is powerful and meaningful? Once you're done being intentional about the space, the next step is how can we convey to the community that something meaningful and powerful is happening?

BRETT: What is your thinking behind creating virtual spaces?

JOSH: This is something I'm thinking about all the time because right now we're gathering virtually. How are you going to do that in a way that feels really impactful for people? I think about the arc of our time together and the ways in which we enter this space. I know that whenever I'm entering a class that Ron's teaching, we're going to start the first fifteen minutes schmoozing. I don't need to think about how we're going to enter this space because we're going to be entering in a space that feels welcoming already. Usually, when I'm entering into a space that I'm leading, I'll post a question so people can type in the chat and let each other know that they're here while I'm playing a niggun. It sort of fulfills that schmoozing moment, but it doesn't feel awkward because they don't really know each other. A lot of times I think about how we can make sure that everyone sees each other. I like to do it like that instead of sharing my screen with a PowerPoint slide that says it, because if you do that people can't see each other. So I want to find a way so people can look at each other in gallery mode, but also be able to add on some of their own conversations.

Something else I'm thinking about a lot right now is the fact that we're in the same spaces all the time, right? We're here sitting in our homes, Zooming all the time, and it's just our regular *makom* [space] all the time. So how can we turn our *makom* into a *makom tefillah* [prayer space]? How can we turn the place where we are all the time into a place of prayer? Or the other way to say it is how can we turn our *makom* into a *mikdash* [sanctuary]? In other words, how do we turn this regular profane space into a holy space? If you were just looking at me right now, you would see this, which is just me with my green screen behind me, but I got a green screen because I wanted to make sure that people would feel like we're entering a holy space. This virtual background is one of my favorite places to pray. It's the sanctuary at Adas Israel in Washington, DC. When I was praying with Temple Beth Am for the High Holy Days, I put up their ark right behind me, because I wanted the people to feel like we were in their sacred space. So even if we're virtual, there are ways to make it personal. Zoom is a great platform, but it's just a platform. What are we going to put into it in order to make this space feel meaningful for people?

BRETT: You got me thinking about informal spaces at Camp Ramah in Wisconsin, and the one that was most energizing for me was Mishmar (celebration) on Thursday nights in the *sifriya* [library]. For the non-Wisconsin folk on this call, it was like the jelly donut model. I just remember being fourteen and going there for the first time voluntarily.

I forgot my kippah, of course, because I was a camper, and I remember sprinting back to my cabin, because I couldn't miss five seconds of being in that room. It was like this whole world opened up to me. And I'm wondering: I don't think it was about the jelly donut. I think it was about the charismatic personalities in the room, like Rabbi Josh Cahan, Aryeh Bernstein, those guys who were leading it. I'm just wondering if oftentimes, the way we set up the room also has to do with who we are and the kind of charisma, the kind of energy that we're working with.

JOSH: Absolutely, yeah. That's a huge part of it. I think in a similar way with Nava Tehila, they put their energetic, charismatic person in the middle, and even though you might be looking all over the space, you are riveted by what's happening in the center of the room because of the kind of charismatic leader that you have. And a lot of that has to do with the kind of preparation that they've done to cultivate that experience. Mishmar didn't come out of nothing, right? They spent a lot of time engaging with some of the campers to bring them in. And have you ever seen the first follower video? It's one of my mentor's favorite videos. There's a big festival outside and there's one crazy dude just dancing by himself. And there's this guy narrating it like it's a National Geographic video. But then another person comes over and starts dancing with him and mimicking his moves and doing the same thing. And then suddenly, that second guy calls over to his three friends and says, "Hey, you guys got to come over here and try this." And now suddenly, there are four people. And once you got four people, you got momentum. So then, like ten more people come, and then one hundred more people come. In some ways, Rabbi Josh Cahan or Aryeh Bernstein created that space and allowed it to be filled up but then made sure to bring along three or four of their closest students, who then brought their friends, who then brought their friends, and then the culture built around wanting to be there, because people were so excited about it. And that's, I think, a huge component of what it looks like to create sacred space: building a cohort of leaders, right? It can't just be one person. For my artist-in-residence weekends, when I'm in person, I come on a Thursday, because I want to meet with people in the community before Shabbat starts. And I say that anybody who's a worship leader, anybody who loves music, I want them all to come on Thursday night, because we're going to sing some of these melodies that we're going to use on Shabbat. Now we're going to sort of have our own practice service, so that we can get in the mindset of what this feels like. So tomorrow, when Shabbat comes, it's going to feel like the melodies are coming from the community as opposed to just from me, right? No matter how energetic or charismatic I am, if there aren't two or three people who already feel like they're into it, nobody else is going to get into it, because that's how humans act. But if I planted some people to be the first ones, and those people are very excited about it, that'll add to the energy.

RON: Yeah, just to underline a point here for all of us, it's not just charisma. Charisma is great, but a leader has to actually be davening. This is a big revelation. You know, in our work in Synagogue 2000, we saw so many cantors and rabbis who were performing the service but weren't davening the service. The first time I saw this was at B'nai Jeshurun where Roly Matalon and Ari Priven were davening, and it was so clear that they weren't there just as emcees, but they were actually davening, and that invited me into my own davening experience. Whether you're charismatic or not, you have got to be authentic. It's got to be a davening experience that you love and that you can lead, and not just be a page announcer.

SARA: I totally agree with everything you just said, Ron, but I feel like there's a spectrum where it's possible to have a rabbi or cantor daven too hard. Have you guys ever seen that, where it's actually distracting because it almost looks like they're performing to try to make themselves seem like they're so spiritually "in it"?

RON: Sometimes it's even good comedy! You want to have a prayer leader who leads you, but if that prayer leader is only thinking about their own experience or they can't recognize what's happening in the space around them, that's not going to help you. I think you're absolutely right that if you're a prayer leader, you have to mean what you say, right? But you also have to be aware that you are facilitating an experience more than having the experience yourself. You want to be into it, and you want to make sure that you're having the experience too so that you're authentic, but you're facilitating the experience for more people than just you. In fact, we had a cantor come up to us during the first Synagogue 2000 conference and he said that "none of this works." I said, "What do you mean?" He said, "We teach our congregants how to use the word 'watermelon.' We just teach 'watermelon, watermelon, watermelon, watermelon.' We'll be doing the *Amidah*, and if you don't know the words, just say, 'Watermelon watermelon.'"

JOSH: Heschel has this amazing quote about being a text person. We need to learn more from text people than we need to learn from textbooks. And I think that's the kind of leader that you're talking about here, right? It's somebody who means what they say. That's the kind of experience that we want to see. I grew up at a synagogue that didn't have a cantor, so there was a rotation of people who would lead the service. I got to see tons of different examples of people who really cared about this, who were sharing their melodies and sharing themselves. And so that was the reason that I wanted to get up on the bimah, because I saw so many amazing examples of people on the bimah. I knew that it wasn't just one person. I knew that I could get up there too.

BRETT: I am somebody who believes very strongly in the divine and divine presence. But I think I feel the way a lot of other Jews feel in terms of accessing the prayer service. I like praying, but the whole idea of the performative aspect I don't like at all. I don't want to put on a show. And I'm not saying that's what it is, but I'm just saying that's my fear. But there's a great opportunity that you actually do have with being a pulpit rabbi of holding that presence for other people, which means you have the power to bring God into people's lives. That's an enormous responsibility. And if you're successful at it, what higher thing is there to do for a person? I feel like it's time to stop being afraid of the synagogue.

JOSH: That's super important. I think what you're saying also is that people don't know that they're coming to the synagogue to experience a relationship with the divine, because they're coming to be with each other or they're coming to have a moment for themselves. But that's another really powerful thing that happens. It can happen anywhere, but it can also be facilitated in the moment of prayer, if you have a facilitator who can help you with that. And a rabbi's role is essential to what we're trying to do in creating moments of holiness for people to connect with something that's bigger than just themselves.

I was studying this amazing midrash last week about *Parashat Beshalach*, thinking about Shabbat Shirah. Last Shabbat was where we crossed the sea. What was the first thing that the people of Israel did as a free people? They sang. There was this powerful moment, this transcendent moment, and they didn't know what else to do, and Miriam led them in songs. Rashi says that she had belief, she had true *emunah* [faith], and that's why she brought her timbrel with her. Everybody was leaving Egypt. They didn't have time to take anything with them, and still she brought her tambourine because she knew that they were going to need to sing at some point really soon in the future, when they were going to need to bring the people together. The midrash says that when Israel was crossing the sea, the angels came to sing songs before God, but God said, "You can't sing now, angels, because the people of Israel need to sing first." And so the rabbi says, "Why do the people of Israel need to sing first?" And the answer is, "Because the angels are always ready to sing," right? Angels are primed. They're always in the right mindset. They're always in the mood, they're always ready to sing. People are not always ready to sing. We're not always in the mood. We're not always ready to have this kind of experience. We're not always ready to be gathered together. When the time arises, when they're ready to be in this moment, we have to capitalize on it. We have to jump on it right in the time when it stirs up inside of them. It awakens in their soul, this need and desire and emotion to sing out, and we can't let that moment pass us by. And when we can prepare for those moments, we will help those moments become more frequent. The more that we can gather with people and help them understand what's going on in prayer, reach out and share melodies, reach out and encourage people to come, reach out and encourage people to bring their friends, the more that we can set up the space so it's ready for people to have an experience in, and the more people will then be able to have an experience there. If we can prepare and continue to be doing this during this time, especially, then all the more so we're going to be empowered to be able to do it when we can come back together. The more that we can create these spaces and engage people and be intentional about the way that we're crafting them, the more I think people will find meaning and inspiration in the music, the liturgy, and the wisdom of our amazing tradition.

RON: Josh, thanks for bringing your *ruach* [spirit] to our seminar!

> ### Questions for Creating Your Sacred Community
>
> 1. Answer Josh's guiding questions for your own community:
>   a. **Who** is coming into our space, and from where?
>   b. **What** are we: the same group of people who can work over time to dive deeper into the prayers, or are there newcomers who need to be taught the basics?
>   c. **Where** are people coming from beforehand, that is, from work, home, school, sleep?
>   d. **When** are we meeting during the day/week, and how does that influence what we do during the service?
>   e. **Why** are we doing this? What are our goals?
>   f. **How** is our space set up: what is the medium and how are we using our equipment and various skill sets?

CHAPTER 4

Welcoming Membership

Rabbi Jonathan Bernhard

Rabbi Jonathan Bernhard began his career in 1996 as assistant rabbi at Adat Ari El, a Conservative synagogue in Los Angeles, California. In 2006, he became senior rabbi, only the third senior rabbi in the history of the congregation. Rabbi Bernhard served as president of the Board of Rabbis in Greater Los Angeles and on the boards of several communal organizations.

JONATHAN: I've been the senior rabbi at Adat Ari El for fourteen years. We've been very fortunate to have some very strong professional staff and very good lay leadership. I say that because if you're going to try to do something like changing from traditional membership dues to a new sustainability model, you've got to know what your congregation is capable of. It's a kind of cool and groovy thing for a congregation of our size to pull this off. We're one of the bigger congregations to move to what we call a <u>sustainability model</u>.

It was completely obvious that the traditional dues model had completely broken down for us. Other congregations may be able to manage it better than we managed it, but for us, the dues model was an utter catastrophe. So, why not try something new? Honestly, what do we have to lose? This was the argument that our executive director Eric Nicastro made to me. I said, "Eric, what happens if this goes south?" He says, "Jonathan, how many years in a row has the budgeting process from dues membership gone south? Whatever money we lose on this, trust me, we will have lost the same, if not more, the way we are currently doing the budgeting process." So, we did our due diligence and brought it to the board of the congregation before we pulled the trigger.

This idea is incredibly anxiety provoking for many congregations, a truly scary thing. It feels like taking a leap off a financial cliff. But the truth is, we had already taken the leap; we just didn't know how fast we were falling.

What's the problem with the traditional dues model? There are both practical problems and psychological problems. The practical problem begins with the financial process itself. Let's say a young family with two kids wants to join. We put them into a specific category that has a number on it. And they say, "We can't afford that." Then we put them through a process where we ask them for financial records or other things to evaluate what we think they can pay. We come back with a lower number, because we know we're not going to turn people away. So, the only question was how much lower the number would be. Sometimes they can make the number and say, "Thank you." Sometimes they say, "It's not enough; we can only pay this amount." And we say, "Fine," anyway. What's the point?

Most congregations have fifteen to twenty "categories" of membership. We had about ten categories. So, you try to budget based on your expectations of what each category will bring in. But what if you don't meet your numbers? It's all guesswork. Then your budget is off if your guesses are wrong. We were very bad at assuming how much money our school families would pay. We were pretty good about understanding what our older population was going to contribute. But there could be fluctuations there, too. On top of all this variation, we never knew the absolute number of people or families that would join the congregation. Bottom line: our budgeting process was all messed up.

Even more concerning was the psychological problem with the standard dues model. We are a religious organization, not a business. It was uncomfortable. Uncomfortable for the members to have us looking at their financial records . . . and uncomfortable for the staff, who don't want to be doing this. The relationship between the congregation and its people should not be a transactional business relationship. When it is, it impacts a person's feelings about religion itself. It becomes a negative association with Judaism.

The whole thing had a bad vibe about it. No one was happy. No one felt good. When we really looked it, there were no positives to the traditional dues structure model. Even practically speaking, it took up a tremendous amount of time, we almost never could get the number right, we were always too optimistic. So, there's no win from our perspective.

As we began considering and then implementing a sustainability model, we paid special attention to the psychology of giving. The best way to distinguish the dues model and the sustainability model is that the former is like paying taxes, while the latter is like giving a charitable donation. When people are hounded by an organization with phone calls and reminders to pay their taxes, they don't feel so good about it. When people make a charitable donation, they generally feel good about it. They feel good because they're able to do it freely from their own heart. It just feels good to them. Right? Interestingly enough, no one says paying taxes feels good. Right? Look, it doesn't take a brain surgeon to know which one you want in your synagogue.

Moving to a sustainability model where we suggest the number that will "sustain" the congregation but each person or family decides what to give has completely changed how everyone experiences this. I was talking recently with our community outreach director, Jessica Bieber. She reports her experience with congregants is so different now. It's good for the congregation. It's good for the congregants. It's good for our staff. It has changed how people relate and feel about the place.

BRETT: How did you make this happen?

JONATHAN: We did the things that organizations do: we set up a specific ad hoc committee to examine different financial models. We looked at how other synagogues do versions of the traditional dues model, just to make sure that we weren't doing something totally wrong and different from everybody else. We quickly realized, yes—there were some areas where maybe we could do this or maybe we could try that. But we weren't hearing from any congregation that was having such marvelous success in this way. And then, we began to read about and hear about the benefits the congregations that had implemented a voluntary sustainability model reported, especially the way the congregation itself felt. We did our due diligence.

Then, we looked at an amazing packet of information that the New York UJA Federation put out, a study of forty congregations that all did this and the different ways in which they've done it. That was invaluable for us. That was our Bible; that was our road map. We learned that not every congregation did this the same way; they all tweaked the model a bit. But all of them reported the psychological benefits, how much easier it was to do, how people felt positive about their relationship with the congregation. And most of the congregations reported a bump in membership.

This is exactly what happened when Adat transitioned to the sustainability model. We met our financial goal ... and we achieved it in May, not in the usual rush in the run-up to the High Holy Days. That enabled us to budget precisely for the coming year; the guesswork was eliminated.

RON: Jonathan, please describe what you did to engage former members with this new model.

JONATHAN: We reached out to all the people who had resigned from the congregation. We began with those who live in the San Fernando Valley, closest to the shul geographically. Then, we sent emails to those in Los Angeles and beyond. We eventually sent emails and followed up with phone calls to everyone who had left with the news of our new sustainability structure. The message was "If this allows you to feel comfortable coming back into relationship with the congregation, please do so."

RON: So, what happened?

JONATHAN: We had something like seventy-five or eighty former members come back to the congregation.

RON: That's extraordinary! I tell the story in *Relational Judaism* about a congregation near Boston where the rabbi invited former members to meetings in his home, where he did a full-court press asking them to return ... and it failed. It was too late. The point I make in the book is that many congregations wait too long to build a relationship with their people. When they're gone, they're gone. But you have proved the opposite. You have shown that there's still a reservoir of fondness for the community and a willingness to come back on this model of voluntary contribution.

JONATHAN: And we picked up another 80 new members who heard about our new financial model of contributing what you can, whether or not you hit the suggested sustainability number. So, we gained close to 150 members in the first year of implementing this model—a huge number for us. Now, some of the new members may have joined anyway. But to us, the really impressive thing was the number of people who rejoined, because that tells you, more than anything, that their connection to the synagogue was influenced by the finances.

RON: There is no mystery about how to do this. Rabbi Dan Judson at Hebrew College in Boston did the first studies of voluntary dues models, and more and more congregations are adopting some form of the process. The New York Federation established a "Synergy" project that brought the concept to their local congregations. Not everyone has adopted it, but many that did are finding success. So, Jonathan, once your committee did the due diligence, how did you make the move happen?

JONATHAN: By the time we got to the executive committee of the board, we had a full understanding of what this model can do for us, what we've seen it do for other congregations, and how we would actually implement it. We got feedback, there were questions; it's a process. We'd have another meeting; we would tweak it and so forth. We had good suggestions from people on how to strengthen the presentation, but very few details were argued. By the time we got to the entire board, we had talked with lots of people. There were some who were resistant to change; you always have those who like things the way they are.

We had to do a lot of explaining. Once we had everyone philosophically on the same page, once we had the approval of the executive committee, we felt prepared to bring it to the board meeting. It was adopted ... and we were off and running.

BRETT: Is this an educational process? A political process? And what kind of Jewish values were used in the argument for doing this?

JONATHAN: It was both an educational process and a political process. Yes, it stimulated a significant conversation about money, about transparency, about what it really costs to operate a congregation. In terms of the Jewish values perspective, that's actually a fairly easy one. We understand our mission is to make Judaism as accessible as possible to as many people as possible. Someone will say to me, "I need to speak to a rabbi, but I'm not a member." I say, "You don't understand. I don't deal with 'members.' That's the executive director's job. I deal with *congregants*, and everyone who walks onto the grounds of the synagogue is a *congregant*." It just kind of works. I get to say that because that's the way the congregation approaches this. In the eleven years I was the associate rabbi to Rabbi Moshe Rothblum, I learned what the congregation expected. From our perspective, we want to be able to bring in as many people as possible.

There is always a good source for this message, right? The best source would always be Abraham's tent. The Midrash teaches that Abraham's tent was open on all sides. We wanted a financial model that embodies that—that makes synagogue membership accessible and welcoming. This model does that. At the end of the day, the board is the fiduciary responsible for the financial well-being of the congregation. Was there some hesitancy to try this? Yes. Was there some anxiety about whether it would work? Yes. But we had a backup plan. If this didn't work, we were prepared to go back to the traditional model.

SARA: How did you determine the sustainability number?

JONATHAN: It's very easy to do. We basically say to the congregation, we have two numbers: the "sustainability" number—what it costs to make our annual budget—and the "minimum" number, which is $500. We make it clear that if someone cannot afford the $500, they are still welcome to be a member and give a gift from the heart. We make it very clear what we need to keep the congregation functioning. And we also make clear that this is not the only time we'll be asking for money; there will be fundraising, as most congregations do. We put all this in writing on our website, our membership materials, and other communications.

RON: So, I cannot wait to ask: what happened in the first year? Did you make your budget?

JONATHAN: Yes, we did. Everyone was amazed. And we've come close to making budget pretty much every year. I say that because this past year with COVID, it's a bit unusual. Our schools weren't open in the usual way, so we lost some members. Again, we don't build membership around the High Holy Days. We build membership in May, so we know the size of the congregation then.

By the way, we try not to use the word "membership." This was one of the more interesting/heated arguments. Some of us thought since we were presenting a totally new way of thinking about the relationship between our people and the congregation, we should come up with new language, like "partnership" and "covenant." Others said if you change the language, people might get really confused. It was so interesting to me. Here we are radically changing the way we engage our people, but some thought it was important to keep the concept of "membership." Here's the thing: they were right. People didn't mind the use of the word "membership," even when talking about this new model. Eventually, they come to understand it. We are still educating folks, to remind people just what this model is and how it works.

RON: Some synagogues have different language for this: "voluntary dues," "gifts from the heart . . ." Some refer to the Torah's instruction that everyone contributes a "half-shekel," so this is our version of everybody needing to contribute in a variety of ways—bring your talents, your passions, and yes, your financial contributions to sustain our community.

What I really want to underline is the wonderful way this model turns the psychological obstacles on its head. I used to hear horror stories of "dues abatement committees," demanding tax returns and trading in gossip. "Did you hear about so-and-so? He wants a dues abatement, but he took his family on an expensive trip to Aspen last summer. Look at the car she drives." That's not the kind of stuff you want happening in a sacred community. All that goes away automatically with this model. And that is wonderful. Do you have any sense, Jonathan, about how many synagogues have adopted this sustainability model? I know when there was a *Jewish Journal* article about your congregation, you must have heard from your colleagues.

JONATHAN: I'm not up to date on the number of shuls that have adopted some form of this model, but I'm sure it has grown ... especially now with COVID. We'll need to work hard to get back people who have not engaged with us in person for all this time. I think it will be even more important to be transparent about the financial impact of the pandemic and appeal to our members to step up. And there are likely some synagogues that are simply afraid to go in this direction. Too risky.

RON: I was at a seminar that Dan Judson did at the LA Federation, sitting next to the senior rabbi of one of our largest synagogues in town. He whispered to me, "This would never work in my congregation." There is resistance among colleagues to it; they feel it's too frightening. My sense is that medium-size congregations of 400 to 600 membership units or even smaller are more likely to adopt this model than the big 1,500- to 2,000-member congregations.

JONATHAN: That's very consistent with my experiences and conversations with colleagues. We are one of the largest congregations to try this. I think over the next twenty years more and more congregations are going to do it, because they just don't have a choice.

RON: Why do you think that's true that they don't have a choice? And could you reflect a minute on how the pandemic is affecting your congregation and your colleagues? What are you hearing on the street?

JONATHAN: A lot of my colleagues and I feel that the pandemic has shown the financial fragility of the Jewish community, not just in synagogues but in Federations, JCCs, the whole gamut of our organizational structures. Many synagogues have gone into debt. Keeping the schools open—even the preschools, which are normally a revenue generator—has been challenging. We'll definitely see some mergers. Look, Wilshire Boulevard Temple and University Synagogue here in Los Angeles have merged, and there are a couple of Conservative synagogues that are merging their supplemental religious schools as a first step toward a merger.

There are serious challenges out there. I've told my community that I'm stepping down from the pulpit. I say this with love for my congregation. I truly do. When people ask me why I'm leaving, I say, "I'm leaving for a lot of reasons, but I'm not leaving because I'm going to find a better place." Right now, I may want to strangle half of my congregants, but I think that's healthy. I think a rabbi who doesn't think about strangling half of his congregants or her congregants might not actually be awake to what they're doing. That's what congregants do—they drive you crazy? It's nothing wrong; that's just what it is. I talk to my minister friends and describe some of my stuff, and they have the same kind of stuff. This is just the nature of the work.

We Jews in the liberal community do not prioritize synagogue life enough. For religion to work, it's got to be your one, two, or three. Otherwise, it's not that you don't care; it's just you care about other things more that take priority and take your time and energy. Religion requires people to prioritize it; the religious community requires it to be a priority on some level. And while I have been blessed with a lot of congregants for whom it is one, two, or three, the number of people for whom it's more like seven, eight, nine . . . or fifteen . . . gets bigger. That's why the sustainable financial funding model is so important; it lowers the barrier of engagement and raises the possibility that more people will think of their commitment to religious life as one, two, or three.

RON: Jonathan, thanks for sharing this bold and successful initiative!

Questions for Creating Your Sacred Community

1. What is your current membership revenue strategy?

2. What are the strengths and weaknesses of the traditional membership dues model?

3. Does your community have a retention problem?

4. Have you attempted to reengage lapsed members?

5. How might your community study and consider the "sustainability" revenue membership model?

CHAPTER 5

Building Organizations through Relationships

Janice Kamenir-Reznik

Janice Kamenir-Reznik retired from the active practice of law to cofound Jewish World Watch, a Jewish response to genocide and mass atrocities, with her rabbi, Harold M. Schulweis (z"l) in 2004. After practicing environmental law for more than two decades, she has served as a leader of many Jewish, feminist, and legal organizations, directing the Commission on Soviet Jewry for the Los Angeles Jewish Federation, becoming a Los Angeles County commissioner, and cofounding Jews United for Democracy and Justice.

RON: Welcome, Janice! Thanks so much for joining us. You have been an extraordinarily successful organizer of sacred communities, especially in your work with Jewish World Watch. I'm particularly interested in how you developed such a powerful partnership with Rabbi Harold Schulweis as a lay leader to make Jewish World Watch such a successful network of synagogues dedicated to addressing the terrible situation in Darfur. How did this happen?

JANICE: Nice to be with you, Ron, and lovely to meet you, Sara and Brett. The answer is simple: Rabbi Schulweis tapped me on the shoulder and asked!

RON: I know he spoke about the Darfur crisis in his big High Holy Day sermon—"As Jews, we cannot stand idly by in the face of genocide." But did he have a plan?

JANICE (laughs): He had no specific plan. Rabbi Schulweis was a moral visionary. He was not afraid to speak his mind or to admonish people to wake up to their responsibility. In this instance he called me and told me, "I'm going to be bringing something up at the High Holy Days, and I want you to be listening really closely because I want you to take the ball and run with it." I asked him what he would be proposing. He told me, "It relates to a place called Darfur." I had never heard of Darfur; this was in 2004, toward the beginning of the Darfur genocide. And I responded, "Well, I'm listening, I'm listening." And I did. The words he used were so profound and really struck me. Especially compelling to me was when he talked about our silence in the face of atrocity. For decades Jews have bemoaned the silence of the world when we were being targeted and slaughtered by the Nazis; we know how that silence feels and how devastating it is to be abandoned. We must start a movement to counter Jewish complacency about the genocide and atrocity done to "others." You can read this sermon on our website (jww.org)—it was the founding sermon of Jewish World Watch.

RON: What was the reaction in the congregation?

JANICE: Among some members of the congregation, his proposal to mobilize the Jewish community to address genocides of "other" (non-Jewish) groups was controversial. To my mind, it shouldn't have been controversial. But there are those Jews who believe that if the horrors are not happening to us, it does not justify our energy and resources. But Rabbi Schulweis was unafraid to address that contingent. He used a big word—he liked big words—"solipsism," which is a sort of narcissism of the soul. Rabbi Schulweis always fought against solipsism; he was never shy about admonishing his congregation to inspire them toward increased moral conduct. If you read Rabbi Ed Feinstein's book about Rabbi Schulweis, you'll see what happened to Rabbi Schulweis when he was the rabbi at a congregation in Oakland when there was a citywide protest against unfair and substandard housing, and particularly against "slumlords." He knew that there were some of his own congregants who might be what people would call "slumlords"; Rabbi

Schulweis decided to call them out and talk about the obligation of property owners to treat their tenants respectfully and fairly. I am sure it was not a decision he made lightly, but Rabbi Schulweis put ethical conduct at the very top of his list of what it meant to be a rabbi and a Jew. No doubt, he risked relationships and maybe even his job when he admonished his congregation, but that's what it means to have a moral soul and believe in yourself enough to know that if you think it's wrong, you need to do something to try to correct the wrong. Another example: At the beginning of his rabbinate at Valley Beth Shalom, he was getting really disgusted with the outsized Bar Mitzvah parties. So, he gave a sermon, I think it was during the High Holy Days, in which he chastised the congregation for these outsized Bar Mitzvahs. And, he also knew that some congregants wouldn't stop having them; so he implored people to at least combine the lavish parties with tzedakah projects. He suggested contributing 3% of the budget for the celebration to tzedakah. At our synagogue, that is how the notion of a Bar Mitzvah "Mitzvah Project" was initiated, which is now part of the planning of every Bar Mitzvah in most synagogues.

RON: This is when he and Leonard Fein came up with MAZON: A Jewish Response to Hunger.

JANICE: Right! In the parking lot of VBS. Their idea was to raise money to feed the homeless by contributing a portion of your Bar Mitzvah budget to the charity and in some way teach your child the value of tzedakah.

Rabbi Schulweis picked his battles. He picked issues that went to the core of what it meant to be a socially aware Jew concerned with the poor, the widowed, the orphaned, etc. In a way, in the best sense, he used the pulpit as a weapon, to garner the support of his army of congregants to fight the moral fight. I think rabbis need to understand their power to be an influential moral voice. Even if it doesn't always produce the desired result, the rabbi must embrace that moral power. The title "Rabbi" means a lot and carries with it a huge responsibility to persuade, to educate, to uplift, and to create impact.

RON: Janice, another important thing Schulweis did that was brilliant can be said in one Hebrew word: *u'lechein*—"therefore." He always ended his big sermon on the High Holy Days with a *u'lechein*. I've presented the issue; now we're going to do something about it. Then, he announced a meeting: "Join me next week on Tuesday night if you want to do something about it." He intended to mobilize his congregation around the issue he was talking about. He used the power, but he was not a detail person, but he certainly knew how to take that first step beyond the sermon by inviting those in the congregation who were moved by his words to gather to plan the next steps.

BRETT: But what if he makes this big *u'lechein* call every year?

JANICE (laughing)**:** It's funny you bring that up! I begged Rabbi Schulweis for the first few years after we started Jewish World Watch to not propose any new organizations or mobilizations on Rosh Hashanah so that we would have the time we needed to sink the roots of Jewish World Watch. Part of the power of the rabbi's voice is that many congregants will do what their beloved rabbi suggests they do. For example, if he made a sermon and a call to action about public education, some in the congregation might conclude (erroneously) that Darfur was last year's news. In a congregation our size, let's say there are only three or four hundred people that the rabbinic leader can inspire to engage in an issue. I thought it was important that for the first few years after establishing something as big and far-reaching as an anti-genocide movement, we focus on that for a while rather than enticing the active participants to turn to a new social issue, as important as it might be, until we had firmly established JWW. It took a lot of restraint on Rabbi Schulweis's part, but he did follow my suggestion. In fact, for many years Rabbi Schulweis would sermonize about genocide and atrocity, which substantially helped JWW grow and flourish in its work.

My goal for Jewish World Watch, which was likely different from the original intention of Rabbi Schulweis, was not to limit the mobilization to our temple. He was very delighted with that strategy and very supportive of our temple being the "instigator" of a bigger and more powerful movement. The model we were using to mobilize our temple could be applied to mobilizing many additional temples. I understood the power Rabbi Schulweis had, to call other rabbis to inspire them to get interested in fighting genocide. For the first year of Jewish World Watch, I would physically pick him up, and he and I would just go from rabbi to rabbi, meeting with all the rabbis in town, to pitch our idea. We'd ask the rabbi to embrace the concept and assign a congregant who could actually establish a committee and send a representative back to the central organization at VBS. One by one, we built this organization. It took us about a year and a half to get more than eighty non-Orthodox LA synagogues engaged; we did succeed in recruiting one Orthodox shul.

Then, it was just a lot of hard, very hard work. I don't know that we could have done it before the email days; the email made everything much more efficient. My husband, Ben, likes to say we started this organization from our bedroom, because it was a 24/7 thing for about a year of following up, keeping the momentum going, and not letting people fall through the cracks. As soon as Rabbi Schulweis and I met with them, we'd ask them three days later, "Who is the contact person in your congregation?" Then, contacting that person to say, "Okay, we'll help you set up a committee, here's what you need to do, here's the programming to inspire them." You can get the rabbi interested, but unless the rabbis use their power to inspire their leaders, it's not going to happen.

SARA: How did you motivate people to raise awareness of the Darfur genocide?

JANICE: Stories. Just like Brett has done with *The Tattooed Torah*, you must tell a compelling story. That's why I decided we must travel to Darfur, to meet the people, to hear them and bring their stories back to these congregations. That was what enabled us to actually inspire the people to do the work and to donate the funds and to really engage. Without those direct stories, we would not have been as successful in inspiring the community.

BRETT: I'm learning more about you and your work and reading up on Jewish World Watch. I'm really excited that we're in this conversation, because the second project I'm working on currently is a documentary about this exact topic. We're doing a whole documentary about genocide and dehumanization. We're asking the question, "Is empathy the proper antidote for these negative forces that repeat throughout human history?" It sounds to me like this is what your work is, so I would definitely like to continue this conversation with you.

JANICE: Absolutely. I can connect you with our current executive director, who would be happy to help; we all will be happy to help you in any way. The power of storytelling is profound, especially for rabbis and communal leaders.

If you've met Rabbi Ed Feinstein, then you know that he is the ultimate storyteller. As writers and filmmakers, you know the power of telling stories. That's what you do. Whether in writing or on screen or from the pulpit, stories are the way to influence, inspire, and make change happen. Jewish World Watch is in our seventeenth year now, and we became the conscience of the LA Jewish community on the issue of genocide and mass atrocity, be it in Darfur, Congo, Myanmar, Syria, or elsewhere. It wasn't always this way. Many asked why we're investing Jewish dollars and energy in something that doesn't affect Jews; those people might have forgotten why we bother perpetuating Judaism to begin with. If everybody was perfect, we wouldn't need any religion, right? But because none of us is perfect, we need these moral codes that help guide us. The core of that code is the holiness and dignity of each individual. If you're not going to apply that to the "other," then why do we "practice" Judaism? The point of sustaining Judaism is not simply to sustain our temples and organizations. To me, it's the bigger picture. Maybe because I was schooled by the likes of Rabbi Schulweis and by parents who taught me that all issues, be it the environment or politics, are all Jewish issues and require our vigilance and attention. To me, that is what it means to be a Jew—to be fully engaged in the world and implementing our values with the goal of repairing the brokenness.

It's odd to me that it took till 2004 for us to address the largest genocide since the Holocaust; the genocide began a year earlier. We should have been on the forefront of mobilization immediately, in 2003! But, American Jews were not always confident to speak up; with the post-Holocaust mentality and the antisemitism prevalent until more recent times, perhaps we didn't have the bandwidth or the confidence to be able to use our voice. Now, I feel that we outgrew the sense of victimhood and have taken our rightful role in America's tapestry. We must use our voice and whatever power we have to fight the moral fight . . . especially when it comes to genocide.

BRETT: I am really interested in the whole genesis of Jewish World Watch. I do envision wanting to start my own thing one day, and I wonder what the first steps are.

JANICE: It was very nitty-gritty. I mean, it's not sexy at all. It is all about persistence. We organized with phone calls, meetings, and emails, phone calls, meetings, and emails. I had to learn about the issue, which I knew nothing about; I had to learn enough to be able to go in front of people with confidence. So, I learned about Darfur and what was happening in the conflict. But that was the easy part. The hard part was how many calls, emails, and meetings can I do in a day? Not all of them yield a result, right? I wanted to be productive. So, after I got educated, I created a PowerPoint to take with me when I went with Rabbi Schulweis. I offered to speak to any congregation, on Friday night, on Saturday morning. If you didn't want a PowerPoint, I would just speak.

I got as many speaking engagements as I could. I was making an emotional argument about why we should care about Black African Muslims in Sudan who were being raped and murdered. I could spend two minutes telling you basically about the geography, history, and politics of the Sudan, but that's not going to emotionally reach people. So, most of my talk was about my feelings about the silence of the world during the Holocaust; initially, until I myself went to Darfur to gather my own stories, I would tell stories about some of the people Nick Kristof of the *New York Times* had written about on the Human Rights Watch website. But, once I started making trips to Darfur a couple of years later, I came back with the stories I heard personally, and they had much more impact because I had experienced something personal and profound. Once you do that, you can tell your story with your words and it's just going to generate more emotional response than telling somebody else's story.

So that is the most important thing. And the other thing, Brett, is something Ron said in a meeting recently that really resonated with me because it's what I always try to do: hang out with people smarter than you, more famous than you, with people with more access than you, and then do things together. I recognize the power that Rabbi Schulweis lent to this cause. He was really healthy for the first seven or eight years of Jewish World Watch and extremely engaged with us. He didn't have to plan anything; all he had to do was say "yes"... and, he always said, "Yes." He came with me to meetings, he would come with me when I was speaking, he would make the call to get a rabbi to respond. Then, as I gathered people, in every community that I went to, a couple of people would stay afterward to talk with me and really show interest. I would invite them to come onto the advisory committee representing their temple. In the end, it was person-to-person, very intimate, labor-intensive engagements that built this organization.

RON: It's all about relationship building.

JANICE: That's true. It's all person-to-person; nothing happens magically or without hard work. You have to be able to collaborate with people; to do that successfully, you need to realize that you do not have a corner on every good idea. Exercising humility, but always plowing forward to build your base. Sometimes you compromise; sometimes your idea is the best idea. You just work really, really hard and gather good, like-minded people. Never being discouraged by the nay-sayers; always embracing the "yea-sayers." Eventually, we built a great board for Jewish World Watch; but it doesn't end there. Bringing in new blood all the time is critical and challenging.

BRETT: I resonate with the hard work point. Our twenty-one-minute film took us over four years to make. I think if you really want to launch something, you really just need to believe in the mission.

JANICE: There is a whole other conversation about founder's syndrome, ensuring that you, as the founder, know how and when to move aside and let other people lead. Hogging the organization is the death of the organization. One of the things I always do when I come in as a chair of any organization is to identify who my successor is going to be within the first six months. Then, I can groom that person, know they are up to the task, and ensure that they will be ready to take over. I came really close to falling into a founder's syndrome trap with Jewish World Watch. It was clear that people saw the amount of work that was involved in starting the organization and concluded that they might not have the time to devote to it. However, once a few additional people began to join us in traveling to the remote and pretty dangerous places, like Darfur and the eastern regions of the DR Congo, where the survivors we serve are living, additional committed and willing leaders emerged. But it's a challenge; to date, there are about eight of us who have taken the trips. As a cofounder, everybody deferred to me, because it was seen as mine and I was willing to work for years fifty hours a week (at least) to create the organization. I left my law practice to start Jewish World Watch. I wanted it to be done as well as it possibly could be done, not only because the issue we were dealing with deserved excellence and optimal effectiveness, but also because I was dealing with the legacy of Rabbi Schulweis. I wanted it to be successful for the cause, but I also wanted it to be successful for him. I took this on as a full-time, unpaid job. Still to this day, our budget is about $1.5 million and I have a great deal of responsibility for raising a lot of those funds. Even though we are about to embark on our eighteenth year, we are still a young organization in that respect. We continue to work on diversifying our leadership. We have a new executive director, a millennial, who's going to work really hard to create a young board.

SARA: Why did you leave your law practice to start an organization that didn't exist yet? Was it just that a really charismatic rabbi recruited you? It seems like what he said to you was a wake-up call that sort of started this journey.

JANICE: Yes, it empowered me in a way that I hadn't been empowered before. Let me make it clear that law was not a perfect fit for me. My interest and my passion is in social justice. In fact, before I became a lawyer, I was a community organizer. Representing clients as a lawyer is a micro undertaking. As a community organizer, I am more attracted to macro systems and work. So, I decided in 2004 to give it up and to dedicate myself to this. It was just more important.

RON: I'd like to make a comment about meaning in the work. Janice is a great example of this. She put her finger on it: how do you motivate people to volunteer for your cause? It's got to be more than work. As hard as the work is, there's got to be meaning associated with the work, one of the things we're going to learn from Rick Warren if he accepts my invitation to Zoom in. An important part of Rick Warren's genius in creating a sacred community is that he taught his people who are volunteering, whether they are directing traffic or stamping envelopes, they're doing God's work. And they are, they are. Many congregations miss that point of telling their people that all of this work is a calling. You're doing God's work on earth. I know that Janice feels that way about the work she did.

JANICE: I do.

RON: It's an important role for a rabbi to make it clear that this is not just helping out building a community, this is God's work. This is what you can do with your God-given talents and gifts. This is what God's work looks like.

JANICE: That's why I keep making the point. It's often not glamorous. Sure, you get out there and give a rip-roaring speech; people respond enthusiastically. It can all look so glamorous. But the reality is everything that goes into getting you to the point of having an audience willing to listen to that speech; and the reality is what you do with their enthusiastic response if you are effective enough to generate such a response. That's the real work! I think one of the problems for synagogues now is that many of the things that used to be done by volunteers, who found meaning in their volunteer work, are no longer being done by volunteers. For example, it used to be that the sisterhood prepared the tuna fish for the *Oneg*? Well, most women today work, or even if they don't work, the culture has changed and today's women don't want to prepare tuna fish for an *Oneg Shabbat* at temple. That work used to be infused with a lot of meaning and engaged the women and their families in the synagogue in a much more intense way than seems to be the case today. When I was growing up at Sinai Temple in West LA, my mother was at that synagogue every single day, often doing what we would call grunt work. She was an educated woman, having been a teacher. She's still around, ninety-seven years old! Ronnie knows her well. She would lick stamps, she would address envelopes, she would cook in the kitchen, she would schlep, driving other people's kids to Hebrew school, if that's what was needed. The temple was the focal point of our life, every single day, and it all seemed so meaningful. The synagogue could have hired somebody for minimum wage to do the work, but they didn't. They had the volunteers. <u>Volunteerism is a serious problem right now; we've lost some of that passion</u>. I think the mentality as well as the commitment of people changes when you no longer rely on volunteers; the fabric of the organization changes—and it's not just about who is making the tuna fish! Professional staff cannot take the place of the passion of volunteers in the long-term sustenance and health of an organization. That passion should be so explosive that they should be willing to do the grunt work of planning a gala, making collection calls, all the stuff that makes a community organization work, as well as what is seen as the "loftier" work of implementing programs, sitting on substantive committees, and the like.

RON: I have another question for you, Janice. How do you get four thousand people to come to a lecture you're doing tonight?

JANICE: Well, that brings us to the next organization I've been working on. It's called Jews United for Democracy and Justice. When Trump issued his first Muslim travel ban, it struck a group of us as so horrible, so reminiscent of what happened to the Jews trying to escape Eastern Europe during the '30s and the '40s; it struck us as so unjust and so dangerous that we mobilized a small committee of people to do something meaningful in protest. Overnight, literally, from a Friday to a Monday, we were able to garner about twenty-five hundred supporters, to sign on to our statement, the gist of which was that we were angry that the organized Jewish community didn't come out strongly against that Muslim ban. We were asking them to take a moral stand on an issue that we, as Jews and as Americans, found to be reprehensible. Our community's answer to our plea was "We don't take political stands or make political statements." So we decided we would be that voice. We were not organized, we had no staff, but we put together this small steering committee of six people. We did some dialoguing with the Arab community and the Muslim community in LA and started an in-person lecture series to bring really prominent voices to discuss the issues—to make people think more deeply and to be more reflective. We raised the money to pay the speakers, to fly them out to California, and to speak at different synagogues in the area. We had good attendance—like 700–900 people attended each lecture. But, along came COVID and the quarantine. We decided to use the power of the Internet and Zoom to put the lectures online. David Lehrer, a former regional director of the ADL, and I thought we would do a weekly series for the month or two that people are going to be at home. We had no idea this was going to go on for months and even years! We started calling these *New York Times* reporters, former senators, sitting congresspeople, and set up these weekly programs on Zoom. Almost immediately, we got 1,000 people. We thought, "Oh my God, 1,000 people!" Well, over the months of doing a one-hour program every Wednesday at 5:00 Pacific, 8:00 Eastern, we kept growing and growing. We are in our forty-fifth consecutive week of programming. We have a 20,000-person email list. We get a 50 percent open rate on our three weekly emails ... unheard of. We get between 3,000 and 5,000 people attending every single week. We have a national, even international audience. We are a nonprofit. We invite people to donate what they might spend on a lecture. The speakers are doing this for a fraction of their usual fee. There are no travel costs. We still have no staff. Our "secret sauce" is first and foremost, <u>the high quality of the speakers speaking on the most compelling topics related to preservation of our American democracy</u>.

RON: Janice, you've been fantastic. A few questions and we'll let you go.

SARA: Trailblazing definitely seems like a theme in your life. And I really relate to that. I feel like I'm a trailblazer in becoming a rabbi; no one in my family has ever done this. Do you have role models to inspire this trait? Is this a quality in you? How did you become a trailblazer?

JANICE: That's such an interesting question. My parents were both very, very involved in community life. They were passionate Americans and passionate Jews. My father had been the president of our synagogue; as his final project before he died, he actually spearheaded the building of the new Mount Sinai Memorial Park in Simi Valley. The chapel is named for him. He was a comfortable, though not a wealthy man; he was a dentist who became a lawyer. He was entrepreneurial, a real Renaissance man in a lot of ways. He studied with Rabbi David Lieber, may he rest in peace, the former, longtime president of the University of Judaism. My mother was also a role model, so active in so many causes and organizations. I learned from my parents that each of us can make a difference. I have a very supportive husband, always encouraging me, and supportive of what I do. And, I admit, I have repeatedly been told that I have an unusually high amount of energy. I need to be busy, I need to be working, I need to be productive. That's ingrained in me from my family. I believe in doing what I can to make the world a better place.

SARA: I'd like to follow up. Can you speak to the obstacles you encountered when you were starting Jewish World Watch?

JANICE: Detractors were never important. I just never got depressed by those people who didn't want to engage. Do what's important to you; I'm going to continue to do what's important to me. As I said, there were people who didn't want to spend Jewish money on things that didn't benefit Jews. There were people who wanted proof that none of the donated money was going to corrupt causes in Africa. These Darfuri women were being raped and murdered as they went out to collect firewood. If that doesn't move someone, then I would move on to people who were moved by the stories we told. I never got angry at people; I just focused on those who understood what we were trying to accomplish and who wanted to help. An example of what I am trying to say is when Rabbi Wolpe would invite me each year to speak to his congregation about Jewish World Watch and the crises in Darfur or Congo or other places we were working. When Rabbi Wolpe invited me to speak from his pulpit on a Saturday morning when there's a thousand worshippers present, that's a very big deal. It's akin to endorsement by him saying, "I think what you have to say is important." I knew that many present in the congregation did not feel that the work we were doing resonated with them; but if I could move a small number of worshippers to become inspired to get involved, I was thrilled. That is exactly what is involved in building an organization. Never focusing on those for whom your cause or message does not resonate; always focusing on those for whom it does.

When I would solicit Federation or other sort of more establishment sources for funds, my message about Jewish World Watch was this: JWW is an avenue to engage Jews who aren't otherwise engaged in Jewish life. There are young people for whom most Jewish causes do not resonate; many young people gravitate to environmental causes, to human rights causes, to homelessness causes, to the kinds of issues that are not typically seen by the establishment as Jewish issues. We have received funding through the Federation for teen programming based upon that argument. It may not be the most perfect motivation on their part, but it is support for our work and that is good enough. We have moved the agenda forward and touched these teens who will grow up, because of Jewish World Watch, seeing genocide-related work as being a Jewish cause that requires their attention.

Of course, to me and to Rabbi Schulweis, when people would say to us that combatting genocide is not a Jewish issue, we both had the same reaction—namely, there is no issue that could be *more* Jewish than intervening in a genocide or helping its survivors. Not everyone sees it that way; we are looking for the people who are receptive to our cause and our mission.

RON: Fabulous. Any last thing from you?

JANICE: No, thanks. This is really great. Thank you so much. Call me anytime; Ron will give you my contact info. I'm always really delighted to talk to you and to help you. And I just want to give you both a big mazel tov on graduating, and let me know where you land.

RON: And thank you, Janice. Amazing!

BRETT: Thanks so much.

SARA: You're inspiring!

Questions for Creating Your Sacred Community

1. How do you recruit volunteers to serve your sacred community?
2. Has your community been challenged with a *u'lechein* call to action?
3. What are the principles of community organizing outlined by Janice?
4. How can you discover the passions of your people?

CHAPTER 6

Relational Engagement Campaigns

Rabbi Nicole Auerbach and Rabbi Lydia Medwin

Rabbi Nicole Auerbach is the director of congregational engagement at Central Synagogue in New York City, where she helps people build deep and sustaining relationships with one another, with Jewish tradition, and with God. She is the coauthor, with Dr. Ron Wolfson and Rabbi Lydia Medwin, of The Relational Judaism Handbook: How to Create a Relational Engagement Campaign to Build and Deepen Relationships in Your Community *(2018). She was ordained by Hebrew Union College–Jewish Institute of Religion in 2016.*

Rabbi Lydia Medwin is director of congregational engagement and outreach at The Temple, a Reform synagogue in Atlanta, Georgia. Ordained by Hebrew Union College–Jewish Institute of Religion in 2010, Lydia served as a pulpit rabbi at Stephen S. Wise Temple in Los Angeles for four years. She is the coauthor, with Dr. Ron Wolfson and Rabbi Nicole Auerbach, of The Relational Judaism Handbook: How to Create a Relational Engagement Campaign to Build and Deepen Relationships in Your Community *(2018).*

RON: Lydia and Nicole have joined us today because these are two rabbis who know more about relational engagement than anybody in the universe. They are pioneering a whole new category of rabbinic work in congregations and beyond. We've written *The Relational Judaism Handbook* together. What do you think are the keys to doing the work of relational engagement?

LYDIA: A lot of the tools that we use in our engagement work were borrowed from our training in community organizing—finding out what is most important to people, what moves them, what they're passionate about, what their gifts are, and then connecting them with other people who share those passions and gifts to make things happen in the world. It's the same with engagement. It's just that the thing you're trying to make happen is community instead of passing legislation. The power of organizing congregational small groups is that once people are used to interacting with each other in this way, it's much easier to do turnout for things like political action. People think, "I'll reach out to my group," right? "I actually have ten people who I have deep relationships with, who I can vouch for on this, and say to them, 'I really want you to show up.'"

RON: What's it really like on the front lines of trying to do this work of engaging people in the life of a spiritual community? What are the most important lessons learned so far in the work you've done?

NICOLE: My overarching tagline at this point would be "It's not complicated." It's just hard, especially at first, because it's just slow, retooling a synagogue or any community to really focus on relationships. Humans are humans. It takes time to build relationships. So, the fruits of your labor are just delayed. You're not going to see a bazillion people who are excited and engaged right out of the gate. It just takes time. Nothing that we teach is outside of what humans naturally do, but to do it with intention and organization and thoughtful Jewish content—that takes time.

LYDIA: I have a very similar take, which is "There's no getting out of the one-on-one conversations." I've talked to a lot of folks who want to do this work, and they ask, "But there must be a more efficient way to do this?" Nope, there's actually not a more efficient way to help people feel seen and heard and known than having a one-on-one conversation with them. I recently did a webinar for the Melton adult Jewish education school. We were talking about what would happen if they measured their success in terms of relationships, rather than "butts in the seats." I asked, "What would it be like if when someone new signed up for Melton, you called them up and scheduled a half-hour conversation to figure out what was really important to them and what they cared about?" I must remind the folks who are on our political advocacy team, people will show up to events, and now you have a list of new people to organize one-on-one conversations with.

RON: My experience in talking with congregations about this is that they often just don't get it. They'll say, "Oh, you mean, I'm supposed to call somebody and invite them to serve on a committee?" Or "I'm supposed to call somebody and tell them about this great program that we have, that they should really, really, really, you know, come to?" The default is "Aren't I supposed to be selling the congregation?" I think it's the exact opposite.

LYDIA: Right. In our culture, people are so used to people having an agenda for wanting to talk to them. When we did our check-in calls during the beginning of COVID, we had to start by telling people we weren't calling for money. People expect interactions to be transactional. It's countercultural to actually say to someone, "No, my only agenda is I want to know who you are." People aren't used to it. They feel like they want the crutch of "But what's the ask at the end? What are you asking me to do?" But you're just asking them to be them!

NICOLE: There's sort of like an alchemy that ends up happening, cumulatively over the course of a bunch of conversations, either with one person or with multiple people. There is a kind of an ask, but the ask is more like "What is going to serve you?" Over the course of a bunch of conversations, you hear these themes, and then the ask is "Would you like to join me to help create this thing that you want? For yourself!" It's not about selling. It's also not about interviewing; sometimes people default into thinking, "Well, if she's not selling something, then she's going to drill me on my biography." It's not that either. This is totally countercultural, as Lydia said. To be really just curious about someone else's life—what inspires them. I've had hundreds of these conversations. People often weep; not every time, but it does bring people so much emotional response to be really truly seen. It just doesn't happen that much in our world.

RON: So, after you've had a conversation with somebody, what's the next step? How do you organize these small groups, as we call them?

NICOLE: It can look like a lot of things. Maybe you learn that there's a huge number of people who all really share an interest, and that might take you down one road and you create a group. But often there's a little bit of matchmaking. Here's an example: I have a member who wants to put people with different political views together. At Central [Synagogue], we're a politically diverse congregation in general, but particularly on Israel. We span JStreet to AIPAC. So, this member is one of our JStreet guys, but he's always been really interested in having conversations with people who are politically different from him. I'm thinking right now, who are my conservative folk who are similarly really open and interested in having conversations across the aisle? And how can I put both groups together in a room and help them have a conversation? And an important part of this process is identifying leaders—people you think have the sort of social skills and listening skills to be able to facilitate a conversation well. Sometimes these leaders emerge. Last week someone said, "I love films and I really want to be able to talk about films with people. Can we do a film group?" When someone asked about this in the past, I've said, "Do you want to lead the group?" And they say, "No, no, no." And I say, "Then we cannot have a film group because we need a leader." This time, my member said, "Yes. I'll be the leader." So, now we have a film group.

LYDIA: That's what I would have said also. Small groups are the most basic form of community. At The Temple, we wanted to create a culture where small groups were the natural outcome of any good idea, because that's where people are seen and heard best and loved best. Our friends at Saddleback Church always ask, "Are you a community *with* small groups . . . or a community *of* small groups?" To transform a congregation into a community of small groups requires a campaign, another tool borrowed from community organizing. Actually, a campaign fits naturally within the life cycle of a synagogue or a Hillel. The programmatic year is a kind of natural campaign length—six to nine months. I might do a listening campaign in the first month. When the listening phase is over, collate everything and then present people a summary of what you've heard, what the options are. And then you move into idea implementation—let's see how we can launch this thing that we all want, for ourselves and for each other.

RON: I'd like to underline a couple of key points. First, Nicole's point that if the layperson doesn't take the leadership role in the idea for a small group, it's not going to happen. That's totally different from a program-directed synagogue or a staff-driven synagogue, where the staff decides what groups we're going to have, what programs we're going to have, what committees we're going to have. A relational model is an empowerment model. It's really saying to a potential group leader, "If you think your community has people that would love to be biking through New York City, or studying Torah together, or watching and discussing films together, then that's great. It's going to be up to you to organize this group and sustain it, because we don't have enough time on the staff to socially engineer and direct all these different groups." I mean, how many groups have you developed over the years?

NICOLE: I would say a hundred. Some groups stick around for multiple years and other groups come and go, but here's what's been interesting. We've started a lot more groups during COVID than we had in previous seasons. For years, we've been trying to convince people that they need relationships, that isolation is bad, that it's not good to be alone. All of a sudden, people really have this visceral experience of "Oh, wow. I feel really alone. And I need to be connected to other people." So, it's both easier to recruit people into groups, but it's also changing the kind of groups that people have asked for. Some are saying, "I don't want to take the subway or the bus. I'm not comfortable doing that. I really want to know if there are people within walking distance of me who I could grab a coffee with or go on a walk with." We had previously tried to do neighborhood groups, but they had totally failed because people felt living close to someone was not enough to have in common. But suddenly with COVID, it's salient because you don't have to get in a taxi. What's really been fascinating is that almost all our small groups have moved online really easily. Most of them are meeting more frequently now because they don't have to come to each other's homes. We've had a surge in people being interested in them.

LYDIA: I would say about half of our groups continued online. For those people in the group, this has been essential. I mean, it has saved their lives. Those are their words: "The small group saved my life." My prediction is that as the weather gets warmer and more people are vaccinated, we'll see much more engagement. They are like a tightly wound spring that gets a release. So, we're setting up for this summer to be one where we are trying to serve that need for people. We've partnered with OneTable to white label their peer-to-peer engagement platform to help people do Shabbat dinner together with safe distancing.

RON: We've identified four ways to organize small groups: affinity, demography, geography, and availability.

LYDIA: We've started to subdivide our groups because there's so many different types. Food is a big one. Culture arts and games like mah-jongg and canasta. Outdoor sports—biking, hiking, tennis. Then there are groups interested in Torah study and spirituality. And we have a number of support groups for various issues. Oh, and the Ben Franklin Circles, an idea pioneered at the 92nd Street Y. Ben Franklin brought small groups and challenged them to develop their character, circles of accountability, and learning together. The Y developed a Jewish values version of these circles, and the curriculum leads to really sweet conversations people have. At The Temple, we have four or five of those circles. A couple of the groups that finished the Y curriculum two years ago have continued to meet using Musar texts. At each session, each person takes turns bringing up one of the values, like compassion or empathy, justice, mercy. This year, they are doing social justice stuff. So, they're learning about civic issues and then, you know, what, how to address them. This year, we started a couple of new groups that were really interested in racial justice; they are developing their own sort of reading list. We have a new group of mental health professionals who want to look at Torah and Jewish tradition through a clinical lens. They are looking at the characters in the Torah to consider what was going on with them psychologically.

NICOLE: We have a group of dads with young kids talking about parenting. We have a group that has been going on for about six years; this year, they're really interested in Jewish identity.

RON: I would add a couple from some of our other colleagues. Rabbi Elie Spitz in Orange County, a Conservative rabbi, is in his seventh year of doing small groups based around a book that the groups read together. And then, Elie provides daily prompts and occasional videos for the small groups' members to think about. He launches the small-group campaign on Yom Kippur. He gets an angel to buy the books for the people in the small groups. He hoped to have thirty hosts the first year; instead, ninety-two people offered, and about eighty of them actually met. They read Elie's book on increasing wholeness. This year, they happen to be reading my book *The Seven Questions You're Asked in Heaven*. The groups meet for seven weeks—each week discussing a chapter. At the end, Elie invited me to meet with the groups on Zoom. It was thrilling. It's important to note that these small groups have on-ramps and off-ramps. They are not like the 1970s' era of *havurot*. Susie and I have belonged to a *havurah* for forty years. We've raised our kids, we took trips together, we celebrated our kids' Bar and Bat Mitzvahs, we were at each other's parents' funerals. Our *havurah* has worked. If the social chemistry is good, they work. But those that are socially engineered by the synagogue often fall apart because they don't happen organically. Small groups are different because they are not a "once and for all your life with the same group of people" commitment. You can meet different kinds of people as you go into these different sorts of groups.

Lydia and Nicole, can you help us out here? Why don't synagogues create demography groups by grade level in their schools?

NICOLE: Because parents are busy. Parents of school-age kids are the hardest people to engage; they feel like they don't have another extra minute in their day.

LYDIA: I think that is part of it, for sure. The goal would be to engineer parental involvement into the learning time, but there are so few hours in the week and we're trying to teach all of Jewish life in that supplemental time frame. At the same time, our teachers understand that if their students know everything about Judaism but don't know each other's names, we have failed. We are training our teachers on how to do what Ron calls "relational moments," to make that part of the classroom experience. We have remade our library into a community space, because parents will sometimes stick around on a Sunday morning. And we have built a café for them. But let's be honest, those parents just need that Sunday morning to either work out or hang out with their spouse for a minute or get more work done.

RON: Well, perhaps we should look deeper into the demography. For example, preschool parents, especially moms, love to have a group of other moms to talk with and share ideas. Bar and Bat Mitzvah parents are going through that experience together. Folks who are retiring . . .

NICOLE: We've had a lot of luck with the Wise Aging curriculum that comes out of Institute for Jewish Spirituality, helping people think about what's important in their lives and how they want to spend this next chapter of their lives.

RON: And parents of juniors and seniors in high school who are looking at colleges—they have a natural affinity and demography at the same time.

BRETT: How do you know you've been successful?

NICOLE: Great question. Hillel has done a really good job developing a system of keeping track of how many relationships their campus engagement workers create. It would be wonderful to have a way to track how many connections synagogue members have made. How many of them know three people who would show up for them in time of joy or hardship? How many people have six people they would show up for in that scenario? And then how many people can name twelve other people who they're not related to in the community? Right? If we measure our success by the percentage of people who could say yes to those questions, we would have a hunch about how good a job we were doing at connecting people in the community.

LYDIA: I have a similar dream. And one of you might be the inventors of this technology! Wouldn't it be amazing if we could be able to map the whole congregation? I actually know schools have been experimenting with this. It would be like the phone network map that shows where everybody's connected. You can see the hubs and you can see the outliers. I want a map so I know who are the folks who are going to be our natural leaders ... and who are the folks who are way out and we need to work harder to make sure they feel loved. Like that would be a dream.

RON: So, what's the impact of this work in the congregation? Has it made a difference at Central Synagogue and The Temple?

NICOLE: We're starting to see our culture shift a little bit, which is great. I hear all the time from people who let me know that someone in their small group had a loss in their family, or someone fell and broke a wrist ... and that the group has been there for the person. That's the best of a relational community. I was talking to a congregation in Santiago, Chile, yesterday. They have a thousand families. They heard my presentation and said, "Oh, you know, it's all nice, but what we really need are people to be members." And they're like, and why, you know? And so, I was like, so why do you think people are members? I asked, "Why?" They said, "Because they want a discount on their burial plot... and a cheaper Bar Mitzvah." And I said, "Okay, but once your kids are done with their *B'nei Mitzvah*, that's not going to be enough, right? Synagogues traditionally have been this space where you do your socializing, you do your programming, you do your praying. But right now, if you go on the My Jewish Learning website, they will give you a menu of adult education seminars from across the world taught by world-class teachers. So why do people need to come to synagogue anymore? Right? If you ask Ron Wolfson, he'll tell you they come for the programs, but they stay for the relationships. The people who have deep relationships are going to stay members of the community. That's the value proposition."

RON: Absolutely. Look what's happened during the pandemic. As soon as everybody went online, it begs the question "Why would I pay $3,000 to my synagogue down the street when I can dip into the Central Synagogues of the world, attend gorgeous worship experiences, for free?" Same thing with Jewish learning. So, what's the value proposition of a local synagogue? It must be a community of relationships.

I have one final question: what does this mean for you as a rabbi? Did you get trained to do this work in rabbinical school?

NICOLE: I was trained by community organizers, political organizers, and our friends in the megachurch world. Those are the people who I think really taught us how to do this. What do you think, Lydia?

LYDIA: I agree. I like thinking about what the Jewish community could be like if it was truly relational. Congregations ask me if it's worth the cost and risk to do this relational work, retooling everyone to focus on this. And I answer, "What is the cost of doing nothing, continuing to do things the way we do now?" I mean, many synagogues are not growing.

RON: I'm hearing from a lot of rabbis that they're really worried about post-pandemic synagogue life. Can we get back the people who have dropped away? Can we think more expansively and creatively about engagement when we are back in person? Some argue that we won't get them back, that the majority of American Jews are finding their

Jewish identity in going to Jewish museums, to the delis, reading Jewish books, doing genealogy. One author says nostalgia is the new religious practice and that's the future of American Judaism. I certainly disagree. But there are lots of donors and communal leaders who agree. Decrying about the death of synagogues is going to be the death of synagogues. We must push back on that, be even more aggressive about the creative things happening in synagogue life, the kind of work you and your colleagues are doing.

One last question: what's one thing that will change in synagogues after the pandemic subsides?

NICOLE: There are a lot of things that we don't need to do in person. We found that people who were unable to attend physically are now able to be included, and there's no going back from that. I continue to want people to feel like they own their Judaism and that they are invested.

LYDIA: I hope that people will continue to plumb their own connections to Judaism. Like the fifty-four-year-old dad whose kids are off to college and says to me, "I heard a TED talk from a rabbi and it was so amazing. I didn't know Judaism was really cool and had so much to say about life." And, then he asks me, "Will you come to my house and teach me and a bunch of guys the Talmud sometime?" And I say, "Yes. Yes, I will."

RON: Lydia and Nicole, thanks so much for your cutting-edge work in bringing the small-group model to the work of crafting a sacred community!

> **Questions for Creating Your Sacred Community**
>
> 1. What small groups are already convening in your sacred community?
>
> 2. How might you envision, organize, and implement a relational engagement campaign?
>
> 3. Based on what you know about your people, what small groups can be organized by affinity, demography, geography, and availability?
>
> 4. Who in your sacred community might be recruited to lead small groups?

CHAPTER 7

The Purpose-Driven Congregation

Pastor Rick Warren

Rick Warren is the senior pastor of Saddleback Church, one of the largest megachurches in the world. He and his wife, Kay, arrived in Southern California in January 1980 and began the church with a meeting of seven people in their living room. Today, over thirty thousand people show up for weekend worship services held at twenty different campuses, sixteen in southern California and four more in Hong Kong, Berlin, Buenos Aires, and Manila. How did he do it?

An evangelical Christian raised in a Baptist denomination, Rick began creating his sacred community by first talking to thousands of nonbelievers. In 1980, before holding their first worship service, he spent twelve weeks knocking on the doors of neighbors in the Saddleback Valley community of southern Orange County, California. He introduced himself and announced he was taking a three-minute opinion poll that had no right or wrong answers and that he was not there to sell them anything or convert them to anything. He just wanted to know their opinion. The first question would determine if he asked his other five questions: "Are you an active attender or member of a local house of worship?" If the person said "Yes," Rick responded, "God bless you," thanked them, and moved on to the next house. He explained that he was only interested in the opinions and needs of unaffiliated or irreligious people. But if the person said "No, I don't attend ANY house of worship," Rick wanted to know why.

After surveying thousands of homes, he summarized the biggest complaints people had about religious congregations. "The members are unfriendly to visitors and new people." "The sermons are boring and don't relate to my life." "The music is outdated. They sing tunes I don't know with lyrics I don't understand. It seems that congregations are more interested in my money than in me." "I'm not sure that I can trust my children to the children's program." Rick noted that none of the barriers to worship attendance were theological. For instance, only a few said: "I don't believe in God." Instead the barriers were cultural and sociological.

So he set out to reach a "church for the unchurched" that would specifically counter these and other common obstacles to religious participation:

- *He posted greeters in the parking lot and everywhere on the church campus.*
- *He provided free name tags, Starbuck's coffee, and donuts for every attender.*
- *He taught practical messages based on Scripture on Sunday that he knew would apply to people's real lives on Monday morning.*
- *He handed out a fill-in message outline that helped people remember the message; it included all the scripture verses for people without Bibles.*
- *He replaced the choir with a contemporary music band and singable songs which were easy to learn.*
- *The church had no dress code. It was casual. Rick wore jeans and sport shirts, noting that the people he wanted to attract to church tended to "dress down" in Southern California.*
- *As the church grew, it offered multiple services times (six) each weekend, with different styles of music.*
- *The children's Sunday school curriculum was written by staff and volunteers, and built around interactive videos, music bands led by the kids themselves, puppets for the youngest ages, and challenging games that teach Bible content.*
- *The church uses no fundraising, fees, or dues. Instead, weekly giving is taught as a worship habit and generosity is modeled with testimonies as a part of righteous character.*

Word spread throughout the community about this dynamic pastor and teacher. Rick structured the church around six levels of deepening spiritual commitment and engagement explained as six concentric circles where one moves from the outer circle (the least committed) to the smallest inner circle representing the deepest level of commitment. This "purpose-driven" assimilation process moves people intentionally and incrementally through these levels of increasing commitment: from the Community (the largest outer circle where there is no commitment to the church) to the Crowd (those committed to attending services) to the Congregation (those who commit to the membership covenant) to the Committed (those who commit to participate in a weekly small group, daily prayer and scripture reading, and weekly tithing) to the Core (those committed to serving the community and the church family) and to the Commissioned (those who commit to serving needs overseas). A four-hour class and a signed covenant are a part of each of these movements to deeper spiritual growth and righteous living.

Rick developed a number of spiritual growth tools that are now used by congregations all around the world: Classes, Covenants, Campaigns, and Cell groups. Over one million pastors and priests have been trained to use these tools in 164 nations in the past forty years.

The Life Development classes are a series of classes he wrote to assimilate and mobilize every member for their personal ministry and mission in the world. People move from membership to maturity to ministry and finally to their life mission in the world.

As the congregation grew larger, Rick used the management advice that Jethro gave to Moses in Numbers 18:17-24 where his father-in-law showed Moses how to meet everyone's needs by gathering people in small groups of ten, so that the span of control would be manageable. Rick cancelled the weekly Wednesday night Bible study meeting (which was averaging over a thousand attendees) because he believed it was a bottleneck. "We wanted EVERYONE in a weekly Bible study so we canceled the centralized 'come to the church building' study and decentralized it into a thousand small group Bible studies." It worked. Today, Saddleback has over 7,000 small groups that meet weekly in homes, offices, parks, and restaurants for fellowship, the study of Scriptures, prayer, fun, and ministry projects that are done as a group. Saddleback is unique in that it is the only church in America that has more members attending home-based small groups each week than attending the weekend worship services. Saddleback small groups meet in 196 Southern California cities—from Santa Monica (north of Los Angeles) to San Diego at the border with Mexico.

Because of this, Saddleback church stayed strong during the two-year COVID-19 pandemic—even when they were prevented from having large, corporate worship services inside the Worship Center for 22 months. The members kept meeting in their small groups during this time.

Rick wanted to prove that you don't need to own a church or synagogue building to grow a congregation. He often says: "A congregation is PEOPLE, not a PLACE," so at the first service in 1980, held in a rented high school theater, he announced that Saddleback would not even start looking for land to build a building for the first five years. Rick explains: "Most churches build too soon and too small. They get in a hurry and build what they can afford at the time, and then the shoe tells the foot how big it can get! So we waited until the church was averaging over 10,000 people in attendance before we built our first permanent building. If we had built sooner, we would have never grown to the size we are today." The congregation ended up using 79 different rented facilities in the thirteen years that they delayed building a permanent home for their spiritual family. "We were the church on the move," said Rick. "If you could figure out where we were from week to week, then you got to attend!"

He added, "Remember, the Temple was David's idea. God's idea was the Tabernacle! It was portable and mobile!"

Eventually, Saddleback built a magnificent 120-acre campus with a simple but functional Worship Center, a children's Sunday school building designed with help from Disney Imagineers, adult education space, and a P.E.A.C.E. center which offers a free medical clinic, a free food pantry that typically feeds 40,000 a month, free legal aid, tutoring, English as a second language, and two dozen other community ministries. The campus also includes "The Refinery," a building for teenagers which includes sports facilities, a skate park, and an outdoor concert arena. There are three large outdoor baptism pools where over 52,000 adults and youth have been baptized. (Saddleback baptizes only those old enough to choose to believe; they do not baptize babies.)

Breaking nearly every stereotype of a sleepy church, Saddleback hums with spiritual energy. There are over five hundred community ministries led by over thirteen thousand volunteers working on everything from social justice issues, orphan adoption, mental health, mission trips to 197 nations, a community forum that offers lectures on topics of the day, and yearly "spiritual growth campaigns" centered around a theme of interest. Everything is presented with style, creativity, and excellence. During COVID-19, when over 120 food banks closed down in Southern California, Saddleback took up the challenge by inventing 420 "Pop-Up" food distribution sites in Southern California. They partnered with school districts, hospitals, parks, and the county Board of Supervisors. Over 13,600 Saddleback volunteers fed over fifteen million pounds of food to over 620,000 hungry residents. The church became the leading food distributor in Southern California due to its values of "Find a need and fill it," "Be fast, fluid, and flexible," and "Work with anyone who will work with you!"

Perhaps one of the most important values behind this congregation's amazing impact is Rick's commitment to "lowering the barriers, while raising the bar." Visitors are treated as the most important people at weekend services. Members are trained to befriend strangers sitting nearby. There are places to watch the worship service outside of the Worship Center. It is livestreamed across the main campus to dozens of other outdoor and indoor locations. A "family room" is reserved for nursing mothers. In the early years of Saddleback, visitors could pick up a cassette recording of the message to take home immediately after the service; today, every service and every message is available free online. No one is asked to identify herself/himself. As Rick explains "We want people to feel welcomed and wanted without feeling watched. Fear is often the first emotion a nonreligious person feels when they attend a worship service for the first time. We do everything we can to eliminate that natural fear from the first time visitors. So we never embarrass them, we never make them stand up and introduce themselves publicly, and we treat them as treasured guests. Saddleback was built on hospitality. It's a simple concept but often overlooked: If you want people to come back after their first visit, you must be nice to them!"

Everything is designed to help people take a "Next Step" in their spiritual journey, but they are not pressured to do it. Rick says "We start where people are, not where we want them to be. We say 'Take the time to make the right decision.' But we are always clear on the benefits of growing spiritually. We tell people 'God loves you just the way you are. But God loves you too much to let you stay that way. You were made for so much more!'"

Rick's book, The Purpose-Driven Church, *outlines precisely how the Saddleback sacred community was built. For over 35 years, Rick and his team have held training conferences for pastors, both in the United States and around the world, sharing with them the models and strategies for community building. When Rick wrote a manual for one of Saddleback's annual forty-day spiritual growth "campaigns" on the theme of "The Purpose-Driven Life," the book version became the best-selling English nonfiction book in history, selling over 50 million copies. It became the second most translated book in the world next to the Bible. Due to its success, Rick stopped taking a salary from the church and repaid 22 years of salary back to the congregation. Rick and Kay have now served the Saddleback congregation for free for 42 years. It is part of their testimony about God's faithfulness to bless us when we bless others. When the Warrens married in 1975, they began tithing 10 percent of their income back to God as an act of worship in whatever church they attended at the time. They also committed to annually increase their giving every year of their marriage. Since 2003, the Warrens have given away 91 percent of their income (which comes from book royalties) and live on 9 percent.*

Each year, we invite Rick and two of his staff pastors, David Chrzan, Pastor of Missions, and Steve Gladen, Pastor of Small Groups, to share what they're learning. Here is a partial transcript of a recent session:

RICK: It's always so great to be back with you rabbinical students and with my dearest friend Ron Wolfson. I look forward to our time together every year because what you are doing matters to God and the world desperately needs your leadership. I'm here with two of my staff pastors, David Chrzan and Steve Gladen. Steve knows more about building small groups in sacred community than anybody I know. We call our small groups "purpose-driven groups" because they are built around our five biblical purposes: worship, fellowship, spiritual growth, ministry (service), and mission.

Saddleback is unique in the fact that it is the only congregation in America that has more people attending small groups during the week than we have attending our weekend worship services. Typically, we have about thirty thousand people attending our weekend services, but during the week we have as many as forty-five thousand people involved in over seven thousand small groups. These small groups are the heartbeat of our congregation and they are spread out across Southern California—from Malibu to San Diego. It has been our network of small groups that has held our church family together during the COVID-19 pandemic when we were not able to meet in large group worship for over a year. And even during the pandemic when we were not supposed to meet in person—our small groups still met online through Zoom meetings. The small group of couples that I personally belong to has been meeting together for twenty years! We have supported each other through every problem and circumstance you could possibly imagine. It has kept us connected to each other and to our entire church family during COVID-19.

David Chrzan was my chief of staff for many years, but now he oversees our P.E.A.C.E. program. P.E.A.C.E. is an acrostic for five antidotes to what we call the "Global Goliaths," five giant, worldwide problems that affect billions of people: extreme poverty, pandemic diseases, conflict, corruption, and lack of education. "P" stands for *promote* reconciliation wherever there is conflict. "E" stand for *equip* ethical servant leaders to fight corruption. "A" stands for *assist* the poor by creating jobs and opportunities. "C" stand for *care* for the sick where there are pandemics and illnesses. "E" stands for *educate* the next generation by combating illiteracy. So far, since we launched the P.E.A.C.E. initiative, 26,869 Saddleback members have paid their own way to serve overseas in 197 countries. The former director of America's Peace Corp told us that Saddleback's P.E.A.C.E. initiative has had more people serving in more nations than the Peace Corps!

RON: Pastor Rick is, by far, the greatest creator of spiritual communities I've ever known. And that's why we bring our students to Saddleback every year. We're just thrilled that you guys have been generous enough to join us today. We've read *The Purpose-Driven Church*. So, Brett, do you have a question you want to shoot to Pastor Rick?

BRETT: I have a bunch of questions. I think what really struck me in reading your book was the major role that your personal relationship with God plays in your ministry. You write that you were called by God to come to Saddleback, knocked on doors, and started a church. Did you grow up in a community where everyone speaks about God in this personal, intimate way?

RICK: Brett, I love you already! The fact that you asked that question just shows the deep spiritual sensitivity in your own heart. When we talk about any congregation—whether Jewish or Christian—we must always begin with God, not ourselves! The first four words in *The Purpose-Driven Life* book are "It's not about you." It's all about God. We were created *by* God, and we're created *for* God, and, until we understand that, life will never make sense! I need a bigger reason than my own self-centeredness to get me out of bed each morning.

As David said in Psalm 5:3, "Lord, every morning you hear my voice. I tell you what I need and I wait in expectation." David had that personal relationship with God. We cannot build a healthy and growing spiritual community that honors God without God being the center of it all. In Psalm 127:1, Solomon said, "Unless the Lord builds the house, the workers labor in vain." Building true spiritual community cannot be done merely by human effort. It requires dependence upon God and trust in God's love and wisdom.

During the COVID pandemic, with all of the forced isolation and quarantining, I've tried to use this additional "alone" time to deepen my walk with God. We have to serve God in the times He puts us in, not in the circumstances we'd choose. Right now, when everything is so unsettled, we're going through a season that I call "God's waiting room." It's a time when we are in a hurry for things to return to the way they were before COVID, but God clearly isn't in a hurry!

Every parent knows that when the kids are fighting and not getting along, you sometimes have to say "Okay, everybody. Take a time out! Go to your room and stay there until you've made an attitude adjustment!" During this pandemic, I think God has been saying to all of humanity, "Okay, everybody. Take a time out! You need to work on your attitudes." So let's not waste this time. Use the time to get to know God better personally. As Psalm 46:10 says: "Be still, and know that I am God." You can't build a relationship with God (or anyone else) unless you spend time alone with Him. I developed a daily close relationship with God at a very young age and now I've walked in friendship with God for sixty years.

Rabbi Elie Spitz, whom Ron knows, is a dear friend of mine. Kay and I love Elie and Linda. We have shared many Seders with them in their home over the years. And we don't observe the abbreviated version! It's the full five hour version (laughs)! I want the FULL blessing of that meaningful experience—with ALL the readings and singing and praying. Recently Elie brought me a little oil lamp from Israel that he collects when he goes there. It reminded me of one of the first Scriptures I memorized as a little boy from Psalm 119:105: "Your Word is a lamp to my feet and a light for my path." As a rabbi, you must saturate your mind with the scriptures, not simply so you can teach great sermons, but because it feeds our soul and it gives us direction. Sometimes I hear people say "I just wish God would write in the sky what He wants me to do." I reply: "Why should God write it in the sky when He has already written it in His Word?" The Will of God is found in the Word of God.

The chronic stress and constant changes during this pandemic has drained everyone of energy. Everyone is tired. No one has the same level of energy that they did two years ago. Trauma saps your energy and weakens your resolve. You get tired faster. So how do we get our "souls restored" as David talks about in Psalm 23? Well, Isaiah 40:30–31 gives us the secret to personal renewal, revival, and restoration. He said: "Even young people become exhausted and weak and stumble. But those who wait on the Lord will find new strength. They will soar on wings like eagles. They will run and not grow weary. They will walk and not faint."

At the beginning of the pandemic, I taught the people in our congregation a simple daily habit that would keep "restoring their soul" no matter how long the pandemic lasts. I call the habit "GWFW" and "GWLW." That stands for "God's Word, First Word" at the beginning of the day and "God's Word, Last Word" at the end of every day. Here's how you do this habit. First, put a copy of the Scriptures by your bed on your bedside nightstand. Open it to a book you want to read through—Psalms or Proverbs would be a great place to start. Never close the book! Leave it open! A closed Bible is easier to ignore. Then, each morning, before you get out of bed, pick up the Word of God and sitting on the side of your bed, start reading where you have left the Scriptures open to. The amount of time you take to read is not important. And the amount of verses you read is not important. Here's the rule: READ UNTIL SOMETHING SPEAKS TO YOU PERSONALLY. It may be a truth that CHALLENGES you or it may be a truth that COMFORTS you—both will feed your soul. I recommend that you read it ALOUD and you read it SLOWLY. Once you come to a verse that speaks directly to you . . . you stop! You're going to think about that one idea for the rest of the day.

Then at night, the very last thing you do before putting your head down on your pillow is to pick up the Scriptures again and start reading from the place where you stopped that morning. Again, just read until something challenges or comforts you. Then you go to sleep thinking about that verse and that truth. Remember, you just read until a verse speaks to you. You may have to read an entire chapter or you may just read one verse and stop right there. It's not about quantity of verses. It's about letting God speak to you. Pray Psalm 119:18: "Open my eyes to see the wonderful truths in your law." Many studies have shown that the first five minutes of your day tends to set your mood for the entire rest of the day so DO NOT look at your phone first! Do not turn on the TV or radio first! Do not read the newspaper first! And, this is especially important—do not look at your social media first! Start your day feeding on the truth of God's Word. Remember GWFW and GWLW. It will change your life.

Another key to maintaining your spiritual strength in ministry is to treat yourself the way God treats you. How is that? God treats you with grace! None of us get what we deserve. If God gave us what we deserve, none of us would be alive. Instead, God gives us what we *need*, not what we deserve. Everything we have in life is a gift of God's grace—the air we breathe, the water we drink, the food we eat. Your mind is a gift of grace. Your abilities are gifts of God's grace. So if that's how God treats us—with grace—then we need to treat ourselves . . . and everybody else . . . the same way. Imagine how different the world would be if we were gracious to everyone around us!

One area where we all need grace right now, and an area where we need to show grace to everyone else, is recognizing that the pandemic and all the changes that came with it has left everyone tired, fatigued, and worn-out. No one has the same amount of energy that they did two years before the chronic crisis began. Let me explain it this way: If you have a car battery, and you attach a single lightbulb to it, that battery will last a long time. But, if you attach two lightbulbs, it will burn out in half the time. And if you attach eight lightbulbs to that battery, it will burn out eight times faster. Now here's the point: During all the changes and crises and trauma of the last two years, you haven't had just one lightbulb attached to your battery; you have been being drained in dozens of ways. So has everyone else around you. If you get up in the morning after having a good night's rest and a couple of hours into your day you think "Man, I am exhausted!" then welcome to the human race! That's the way everyone feels right now. So cut people some slack. Don't expect them to work at the same level of energy they had two years ago.

That's what chronic stress and continuous trauma does to people. So be gracious and merciful to others just as God is with you.

Let me mention one other thing that will help you when your emotional tank is running on empty. Plan to connect daily with people you love. That re-energizes and recharges a drained soul. Even if you have to do it by FaceTime or Zoom, put it into your schedule. The very latest neuroscience studies show that when you make contact with someone you love—to encourage them or to be encouraged—your brain gets a huge hit of dopamine and your brain chemistry changes in about thirty seconds. And here's the interesting part: you don't have to have a twenty-minute phone call to get that effect. Most of the benefit comes in the first thirty seconds! Both you and the person you connected with get a lift and energy boost in less than a minute of contact! So do that every day.

RON: One of the things I've learned from you is that a rabbi and a preacher need to say something on Sunday your people can use on Monday. You just illustrated that, Rick, by taking Brett's question, applying biblical principles to his life. You generally shape your messages around twelve to fifteen biblical verses. You are a great text teacher, something we value highly in Jewish education. Our spiritual life is centered around texts. Why is that so important?

RICK: The text is so important because my opinion can't heal a hurt. What matters is what God has already said in His Word. The answers to all of human life's predicaments and the wisdom we need for living and relationships are all in the Word of God. For instance, every human emotion is covered in the Psalms. Psalms is not just about praise and thanksgiving. One third of the Psalms are songs of lament. It was those Psalms of Lament that guided me through my overwhelming grief when my youngest son ended his life after battling mental illness for 27 years. The day that happened was the worst day of my life and I lived in the Psalms of Lament, literally, for a couple years. By the way, the Bible commentators who helped me the most were Jewish scholars, not Christians, because Jews have far stronger traditions and skills for handling grief.

In the New Testament, Paul gives us four purposes of Scripture in 1st Timothy 3:16–17: "All Scripture is God-breathed and is useful for teaching, for rebuking, for correcting, and for training in righteousness, so that the people of God may be thoroughly equipped for every good work."

At Saddleback, in Class 201 (Discovering Spiritual Maturity), we explain these verses like this:

"for teaching"—Scripture shows God's path to walk on

"for rebuking"—Scripture shows where we've gotten off God's path

"for correcting"—Scripture shows how to get back on God's path

"for training in righteousness"—Scripture shows how to stay on God's path!

SARA: I wanted to ask a question about *The Purpose-Driven Church*. If you were going to update *The Purpose-Driven Church* for 2021 after the world has completely changed over the last year, what would you add or change?

RICK: Another wise question! Sara, I would change a lot. Of course, God's "purposes" never change (Psalm 33:11) because they are eternal. The ways we fulfill those purposes MUST change with every generation. Our message never changes, but the methods do change. There are a number of methods and tools and programs that I share in *The Purpose-Driven Church* that were quite effective in 1995, but that is now over twenty-five years ago. The world has changed, of course. For instance, in PDC, I described the typical target we were trying to reach in a profile that we called "Saddleback Sam." Today, our target is very different. But the principle is still true: No congregation can appeal to and reach everyone. You must define your target and know who you are most likely to reach. And you need to admit who you will likely never reach! That's why we say: "It takes all kinds of congregations to reach all kinds of people." In your case you need to ask: "Who can we best reach? Are they cultural Jews who've lost connection to their faith? Or have they not grown in their faith?" Methods are many; principles are few. Methods change often. Principles never do.

In the early years, most people in our congregation looked like me ...young, white, and drop dead sexy! [*Laughs.*] Obviously I'm kidding, but we were a pretty homogenous group. You tend to attract what you are, not necessarily what you want. But today, Saddleback looks like the United Nations because we intentionally went after diversity. Another of our ten values—the first "A" in our S.A.D.D.L.E.B.A.C.K. acrostic is "All-Nation Congregation." We want our church to look like how heaven is going to look! Remember, diversity is God's idea. Racial and ethnic identities are God's idea. We're not all going to look alike in heaven either. So if you don't like people who look different than you, you're going to HATE heaven!

Have you figured out that God loves diversity? Did you know that, for instance, in the insect world, God created over six thousand different kinds of beetles? You would have thought that three or four hundred varieties would have been enough, right? No! God goes overboard on diversity in everything He creates. He doesn't make clones of anything. There's not a single person on the planet who looks like you. Just like no two snowflakes are alike, God broke the mold when He created you. By the way, this is why racism is actually a form of idolatry. It questions God's wisdom by implying "God, you made a mistake. You should have made everyone like me!" Racism is the ultimate arrogance and it is an insult to our Creator.

Today Saddleback is likely the most ethnically diverse congregation in America. We speak 169 languages in our congregation. Most of my twenty campus pastors are *not* white guys. We have Asian pastors (all kinds), Hispanic pastors (all kinds), African pastors, African-American pastors, and pastors from India, Europe, and the Middle East. Our diversity is intentional because we know it would give us far more health and strength than if we all had the same background. Of course, we are now a global congregation, with campuses on four continents.

Sara, another area where I wish I had been more intentional at the start of our church was in hiring staff who were at different ages and stages of life than me. I was 25 when Kay and I "planted" the church. We did not attract many middle age members until I added Glen Kreun as a staff pastor, who was ten years older than me.

As a leader, you'll find that the people it is easiest for you to lead tend to be those within about ten years on either side of your age. That means that, as a young leader, you'll need to add staff (paid or volunteers) to your team who are older than you. As you grow older in your ministry, you'll need to add staff to your team who relate to members younger than you. Regardless, at any age, you need helpers who represent each generation or each decade of ages. As a young pastor, I needed staff helpers who were older than me. Now, I have layered staff of all ages—with people in their 20s, 30s, 40s, 50s, and 60s—helping care for the five generations in our church family. In professional baseball, every team has a farm league of "up and comers" being prepared for future leadership. What I'm talking about is different. These leaders of all ages are ministering to their age groups right now.

It's helpful to think of your congregation like a square divided into four quadrants representing four kinds of people you must persuade to follow your leadership. Some people are older than you and others are younger than you. Then, there are people who joined your congregation before you did, and others who joined after you became the leader. Now, the people you can lead the easiest are those who are both younger than you and joined after you became the leader. In contrast, the hardest group to lead are those who are older than you and joined before you became the leader. The other two quadrants are always watching these two opposite groups to decide how they will react. So how do you lead all four quadrants? You find a spokesperson who matches each group and can represent you to them. You need an Aaron who can speak up for your ideas in each group. This is not only true generationally; it is a key to growing a multicultural congregation. Platform and profile the kind of people you want to attract.

RON: What else do you wish you'd done differently or sooner?

RICK: Another mistake I made in the early years was underestimating the importance of music in positioning your congregation to reach new people. Right now, without knowing anything else about your congregation, if you were to tell me the style of music that you are currently using in worship, I can tell you the kind of people you're attracting and also the kind of people you'll never be able to reach. The moment you choose a music style, you're determining who you'll attract and who you'll never attract. That's why I keep saying that it takes all kinds of congregations to minister to all kinds of people. You cannot get the members of your own family to agree on the best music style, so why should you think one style will appeal to everyone? I have three friends who are rabbis of three different congregations on Wilshire Boulevard in Los Angeles. Although they lead shuls on the same street, they attract different people with different worship styles. Some might wonder "Do we really need three synagogues on the same street?" The answer is yes, of course we do! Why? Because no one congregation can appeal to everybody's needs and preferences. Our differences in personality are God-given.

BRETT: Rick, as you survey what's been happening in the world recently, what is your perspective on ministering to people's spiritual needs during the pandemic?

RICK: Over the past two years, our world has been hit with five giant problems that I call *"social storms."* These storms have created a lot of emotional stress and relational conflict, but they have also awakened a spiritual hunger in many people. The first social storm has been the COVID-19 pandemic. It's a *global infirmity,* a health issue that is impacting literally everyone on earth. A second social storm has been the *financial insecurity* that millions of people have felt when they were temporarily laid off from their jobs or, even worse, saw their jobs permanently deleted. Many without any savings suddenly found themselves standing in line at food distribution centers for the first time. A third social storm has been the examples of *racial inequality.* America saw a disturbing series of deaths of young Black men and women due to racism, abuse, and injustice. Another social storm has been *political incivility*. Our nation is more divided and polarized than probably at any other time since the Civil War. These four social storms created a fifth one: *social instability*. We've seen this instability and unrest expressed in both riots in cities and an attack by our own citizens on our nation's capital for the first time in history. The massive changes that the COVID pandemic brought has challenged all of us deeply. But COVID-19 is just one of five giant challenges that hit the world at the same time during the past two years. Together, these five storms have damaged and disrupted and discouraged and divided people in unprecedented ways.

If you study history, you'll find that people respond to pandemic diseases in the opposite way that they typically respond to natural disasters. Typically, if there is a hurricane or flood or fire or earthquake, people draw together to cooperate in serving and solving problems. Natural disasters typically unify people. Hurricane Katrina was a great example of that. Disasters can bring out the best in people. People are more kind and more generous and gracious with each other. But pandemic diseases create fear and distrust and division. Rather than working together, the fears that accompany a health pandemic can cause polarization, blaming, scapegoating, and demonizing of different groups. We've seen all that happen with COVID. Just like an earthquake, tension builds between different forces. Then at some point, the pressure causes a great fracture and the ground splits. Or, like a volcano, the pressure builds up until it finally erupts.

I recently learned that there are three distinct elements required for an explosion. First, an explosion requires FUEL. Second, an explosion requires CONTAINMENT. Third, an explosion requires a SPARK. I was unaware of the necessity of the second element—containment. If you pour out a gallon of gasoline on a road and drop a match on it, it will create a big fire, but it will not explode because the gasoline is not contained in anything. When I read that, it explained why we've had so many emotional social explosions and eruptions during COVID-19. During the past two years, people have felt contained or controlled by quarantining, social distancing, mask requirements, and other restrictions to their freedom. Concerts and sporting events were cancelled, schools and church services shut down, travel was restricted, jobs were eliminated, and people felt limited and constrained by new boundaries. That's why any little spark seems to create explosions today. People have erupted over all kinds of issues because they feel controlled and constrained. So these are not our happiest days.

God's Word gives us many, many examples of how spiritual receptivity changes in people's lives as their circumstances change. In good times, people tend to forget God, become prideful, and stop depending on Him. But in difficult times, people tend to look to God and ask for help.

God warns us many times about the temptation of success, such as in Deuteronomy 8:11-14: *"Be careful that you never forget the Lord your God, failing to observe His commands, laws and decrees that I give you today. Otherwise, when you're satisfied and build fine houses and settle down, and your herds grow large, and your silver and gold increase, and all that you have is multiplied, THEN your heart will become proud and **you'll forget the Lord your God**, who brought you out of Egypt, the land of slavery."* (New International Version, NIV)

Jesus told a story called "The Parable of the Soils & Seed" to explain spiritual receptivity. It's so insightful, it is repeated in three different Gospels: Matthew 13, Mark 4, and Luke 8. He said there are four kinds of soil that represent four kinds of hearts, or spiritual receptivity. The farmer (God) plants the same, identical seed (God's Word) in four different kinds of soil (human hearts). Although the truth is the same, the results vary due to different levels of receptivity.

Some of the seed gets sown onto *hard soil*. It falls on the hardened pathway between the garden rows. The hard soil represents **the hardened heart** that has been trampled on and packed down over time so that the seed cannot even penetrate it. Before it can even take root, a bird eats the seed. The Word has no effect.

Some other seed gets sown on the second kind of soil: *shallow soil* with a bedrock underneath it. This represents **the superficial heart**. There is just enough soil to allow the seed to sprout quickly, but the hard bedrock underneath it prevents roots from developing. So when the heat comes – hot, dry, difficult days – the plants quickly dry up and die. The initial enthusiasm for spiritual truth doesn't last because they have no roots to sustain them in dry times.

Then some seed gets sown on *soil with weeds in it*. This represents **the distracted heart.** The seed of God's Word gets planted but, as Jesus explained, *it gets choked out by daily worries, making money, and having fun, so they never grow to maturity.* The *things of the world* compete with the *truth of the word* for people's attention. Busyness causes spiritual barrenness.

The fourth kind of soil is the *good soil.* It represents **the receptive heart.** It is the open heart that welcomes the truth of God's Word, and it produces a huge harvest of good fruit (character). Then the seed is multiplied thirty, sixty, or a hundred times over. The result is exponential growth!

What Jesus was pointing out is that at any given moment, three out of four people around you are *not* interested in spiritual truth. That means seventy five percent of the people in your area, at any particular point, will *not* be receptive. You can't reach everyone at the same time. Now, there are three important applications for us as rabbis and pastors:

First, if I'm a good farmer, I don't want to waste time and energy broadcasting seed indiscriminately. It is not good stewardship to waste precious seed. Instead I should focus on planting the maximum amount of spiritual seed into hearts where it is most likely to take root, grow, and reproduce!

Second, it is not my job as a rabbi or pastor to prepare the soil. That's God's job! I'm not the spirit of God. I can't change people's hearts. I can't make people more responsive or more receptive. I have to trust God to do that *in His way and His timing!* He prepares hearts through circumstances that He controls and I don't control. My job, as a spiritual farmer, is to recognize the right place and season to plant. Ecclesiastes 8:6 says *"There is a right time and a right way to do everything."* My job is to always be ready to plant the seed in soil that God has prepared to receive it.

So the question is this: *How does* God turn hard, unreceptive soil into good, soft soil? **He sends a storm!** God softens soil with rain! When the inevitable storms of life come, they can soften even the hardest heart. C.S. Lewis said "God whispers to us in our pleasure, but He shouts to us in our pain. Pain is God's megaphone." Everyone ... everywhere ... eventually goes through pain, because no one gets to live a pain-free life. Job 37:13 says *"God sends storms to correct us (shebet) and show us his lovingkindness (chesed)."* We just have to be patient for God to soften a heart.

So here's the third application: You build a congregation by focusing on people in pain and ministering to them! Focus on the people that God has made receptive through a storm in their life. Don't worry about the hard hearted and unresponsive. Everyone's season of storms is inevitable, and then you can step in with the grace and mercy of God. For 42 years, I've taught this truth to spiritual leaders around the world: If you just focus your energy on people in pain, your congregation will grow.

What kind of pain should you look for? Every kind. Look for a hurt and heal it. Find a need and meet it. Listen for their question and answer it. Understand their fears and relieve them. The past two years have been the most difficult in my 52 years of ministry. But because we focus on people in pain, these two years have been the most spiritually fruitful years for Saddleback Church. We saw more lives transformed, more marriages restored, more families growing in love, and more people fulfilling the five purposes that God created us to fulfill.

So don't be discouraged. This is not the end of the story. Don't give up. Look up! And pray for a spiritual revival in our generation. We need it!

RON: Pastor Rick, thank you so much for spending this time with us to share for your teaching, your inspiration, and your friendship.

Questions for Creating Your Sacred Community

1. Who are you trying to reach? Have you identified your target population?

2. Do your members and guests hear something on Shabbat/holidays they can use in their daily lives?

3. How can you "plant in the soil" after it is softened by the inevitable "storms" of living?

4. Are you ready to say, "Belonging to our sacred community will transform your life"?

CHAPTER 8

Emerging Spiritual Communities

Rabbi Sharon Brous and Melissa Balaban

Rabbi Sharon Brous is the senior rabbi and founding rabbi of IKAR, a Jewish community launched in 2004 to reinvigorate Jewish practice and inspire people of faith to reclaim a moral and prophetic voice. Her TED talk "Reclaiming Religion" has been viewed by more than 1.4 million people and translated into twenty-three languages. Ordained by the Jewish Theological Seminary, Sharon is widely recognized as one of the most influential rabbis in America.

Melissa Balaban is IKAR's founding president and CEO. She focuses on the strategic direction of the community, working closely with Rabbi Sharon Brous and the board to develop appropriate fundraising goals and execute the associated activities. Prior to joining IKAR, Melissa was assistant dean at the University of Southern California Law School.

Together, Sharon and Melissa are among the founders of the Jewish Emergent Network, a consortium of seven leading independent minyanim.

RON: What we are asking in this seminar is "How do we construct spiritual communities?" You, Sharon and Melissa, did it from scratch. So, please tell us the vision and what you've learned about doing this work in the past eighteen years of IKAR.

SHARON: My rabbinate is rooted in the Jewish promise that every human being is made *b'tzelem Elohim*, "in God's image." I learned this Torah from Rabbi Shai Held, who learned it from Rabbi Yitz Greenberg, years into my time in seminary. This idea, this theological commitment, became the core driver of my political, social, and spiritual life: that at the heart of my yearning for a different kind of world was the idea that every human being is intended to live in dignity. The question for me became: how willing are you to actually invest in the building of that reality?

I met Rabbi Yitz several years after we started IKAR, and he asked, "How did you do it? How did you build IKAR into a Shabbat centered, justice-driven community?" And I said, "Yitz, we just took your Torah really seriously." That theology is the heart of the practice for me; that's the driver for every conversation and decision at IKAR. What if you built an organization in which at the center of every conversation was the question of human dignity ... where then do you land on budgeting? On hiring? On program and governance? That's always at the center of the conversation—the idea of infinite worth, of equality and the uniqueness of every single person.

Ron likes for us to tell about how we met. We were introduced by a mutual friend, Daniel Sokatch, who now runs the New Israel Fund. I had moved out to LA after finishing a rabbinic fellowship at B'nai Jeshurun in New York. And my rabbis there, Roly Matalon and Marcelo Bronstein, told me: As soon as you move out to LA, you have to meet with Ron Wolfson. He's thinking about community in a radically different way. Ron had just become friends with Rick Warren and was a careful observer of Warren's work and the whole idea of a purpose-driven church. What would it mean, he was asking, if we applied some of what we're learning from the Christian world into our Jewish spaces? Ron and I sat and talked about these things and quickly became friends. I was curious about what it would take to build communities that would help people have the kinds of transformative experiences I had had at B'nai Jeshurun.

And at the same time, I also got involved in Reboot, a select cohort of changemakers and tastemakers, creatives and intellectuals, all of whom are Jewish, most marginally connected to Jewish life. They were raising questions about why Jewish institutions had done so little to fill their hunger for spirit, meaning, connection, and community. So, I think a combination of all of these influences—the theological foundation, the radical thinking about community that Ron was proposing, and the questions being asked by the Rebooters—in addition to the realities of the time, which were breaking my heart, all of these things had me pretty stirred up.

Then I met Melissa, and there was a kind of magical combustion that every now and again happens in life. Before that night, I was already thinking it was time for me to leave the day school I was teaching in. I love teaching Torah and I love kids, but I knew it wasn't what God put me in the world to do. I was trying to sort out what my rabbinate would be. I also just missed my Jewish community in New York and yearned for community here. When Melissa and I met, there was a kind of sacred alignment. We both felt it immediately: together we could think about Jewish community in a way that I don't think either of us would have without the other.

MELISSA: I'm an ill-educated Jew. I won't tell you which shul I grew up in in the Valley, but mostly I cut classes and caused trouble; I couldn't stand it. I found it boring and useless and not relevant to me at all. I loved Jewish summer camp but felt mostly alienated from Judaism. I was pretty disconnected in college. I felt Jewish, but it wasn't in any way a driving force. I traveled a lot in the world. Part of the reason I was so alienated from Judaism is that I felt like there was a secret handshake that I didn't know, but everybody else did.

My mom sort of dragged me to a service where Rabbi Chaim Seidler-Feller was speaking, and I was like, "What? What?" He was talking about stuff in the Torah that relates to the world. Nobody ever told me that. I thought this was all bullshit for older white dudes. Chaim actually officiated at my marriage with my husband, and that sort of brought me back into Jewish life. So, we sort of found our way. I was a first-year law student at USC, and Rabbi Laura Geller took me out for lunch. And she said, "I want you to chair the Jewish Feminist Center." And I said, "What? Me? What can I do?" And she said, "Here's why I think you'd be really good at this." And she liked to list the reasons. By the way, I've stolen this approach as a way to get volunteers involved, because how can you say no to that? I would never have raised my hand for it, but she reeled me in. And that was how I started getting involved in Jewish life. So, when Sharon shared her vision for what became IKAR, I wanted to make sure that people who felt disconnected like I did could find a way in.

BRETT: I have a clarifying question. This is your strategy for getting volunteers?

MELISSA: I think a lot of synagogues operate under the premise that when they need somebody to work on a project, they just throw it out there: "Who wants to do this?" And the task feels like a bummer. What Laura did was different. She said to me, "I see you. I see your gifts and talents, I want you to do this, this is why you would be really good at it, and it would be so much fun." That was such a powerful lesson for me about how to engage people in doing the work of building community … because I would never have volunteered to do it; it wouldn't even have been on my radar. She singled me out and saw that it was really something I could do. And I owe her now for everything. I'd still be a civil rights lawyer or law school dean if it wasn't for Rabbi Laura Geller.

Later, I had taken a job at USC as the assistant dean of the law school and was serving on the board of the Progressive Jewish Alliance, where Daniel Sokatch was executive director. I had young kids, and we couldn't find a shul that worked for us. Nothing enticed my husband, a sort of curmudgeonly New Yorker, atheist non-joiner, but my kids were approaching the age where they should start studying. And so, Daniel said, "You should meet my friend Sharon Brous." And I said, "Whatever, I don't have time for that. I'm busy." But then, "Oh, maybe she's great. And she can study with my kids."

So, we had this meeting, it was me and my husband, and Daniel and two other women. And Sharon articulated this vision that was so moving; she understood the hunger we had for something deeply spiritual—this idea that there are so many parts of your Jewish and human self and you often compartmentalize them in ways that make no sense, particularly in a Jewish context. She described going to different fancy shuls that were talking with her about doing something different. One said, "We're a davening shul." Another said, "We're a social justice shul." And that just didn't make sense to her. How can you go to shul every week, as a *shomer* [observant of] Shabbat and *shomer* kashrut Jew and not understand your responsibility in the world? At the same time, how can you be a Jew engaged in social justice and not get that your texts and traditions inform that work? This was a revelation for me because I had seen it in pieces, but I had not seen it come together in one vision.

So, we had this amazing meeting. And as my curmudgeonly, atheist, non-joining husband and I walked upstairs afterwards—a man to whom I had just promised I would resign from all my boards and wouldn't be involved in Jewish community work because I was so busy in my new job—and I'm thinking, "We have to do something, but he's going to think I'm nuts." And then he turns around, and he looks at me, and he says, "Our daughters have to grow up with that woman as their rabbi. And we have to do whatever we can to make it happen." And that was coming from the guy who really had zero interest in this kind of stuff. It was really powerful.

Then, we had to figure out what to do. Sharon had this job at the Milken High School. Her husband is a comedy writer. They needed health insurance; it was before Obamacare. She had a six-month-old. We came up with three ideas: one was she stayed at Milken, and we'd spend a year building a business plan and really figure out what this is and what we're doing. The second idea was perhaps she could go part-time at Milken, and we'd do services maybe once a month. And the third idea, which was idiotic—she just quits her job and we start something, maybe even a religious school. We had some cockamamie business plan, which consisted of getting one hundred people to give us $1,000, and we might be able to make something happen. We were sitting around my dining room table, we had the butcher, the baker, the candlestick maker—a lawyer and a movie producer, and somebody who knew how to build websites, a shrink, an event producer, and we were sort of piecing things together. We were trying to create the Jewish community that we all wanted. So, we decided to go for it. I was chair of the board for three years. I then left the country for seven months to travel and volunteer with my husband and daughter—essentially abandoning Sharon. And when I returned, Sharon said, "Why don't you become the executive director?" And I did . . . and our partnership continues to this day.

RON: Well, the first thing to say about this story is the partnership here is remarkable. It's really important when you're building a spiritual community that you have the rabbinic and lay leadership on the same page. What you've done together is absolutely spectacular. But I'm just curious: what's the secret sauce of IKAR? You've gone from zero to hundreds of families and individuals. And you have not compromised one inch of your initial vision, Sharon, which was to meld spirituality and social justice. You are one of the few shuls that is not afraid to say, "If you come and join us, your life's going to be different." Is that still your driving message?

SHARON: Yes, it is. Part of the strength of IKAR comes from the fact that Melissa and I were both Jewish outsiders. Before I went to rabbinical school, what propelled me into my Jewish learning was a profound sense of alienation from Jewish community and Jewish spaces. That's part of my Jewish journey: I felt like I was knocking on every Jewish door and getting kicked out of every Jewish party. Until finally, I realized I had to learn enough Gemara that I could build a space for myself when there was no space that was welcoming. I was alienated by the conventional Jewish spaces, and so not beholden to models that weren't asking the questions I wanted to ask.

Once I became a rabbi, on some level I became an insider. Then Melissa would be the one who would say with every single email, "How will this be heard by the people who are now where you were when you were nineteen? Feeling like there's no place in the world for them as a Jew?" There's something about margin dwellers—"edgers" as I like to think of us—that's interesting. What happens when edges create our own communal spaces? How do we see the world differently?

RON: Didn't Josh Avedon write a master's thesis about IKAR that explored this?

SHARON: Yes, he said that the secret sauce of IKAR was that we lowered the bar for entry and raised the bar for engagement. I had not explicitly articulated it that way, but knew it was right. We're trying to make it so that everybody can feel at home here. But at the same time, we need it to be challenging and meaningful and demanding in ways that I think a lot of Jewish places shy away from. We're asking: what would it mean if we actually ask something of people? What if we said: To be in this space, there's something that we're hoping you'll give us. It's not your cash; it's your spirit, it's your time, it's your love. We're asking you to open your hearts. You're here anyway . . . you may as well try.

When we first started IKAR, a rabbi in the Valley took me out to lunch. He was known as the social justice rabbi. He met the pope, marched in Selma, was on the front lines. He was retiring, and he had some advice to offer me. "Don't build a rabbinate like my rabbinate," he said. I asked, "What are you talking about? You're like a hero. Look at all the amazing things you've done!" He said, "I'm an entertainer. My people are so happy that their rabbi meets with the pope. But it hasn't changed their lives. Build a community whose goal is not entertainment, but transformation."

The first night we met, Melissa said to me, "Go home and write down your vision for what's possible in Jewish life." I stayed up all night with my husband, David, and wrote my vision for what we could build. "We are living in a fraught time, in which religion has failed to speak to the needs of a generation yearning for connection. This community will stand at the intersection of spirit and justice, etc." That statement became our original mission statement (and my TED talk years later!).

A few months later, the professor of a grad school seminar holds up our mission statement, which we handed out at our first service. The professor says, "This is the most audacious, ridiculous statement. Mark my words ... six months from now, nobody will even remember the word 'IKAR.'" But why? Why should we not dream big? Yes, there was an audacity to what we were doing, to say that religious life could be reclaimed. Reanimated. That davening could be transformative. I knew what it meant because I was at B'nai Jeshurun for years. I davened in Jerusalem in the summer every year. I've been in transformative davening spaces. Our goal was nothing short of trying to change the way we think about what it means to be a Jew and a human being in the world. That's what we wanted, that was our ambition. We were shooting for the moon and either we were going to get there ... or fail spectacularly.

This was a big risk. There was no model. I went to a Selah leadership workshop shortly after writing that statement, and Simon Greer was my coach. I told him about the idea behind IKAR. I told him that the reasonable thing would be to start part-time, build a business plan, and launch in a year or two. And Simon said, "This model doesn't yet exist. You have to show people that you are 100 percent committed to this. And if you do, they'll believe it." So, I gave notice at the day school that I wouldn't sign a new contract for the upcoming year, and we got to work. It was ridiculous. But, well, it worked out.

I really aspired to build a Jewish community I'd be proud to raise my children in. I wanted them to fundamentally understand what it means to be a Jew, because we'd be living what it means to be a Jew. I didn't want to tell them about transformative davening; I wanted them to feel it and know it in their bodies. That kind of experiential learning has driven a lot of our decisions at IKAR. For example, we have Limudim, religious school, on Shabbat morning, not Sundays, so that the kids could see their parents actually having a meaningful experience, rather than be taught that such a thing was possible.

Ron actually talked us through a bunch of these decisions—like the importance of language, the way we greet people. Who is at the door when people come into services? Are they smiling? Melissa created a cadre of people called "schmoozers." Their job is literally to schmooze people who come into services, just to say hello and look each person in the eye and smile and say, "Shabbat shalom." "Where are you from?

New York? Oh, so and so is from New York." Their job is to make a real human connection with you so that you feel like you're seen, like it matters that you're there. This is straight out of the Ron Wolfson playbook.

BRETT: I'm resonating with this idea that if you go on the journey, you have to go on the whole journey. What convinced you to go all in, to have a crazy vision of something that didn't exist and then you just sort of make it up as you go? What was the leap?

MELISSA: A little bit of insanity and a little bit of cluelessness. Sharon was a rising star but was not a household name. It was a significant risk to her if it didn't work out. If we as lay leaders, tried this and failed, we go on our merry way, we go on. But for Sharon, this is her career. So, we really had to take this seriously. We had a meeting with a slightly larger group, and one of the wealthier folks said, "Don't worry, Sharon, we won't let you fail." And—since she was one of the few who could write a six-figure check if we ran into trouble—it gave us the chutzpah to take the leap.

SHARON: Ron pointed out earlier that without Melissa, I would have felt like there's no way that it would have happened. It would never have happened without the partnership; it's not something I could have done without finding the person who had the shared dream and the ability to execute on that dream—someone who when we're going through this is actually thinking, "Okay, this is a huge risk for her, and could actually harm her career, so we need to somehow protect her." Melissa could ask in a way that I couldn't. One of the things that happened in that early stage is we knew that without the day school position, I'd lose my salary and lose health insurance. I was not independently wealthy—this was really significant. We realized if we could raise $60,000 for salary, some rental expenses, some food, and other expenses, we could launch the organization. We thought we could make it through half a year or so on $60,000. Melissa and I called our parents, my grandparents, some of the people who were at our early meetings. We did not get to $60,000, but we got to $40,000, which was amazing. Then, that one wealthy person said, "Don't worry, I got you if you need it." I'm like, "Okay, okay, that's enough of a safety net."

There was a lot of concern in the Conservative movement at that time that independent minyanim, like Hadar, which had just started, would be a threat. Right when IKAR started, they actually wrote an official letter saying, if you're a Conservative rabbi, and you start a minyan or community within five miles of any Conservative synagogue, you'll be blacklisted from the Rabbinical Assembly. I was scared. But I also knew this is the way of the future. Thank God, the movement seemed to make a strategic decision that instead of battling IKAR, they'd be better off embracing us. They turned around and said, "Look how proud we are that these seminary graduates are doing this interesting work." And it wasn't just me. Within a couple of years, several other rabbis who came out of the movement started new community efforts.

RON: Let's just put on the record that I offered you a job, Sharon. Roly Matalon called me and said, "There's a dynamic young rabbi coming to Los Angeles you have got to hire for the Synagogue 2000 project." I would have hired Sharon in a second. But I'm glad it worked out the way it did, for sure. Here's what's happened: these innovative young rabbis that have created independent minyanim have joined together in the Jewish Emergent Network, seven communities that have adopted this playbook, something very different from the mainstream synagogue world.

SHARON: The idea was that there was a kind of shared DNA among these seven organizations—a shared sense of purpose—and we were all connected to each other in friendship. Some of the rabbis of the network were rabbinic interns or rabbinic fellows at IKAR, and then they went off into the world. Some of them had no connection to IKAR but were on parallel paths, thinking about community in a similar way.

This connects back to the IKAR origin story: Ron pulled me into a Synagogue 2000 leadership group of interesting rabbis doing interesting stuff. It was an incredible honor to be in the mix. But I realized that these rabbis were asking fundamentally different questions than we were. They were talking about membership categories—I was wondering if we should have membership at all. Maybe instead of asking for money from people, we should be asking for them to make a commitment to show up at our justice campaigns. We were just asking different things.

Then, Synagogue 2000 organized a conference with Christian emergent communities who were about ten years ahead of us. One pastor explained: They didn't want to build a megachurch. They wanted a bunch of friends to sit together in a room and look into each other's eyes, to try to decipher what God is asking them to do in this world. And, I thought, yeah, that's what we're doing too. So, the word "emergent" was planted in our heads; we realized years later, as this network started to form, that's what it was: a Jewish Emergent Network, a group of people who were all thinking at the leading edge of what might be the next iteration of Jewish community and Jewish gatherings.

MELISSA: One of the things the Jewish world does is pit folks against each other. There is not a culture of abundance—more of a culture of scarcity. We reject the notion of scarcity. We firmly believe that the sum is greater than the parts. If we come from a place of abundance, we can focus on how we can help each other and have each other's back. But this is another important lesson that Sharon mentioned: we're going to ask something of you. You can come to IKAR forever for free, but if you're going to join, we will ask you to make four commitments: a justice commitment, a volunteer community commitment, a learning commitment, and a tzedakah/financial commitment. We didn't know what the impact of the pandemic would be, but we assumed membership would go down by 15 or 20 percent. Despite that, we decided to make everything as accessible as possible to give the widest group of folks access to our brand of Jewish life. Everything online is free, no firewalls or passwords (except religious school), zero barriers to entry. And we were surprised to see membership actually increased—by a lot—over two hundred households (we are now at one thousand households). My economist friends would say, this is the perfect free rider situation. You can take advantage of everything we offer and contribute nothing. We are in the midst of the generation that has been given "free" everything: Birthright trips to Israel, PJ Library, you name it. But we found that people did not want to free ride. They wanted to be part of something—to help build this community, even virtually. We created a new membership category to welcome people beyond the geographic boundary of Los Angeles, called "IKAR from AFAR."

RON: Your insight is fantastic. Synagogues should serve the spiritual needs of people but should not be afraid to say, "You join our community, your life will be different . . . because we will be asking you to be part of building this community. Most synagogues give new members a list of committees to volunteer for . . . and nobody does. IKAR starts with the whole notion that you must be seen, you must be heard, and then we can connect you. You've done this brilliantly. I cannot believe that number. I'm shocked, but not at all surprised.

SHARON: I just want to say that one of Melissa's superpowers is changing people's lives by tapping them on the shoulder and saying, "You should be chairing the High Holy Days—you'd be great at this."

From the first week of IKAR, we'd do house parties where we get a small group of people together to hear them and learn with them. For seven years, I did at least one house party a week, in all different neighborhoods around Los Angeles. I would go to living rooms and sit with ten to fifteen people and ask, "What's your story?" When someone asks what your Jewish story is, it makes you feel like you have a Jewish story. And once you know someone's story, you have a point of connection. This is transformational. It is relational. (Maybe someone should write a book about that? Maybe call it *Relational Judaism*?) So much of what we do is about helping people find each other in a space where it matters who they are and what they bring.

At IKAR we work hard to share our stories. We have a really special *Yizkor* book. It's not a list of names. It's a collection of short stories, memories, and photos of our loved ones. The message is: the world is bigger than our own grief and our own loss, our own fear, and our own love and our own gratitude ... because we're in this sacred network of people.

We live in a world where everyone feels a little invisible. And yet, all of us have the need to be seen. When somebody actually sees us, it feels like we're honored in some way, we sense our dignity. We're teaching the community to see each other. To show up at each other's shivas and to pick up the phone and call when we haven't heard from someone. We are trying to train a community to give each other that gift, the feeling that each of us fundamentally matters, because the world sometimes feels like it's conspiring to give us the opposite message. I think that's why so many people joined IKAR during COVID. We're doing these new-member house parties with people from Chile and Japan and London and San Diego, and I'm saying, "You could have gotten IKAR for free!" But what they want is not just access to services, which are streamed during the pandemic. They want to be a part of something that feels purpose-driven, a place that feels like their voice matters, like they are connected to other people standing on the same side of history.

MELISSA: And now, we have a property that we're developing, to have a permanent home for the IKAR community, a space where we can realize our most audacious dreams of what Jewish community and multi-faith justice could actually look like. We're working with architects, potential partners, and raising a massive amount of money, different from anything we've ever had to do before. What is a building that puts human dignity and *b'tzelem Elohim* at the center of the conversation? We are focused on building a physical structure that feels equitable and just. It will be green, inclusive, and radically welcoming. It's going to be amazing!

RON: Thank you both for sharing this incredible story of creating sacred community.

Questions for Creating Your Sacred Community

1. The creators of IKAR began with a vision for the kind of sacred community they themselves wanted to be part of. What is your vision for your sacred community?

2. What expectations do you have of the members of your sacred community?

3. How are your people invited to share their stories?

4. What lessons for building sacred community have emerged from the pandemic?

CHAPTER 9

Rethinking Synagogue

Rabbi Ed Feinstein

I first met Rabbi Ed Feinstein during my rabbinical school orientation week when he came to campus for a lunch and learn. Growing up in the Chicago Jewish community, I had never heard of him before that day. When Rabbi Feinstein began his talk, he started by telling us a story about walking into his rabbi's synagogue office as a teenager and complaining that the services were boring and uninspiring, and he didn't want to go. The rabbi told him to stand up, pull a book off the shelf, open to the first page, and read. Rabbi Feinstein had given us all source sheets, and orienting us to the top of the first page, he said, "And I read..." and began reading the words of Abraham Joshua Heschel about the synagogue, words that he told us would change his life. There was something in the way he introduced the text by grounding us in his story of discovering it for the first time that took me by surprise and made me feel as though I was sitting in his rabbi's office chair as a teenager, learning right alongside him.

During that same talk, Rabbi Feinstein quoted Psalm 23: "Though I walk through the valley of the shadow of death, I fear no evil, for Thou art with me." "You know what that really means?" he asked us. "That means that one day you will be sitting in a hospital room with your loved one when you both hear the doctor say the dreaded word 'cancer,' and you will take your loved one by the hand, look into their eyes and say, 'We are walking this road together.'" I had to look down at the table and hold myself back from bursting into tears, so authentic and sincere and powerful was his teaching.

I had the privilege of learning homiletics (sermon giving) from Rabbi Feinstein for a full year during my last year of rabbinical school and was thrilled to have the opportunity to learn more from him about being a community rabbi during our Creating Sacred Communities class.—BK

Rabbi Ed Feinstein is the senior rabbi of Valley Beth Shalom, Encino, California.

RON: Rabbi Feinstein, would you like to start our conversation about how you shape communities? Then our guests here have some questions for you.

ED: I was raised in a home that was a kibbutz. My parents were *halutzim* [pioneers]. They grew up in a Zionist youth movement, made aliyah in the 1950s, and came back just before I was born. They were not religious. My mother was never a believer, to the day she died, but she kept a kosher home, with Shabbos candles every Friday night with a *b'rachah*. My parents insisted that my brothers and I go to Hebrew school and to Jewish summer camp. They owned a bakery, my dad, the baker, my mom, the "bakery lady." Every Friday night, my father would finish work early, come home, and get a little rest; my mother would come home early and cook. She was a kibbutz cook, and she made up in quantity what she lacked in quality—big meals in plastic bowls. At the Shabbat table, my father held court. He asked a question and conducted a spirited philosophical discussion about the future of the Jewish people, about civil rights for African Americans, about Israel, about Vietnam and the morality of our government. My brothers and I had to be at the table every Friday night. That was the rule in the house. But we could invite friends. So pretty soon all of our high school friends would come over to join us. First of all, because there was always a good dessert. But more, because everyone wanted to join that conversation. Dad asked big questions. He challenged us. It was wonderful. I grew up in a family that loved ideas, loved discussion, loved food, and loved cookies. Ideas were important to me, and Jewish ideas were especially important to me. There was a moral language at my table growing up. So, as I grew into adulthood, I decided that's what I wanted to do in my life—I wanted to live in a world of moral language. So, it was either going to be teaching in high school or college, or the rabbinate. The rabbinate gave me the chance to live in a world of Torah, to speak a moral language, to teach a moral language. The rabbinate gave me a pulpit, literally, to speak to people's lives. It gave me a world where the meaning of life is an active question, an important question. And I learned that if you gain some skills at this, you can talk in such a way that people actually listen to you. And that's a great thrill. So far, it's going okay. Let's see what tomorrow brings.

Modernity has brought us many, many gifts. I'm vaccinated [against COVID]; now I can walk outside. And that's something of a miracle when you think about it. The power of telecommunication, gifts of technology, gifts of travel, gifts of culture and liberation. The fact that Rabbi Himeles is with us today. We don't put women to the side, but we welcome her voice and her soul and her spirit. These are gifts of modernity that I consider tremendous blessings. But there are some parts of modernity that are actually pernicious. One of them is an overemphasis on individualism—the idea that I walk the world alone, that I'm a lone ranger, that I'm an individual in the world. The loss of intimacy, the loss of connection is a tremendous casualty of modernity. How do we create circles of people who desire to become part of something bigger than themselves?

A great truth of the Torah is *lo tov heyot ha-adam l'vado* [Genesis 2:18], it's not right to walk the world alone. Modernity teaches that a claim upon the self is a diminishment of freedom, and therefore a diminishment of the self. And in fact, it's the opposite. We are not diminished when we allow claims upon the self. Our options, our freedoms are not diminished when we engage in relationship. A claim upon the self enhances the self. The bigger the circle around me of those I care about, the more my life has meaning, purpose, and joy.

There's no relationship more intense than the relationship between a parent and a child. If you want to preserve your freedom, don't have kids, because God knows they're going to restrict your freedom in a huge way. But there's no greater joy than raising a child, launching a child, and sharing life with a child—crying, laughing, and loving a child. That's what the Torah is trying to teach us. So, community building, to me, is a great corrective of one of the flaws of modernity. It's enormously difficult to do in the American context, but it's something that's so very necessary. It's one of the things that we're called upon to do. That's my basic philosophy.

SARA: So, you can create a Jewish community, but that can't be the "be-all end-all." Because what if you create a community that is not kind, not in keeping with Jewish values? What goals should we have for the Jewish communities that we create, beyond just creating them?

ED: That's such a very, quite beautiful question. Let's take the first half first. People don't know how to be in community. They don't know how to commit to a community. They're afraid to commit to a community. Once they enter into a community setting, they don't know how to behave. They don't know how to conduct themselves. Being in community is a claim upon the self—it demands a certain degree of discipline. Discipline means *I need to do what the community needs me to do, not what I want to do right now.* The discipline of being a member of a community is that I have to talk in a certain way about people. I have to resist my destructive impulses. I have to contribute. I have to learn to look for the best in people. I have to put up with the worst in people. Not everybody in the community is nice. But they're still part of my community. And I welcome them, because if I'm going to run away every time I meet someone who's not nice, I'm never going to find a community, because not everybody in the world is nice.

So, how do I gain the skills to be a part of a community? We have to teach that to our people. It takes time; it's hard. Sometimes as a rabbi in a community, I've had to go to people and say, "What you just did or said is out of bounds." We have to learn how to offer this *tochechah* (rebuke). And in community, there has to be a process of *teshuvah* (repentance). In community, we're going to make mistakes in what we say and what we do, and we have to be able to come back to the community and say, "I'm sorry I did that, and I hope that you'll forgive me."

RON: To follow up on Sara's great question, the rabbi has to set the norms of the community in terms of kindness and no *lashon hara* (gossip) and so on. That's creating culture. What happens when the rabbi gets up and gives a sermon on Rosh Hashanah, and half the congregation gives him a standing ovation and a few people walk out?

ED: That's going to happen. You need to know as a rabbi that you're not going to make everybody happy all the time—unless you want to be the kind of rabbi who never says anything important. There are rabbis who've made a whole career out of never saying anything important. Stephen S. Wise once said: A rabbi who nobody loves is not much of a rabbi, but a rabbi who everybody loves is not much of a person. Because sometimes, you need to take a stand. You have to be judicious about these things. You're going to anger people and it's hard. We all want to be loved. No one wants congregants to walk out angry and never talk to us again. But that's the price of being a public person. It's the price of taking a stand on an issue. We're here to teach a more moral way of living life. And that requires a certain quality of courage. When someone lets you know you angered them, then you call and invite them to sit down and talk about it. Half of the problem is solved when someone feels they've been heard. And having the courage to listen to someone's rebuke, someone's disagreement, will earn you a reputation as a fair and wise rabbi.

BRETT: Depending on where you serve as rabbi, when you enter a new environment, did you ever feel like you had to change the way you packaged your message? How did you deal with that, of moving into a synagogue culture from another Jewish institution?

ED: You have to learn the culture of the place. You have to learn what they're comfortable with. You have to decide how much controversy you want to stir up. Most of all, you have to gain people's trust. Once you've earned their trust, they may say, "That's not what I believe," or "I don't agree with the rabbi," or "I was taken aback by what the rabbi said. But I know the rabbi to be a decent, responsible, and kind person." So when I first came, I was much more reticent. I was better at quoting lots of teachers and authorities, because I could hide behind those people instead of offering my own thoughts. But over the years, I've built enough trust with people, I can tell them what I think.

Recently someone asked me, "When we have a Seder on Pesach, I have a hard time with this idea that God is in history. So, how do you do a Seder if you have a hard time with God intervening in history?" First of all, that's a really honest question. Most Jews aren't that honest. They'll just read the Haggadah. This is a very sensitive soul. So, we started talking about why it is that we have a hard time with the idea of a God who is in our history. Partly, it's modernity. Partly, it's the Holocaust. It is very, very hard to believe in a God who intervenes in history after Auschwitz. In Martin Luther King's Nobel Prize speech, he states that the arc of history bends toward justice. So, is there a moral order to history? That's a wonderful question to ask at a Seder. But it's a deeply personal question. It is a question that demands a great deal of mutual trust.

RON: Why did you stay at VBS? You could have been a senior rabbi at any synagogue in America. I mean, Brett and Sara, the guy's one of the most talented rabbis in the whole country. What kept you in one place for that long and what's the advantage, rather than hopping around and climbing the ladder of pulpits?

ED: The first reward of staying in one place for a long time is that you build relationships with a community and with its people. When you come out of school, stay in a job for seven years. That's the cycle. Because in seven years, you'll marry a couple and name their first two kids. In seven years, you'll do a Bar Mitzvah and then be there for that kid's graduation from high school. Second—staying in one congregation and building it up established a base from which I could do so many interesting things. Professor Wolfson and I were part of an initiative called Synagogue 2000, which he invented and invited me to join. Joining the faculty of Synagogue 2000 was one of the great joys of my life, because I was part of a team of the most talented rabbis, cantors, and teachers in the world. We went around the country teaching synagogues how to be better. Then I got to be on the faculty of the Hartman Institute and then the faculty of the Wexner Foundation. Most of all, I stayed because I found a home. I found a community of people I loved and respected. I gathered a staff of wonderful colleagues. It was home. And that makes all the difference.

You need to always be growing; always learning something new. I have a policy. I always choose a topic for my teaching that I haven't learned before. That forces me to learn even if I'm two weeks ahead of the class. I'm learning. I'm growing. Every year I spend the summertime thinking about what I want to learn this year, and that's what I end up teaching. One year it was how a Jew reads the Christian Bible. So, I found books, listened to lectures, and I became conversant with the Christian Bible. Then it was the history of Zionism, the traditions of Jewish mysticism, the origins of our denominations, Orthodox, Conservative, Reform. Every year, something new. I'm always trying to grow that way. That's how you stay alive in this business.

I'm also not the kind of rabbi who would say to a family, I'm not available. If they need me, I'm coming. Because that's why I went into this—to be present with people, to be there for people. I spent an hour on Zoom yesterday with a kid who's a junior in college, a kid I raised in my synagogue, who I absolutely adore, who wrote me and said he had some problems. You know, in the book of rabbis, they would say, "This synagogue, let's see: eighteen hundred families, ten thousand people, $20 million budget. What are you doing spending an hour on the phone with a nineteen-year-old kid?" *And the answer is, "Because that's why I became a rabbi: to spend an hour on the phone with a nineteen-year-old kid. That's what I do."* Now, maybe I could raise more money, or write more books, or serve on more committees, or get more famous if I did it differently. But that's not my idea of the job. I'm here to raise souls, not raise money or raise my own ego.

RON: I have another question for you. You do something that I don't think most rabbis are trained to do that you're an expert at, which is to spontaneously speak. You're a wonderful blesser of moments. I've watched you at funerals, at baby namings, at weddings—including the wedding of my own kid. And you'll have stuff that comes out of your mouth that is so powerful, so meaningful, so connects Judaism to the moment and to the people in that moment. How do you do that?

ED: Partly, it's because I've done it a lot, and the more you do it, the easier it gets. It becomes a habit. I have certain themes and certain ideas that I've spoken about so many times that I can go to automatically. A rabbi has to be ready to talk spontaneously about every prayer in the prayer book, because at some service, someone will always ask you, "What's this prayer about?" And we spend so much time at life-cycle rituals, you have to have a sense of the deeper meaning behind each of these moments and these rituals. But the most important thing to remember is this: People are going to tell you that being a great rabbi is about speaking well. It's not. *The greater skill of the rabbi is how you listen.* People who are able to really listen are people who make great rabbis. Listening gives you a clue about the deeper meaning of the moment and what needs to be said.

When I'm asked to lead a funeral service, I meet with the family, and I listen to the way they talk about their loved one. When I go to a funeral, I listen. I try to sense: What does this moment mean for these people? Can I find a way to put this moment into words? What was the Torah of this life? That's the question of every eulogy. What is the deepest truth, the highest wisdom of this life? That's what we're here to do. That's what they asked us to do: express the meaning of this moment to them—at a wedding, at a bris, at a funeral, at a Bar Mitzvah, and at a special moment in someone's life. Just what does this moment mean? You listen, and you let that shape your words.

RON: My point to Brett and Sara is what we just heard from Eddie, which is the flip side of Rick's point about saying something on Sunday that you can use on Monday. That is the main theme of both talks we've heard from these fabulous teachers: you've got to take the Torah, whatever Torah you're teaching, and link it to people's real lives. That's what's important.

ED: The second question of the Seder is the most important question of the whole tradition: What difference does this make to you? How has this changed you? How does this narrative shape you? I told you in class that if you ever start a sermon with the words "Today's Torah portion is *Vayikra*, which is on page 585," my shoe is going to come toward your head. Because what that does right away is say to the crowd, "I'm more interested in what's in the book than what's in your heart." But if you look out at the crowd and say, "Ever made a mistake, a big mistake, like a real Major League screwup, and then you had to go and fix it up good? Now you know what Moses is thinking in today's Torah portion. That's what *Vayikra* is all about. How do I fix a big mistake?"

The Seder asks us to think of ourselves as a community of ex-slaves. If you thought that way, how would you walk the world differently? What would you see that you couldn't see otherwise? How would you respond to the world? Every ancient culture thought slaves were the lowest forms of life. If you were a child of a slave, you were nothing. And we walk around going, "I'm proud of this." Why? What does it do for us? That's the question. *What does it do for me? This is the question we have to be answering all the time.* You have to listen to the text and ask yourself this: What happened to the person who wrote this text that he or she wanted so badly for us to know? How did it change them? *Mah zot lachem?* What does this mean to you? That's the question.

BRETT: So why do we put the wicked child's teeth on edge and get angry? What's the theological significance of that?

ED: Oh, I think that's a brilliant question, Brett. Such a wonderful question. Not just that, but why do we privilege the kid who says, "What are the laws and traditions?" We say that he's the wise one? Why? The answer is really simple: *It's much easier to answer a how question than a why question.* It's safer to answer a how question. You want to know all the laws and traditions? That I can easily tell you. But the kid who says, "What does this mean to you?" You put his teeth on edge, right? Because his question goes right to the heart: Why does the Passover story matter? Why is this Seder ritual so important to you? It's a crime to call him wicked. Rabbi Schulweis used to say that the one of the four children that he didn't understand is the last one, who doesn't know how to ask a question. What kind of Jew doesn't know how to ask a question? At least he asks, "When do we eat?" What kind of person sits quietly through a whole Seder and doesn't say anything? I'll tell you who he is: He is yesterday's wicked child. He came to us and said, "What does this mean to you?" And you know what we said to him? "Sit down and shut up. We're not interested in your question." So tonight, he's silent, withdrawn, passive, and apathetic.

The Pew report in 2013 asked five and a half million American Jews, "What is your current religion?" Thirty-three percent of young Jews checked the box labeled "None." Not Orthodox, not Conservative, not Reform, not Reconstruction, not Renewal, not Zionist . . . "None" Jews. The fastest growing religious group in North America are the "Nones." Why? Because they came to us and asked, *Mah zot lachem?* and we didn't have an answer. We didn't welcome the question. So, what happens the next year when that kid comes back to the Seder (if he comes back!), and he thinks, "I better not ask any questions. They're just going to yell at me"—what happens? He sits at the end of the table with his arms crossed over his chest saying, "I'll come because I'll honor my parents, but I'm not going to participate." That's why our biggest job is to answer that question every single time, every chance you get! *Mah zot lachem?* Why does this matter?

Rick Warren sent out an email to pastors about their Easter preaching. He said to them: You only have one job Easter Sunday. You have to tell your congregants, "What's the meaning of life?" Tell people about the meaning of their existence. How do you live in the face of death and make meaning out of life? That's what Easter is about—a great holiday. Ours is Yom Kippur. Living in the face of death and making meaning out of life. Where I fit into God's plan. Warren is pleading with these pastors: Don't talk about small things! Take the biggest questions and jump right into them, and don't be afraid. You can't fail with this.

In my congregation, I talk to five generations of Jews at the same time—people in their 20s, 30s, 40s, 50s, 60s, 70s, 80s, and beyond. How do you find a language for five different generations, all of whom have very different relationships to Torah, to the synagogue community, to the institution, and to the rabbi? How do I find a moral language to speak to all those generations? How do I talk to them? It's hard, but that's what I loved about Warren's message. It was a reminder to me that whenever we find ourselves speaking to our communities, it's got to be about the biggest stuff. We have to ask, "What's the biggest question I have to answer this year?"

SARA: When you think about the Jewish future and the direction the Jewish community is going in, what is exciting to you, and what most concerns you?

ED: What's exciting to me is that there are lots and lots of people like yourselves who are filled with creativity, coming into the community with big, open minds, bringing new creative language to Jewish life. The creativity of the next generation of Jewish leaders really impresses me. And the diversity of the Jewish community, that we're not just Ashkenazi, but we're also Sephardi and Persian and Israeli and Russian, that we're not just white folks, but we're now people of all kinds of colors and backgrounds, and we're certainly not just men like it was when I trained, but there are wonderful female souls and remarkable differently gendered people involved in Torah. All of that brings me great optimism. A dying people does not produce creative souls. We're not a dying people. We're experiencing a Renaissance. So that's the beautiful thing.

The hard part is that there's an erosion factor of Jewish community life. I worry, for example, about institutions that can't hold their own because they don't have the resources or the membership. I worry about being able to engage people like yourselves who are ready to lead and to teach. Do we have jobs and a livelihood for your life? The community will be smaller in the generation to come. Will it have the resources to provide for a new generation of leaders and support them with the material resources they need? I'm worried about the effect of technology on American life, and I worry about the effect of the kind of moral corrosiveness and moral corruption on our community's life. I worry about the split between Israel and America, Israeli Jews and American Jews. I worry about the huge polarization of American life and about America's future. These are things that concern me a lot.

I really appreciate the question because one of the arguments I've made is *we have to stop telling the pessimistic story*. You hear it so frequently: "We Jews are disappearing. We're assimilating. We're intermarrying." Maybe that's true. But we're also experiencing a Renaissance of Jewish life and culture. So as long as the story is equivocal, I'm going to tell the optimistic story, rather than the pessimistic story. For a really simple reason: Nobody is going to give us a penny or fifteen minutes of time if we tell them we're a dying people. So why do we keep telling that story about ourselves?

Years ago, there was a Broadway show called *Titanic*. It won a Tony Award. So when it came to LA, we went to the Ahmanson to see it. Great show! We go to intermission, and when we come back from intermission the whole row is empty. In fact, I look around and half the theater has emptied out. Now the ship hit the iceberg at the end of act 1. So, you're going to come back for act 2 as the ship is sinking. And guess what? The theater is empty. Why? The dancing is beautiful. The music is great. The sets are amazing. The choreography is wonderful. People left. Why? Here's my lesson: People don't want to be on a sinking ship. If we go into our community and we say that we're vanishing, we're disappearing, the synagogues are closing, there's no future in Jewish life, all we do is send our people away. We discourage them from participating. Why don't we say the opposite? You know Sara Himeles? Brett Kopin? They are brilliant young rabbis who are going to change the Jewish world. And here's Ron Wolfson, who's been doing this for fifty years and he's still writing books. We're a growing people. We're a living people. We're a creative people. Let's tell that story. People will come to us instead of running the other way. I would rather tell a story about the Renaissance in Jewish creativity and spirituality that's happening in America, because that's more energizing and it gets us to a place I'd rather be and into to a conversation I'd rather have.

RON: Thanks so much, Eddie. A fantastic session! Brett and Sara, Rabbi Feinstein is my neighbor in Encino. When we're away from the house, he watches over our home. Thanks for bringing in the garbage cans, Ed!

Questions for Creating Your Sacred Community

1. Rabbi Feinstein says that "in community, there has to be a process of *teshuvah*." What does this look like in your community?

2. How would you describe the culture of your community: spiritually, politically, and socially?

3. What is the learning culture of your community like? Are new subjects being taught each year?

4. What is the biggest question you have to answer this year?

5. How would you tell the optimistic story about Jewish life and peoplehood? How does your community fit into that story?

CHAPTER 10

Chabad

Rabbi Motti Seligson

Rabbi Motti Seligson is director of media and public relations for Chabad-Lubavitch.

RON: I got to meet Motti when he invited me to spend a whole day with him at 770 [Chabad-Lubavitch World Headquarters in Crown Heights, New York], which was remarkable, and I talk about it all the time. And this is a very important man in the realm of Chabad, and a sweet, sweet person. So, thank you for joining us. Hey, do you remember when I couldn't find an Uber in Brooklyn? He literally rescued me! So, I'm happy to have you tell us a little bit of your own perspective of why you think Chabad-Lubavitch *shluchim* ["messenger" rabbi families], in particular, are so effective in shaping their spiritual communities. Then we'd love to just have a conversation with you. I'm sure Brett and Sara have lots of questions.

MOTTI: Chabad is a spiritual movement. There's a philosophy and theology that is hundreds of years old, which is built on Torah as it's illuminated through *Chasidut* [Hasidism], that has real-world ramifications for how communities operate. For *shluchim*, for Chabad rabbis and rebbetzins, their work is their own personal spiritual journey. It's not just a career; it's not just a job.

There are three characteristics that can help one define Chabad's unique approach in Jewish communal and institutional life. The first area is the focus on the individual, the core idea being that we have a responsibility to every single person, and every individual, unique to the community, is the center and focus of everything. The second is understanding the immense importance and almost unlimited spiritual power of even a single mitzvah—the power of the deed—to the individual performing the mitzvah and everyone else. The third is the responsibility that we feel we have to all of the Jewish people, not just dues-paying members in our shul, or even just people who feel they are part of the community, but all Jewish people and indeed, in a broader sense, to all people.

I've spent the last several hours before this conversation being in touch with people looking for help, and all I had to do was call a local *shaliach* [messenger], and the person had a knock on their door within minutes. It's not a question of "Wait, are you going to fund this initiative?" That's not even part of the equation. It is also not about the numbers or the flashy reports.

What's driving a couple to move out to the farthest corner of the world—the frontier of Jewish life? Drop everything—sometimes moving far from family, friends, community—and build everything from scratch: build family, build friendships, and build community. It comes down to dedicating oneself to the Rebbe's mission of *ahavat Yisroel*, love for your fellow.

The centrality of *ahavat Yisroel* to Judaism doesn't need to be repeated to you. What's needed is a real dedication to it, though, not just sermons and talks. It means putting yourself aside and sometimes making sacrifices for the benefit of someone else. The guy on the street corner handing out Shabbat candles or putting on tefillin with passersby is not doing it for herself or himself. It's not like there's a big scoreboard in Crown Heights with the names of the yeshiva or rabbinical students listed with all the numbers of people doing mitzvot. It's the way that they see this as something important and powerful, that's inspiring and important to your life—and may even change your life for good—and they want to share it with you.

And it's not my Judaism. It's not something that I own. This is an inheritance that was given to us through Moses and belongs to every single one of us, every single one of you.

It's all worth it for that one person. I know a rabbi who put on an event with his wife introducing a mikveh, and they were expecting a lot of people. One woman showed up. The joke goes that having one person attend your event is far worse than no one showing up, because then everyone knows how the event turned out. These *shluchim* were very down because they were hoping to teach and inspire a big part of the community, and they wrote to the Rebbe about how they felt that they failed. The Rebbe responded that Moses, Moshe Rabbeinu, had but one mother. You think about that for a moment: the power of the individual, and the impact that is made on a single individual. Each person is an entire world, and it's all worth it for that one person.

The second area is the importance of a mitzvah. While a mitzvah is a good deed, it's much more than that. It's the means by which, through our actions, people are able to connect with the Divine, connect with God. Now, that has ramifications in terms of how we structure our lives and our values. We could have all the Jewish feelings we want, but if it's not put into practice, it doesn't have the impact on us and the world. A mitzvah is the way that we connect to thousands of years of Jewish tradition and generations of Jews who have come before us and Jews who will come after us—it's timeless. So, in shaping spiritual communities, what can be more powerful than building our communities on a foundation of mitzvot?

Our tradition says that our forefathers, Avraham, Yitzhak, Yaakov, Sarah, Rivkah, Rachel, and Leah, did mitzvot. They connected to the Divine. So what changed with Mount Sinai?

BRETT: It was the moment that we received a national covenant. So, they were all a part of the covenant on an individual basis, but Sinai was when the nation really got its identity, got its substance, and its commitment to a large degree.

MOTTI: Brett, what are you saying in terms of that mission and that national direction? Absolutely. On a deeper level God gave us each the power to transform the mundane into something sacred. Spirituality means not something physical. We had spiritual experiences before Mount Sinai too. At Mount Sinai we were empowered to take physical matter and turn it into something sacred by using it for a higher purpose, for a spiritual purpose, a godly purpose, for a mitzvah. We're revealing the godly purpose of mundane things and uplifting them, and thus turning them into something sacred. Every time we do a mitzvah, we're doing this to ourselves as well, we're doing this to the materials that we're using, and we're doing it to our environment. So, when we're talking about building spiritual communities, there's no stronger way of doing that than through building with mitzvot.

Using Torah and mitzvot as our guiding principles to build our communities ensures that we build timeless communities. We can focus our communities around all kinds of fine shiny causes that have the zeitgeist of the moment. Many of the secular pursuits that were progressive only yesterday are seen as antiquated today. It's critical that we don't lose our bearings and get swept up in the moment and build our lives and communities on something that's fleeting and rather tap into the infinite and that's timeless and not going to trend out.

The third area is the responsibility for one another—everyone. There is no such thing as "I don't care, not my problem." That doesn't exist because we have responsibilities for one another as Jews and as human beings. We can't just put up an artificial fence. With communities that define themselves by a paying membership, there's a list and it's very straightforward. And the reality is that if you're running a congregation, you're using wisdom, you're teaching wisdom that doesn't really belong to you any more than the person who is not in that congregation, who is not a "member," yet it actually belongs to them! It is their inheritance—תורה צוה לנו משה מורשה קהלת יעקב—"The Torah that Moses commanded us is the heritage of the Congregation of Yaakov" [Deuteronomy 33:4]. They have an inheritance from God, and it belongs to every one of the Jewish people. It's our responsibility, especially when leading a community, to really internalize the idea that there's no concept that someone doesn't matter, or something doesn't matter, or you don't care. We do care! We care for every single individual! Unless every individual is welcomed and part of the congregation, part of the community, we are not complete.

You may have joined this conversation today to learn more about mechanics of Chabad—like when the couple is really starting their community, literally from scratch, how do they grow? How do they go from just working out of their living room or the kitchen table to these magnificent communities? The ideals are what drive everything.

I remember as a child seeing mailbags—those big cloth bags—being delivered to the Rebbe. And the Rebbe would respond to each of those people. There are dozens of volumes of the Rebbe's correspondences, and it's only a fraction of the complete amount. You could walk into 770 and set up a meeting with the Rebbe, and they would find the time for you. When that was no longer sustainable, the Rebbe began greeting people Sunday mornings and gave them a dollar bill for tzedakah—to do a mitzvah with. Thousands would line up and have their personal moment with the Rebbe and ask him whatever was on their heart. Anyone could show up.

As a child, I had the privilege of meeting the Rebbe and receiving a dollar from him. I remember the line going down the block and wrapping around the corner. It would last hours, and the Rebbe was ninety years old, focusing on every individual. No matter how important you are, every person matters. You have the time to hear them, be there for them, and help them.

BRETT: First of all, I love Rebbe stories. I can listen to those all day. And also, by the way, Ron has some powerful *ruach ha-Kodesh* [sacred spirit]. He laughs, but he knows it's true. I'm just wondering, from the Rebbe's correspondences and the hundreds of thousands of letters he wrote, was he also the main *posek* [Jewish law authority] of the movement?

MOTTI: No. The Rebbe's scholarly output in Torah and halachah is immense. My father wrote an index on all the Rebbe's talks and it's sixteen hundred pages thick, and that's just the index! The Rebbe spoke publicly for roughly eleven thousand hours. There are thirty-nine volumes just of his edited talks. Yet the Rebbe would often advise people, when asking halachic questions, to consult their own *posek* or halachic authority.

SARA: I want to ask you about the future of spiritual communities now that the whole world has changed with COVID. What do you see as the future of the spiritual community online? What do you think it will look like? And what are some opportunities that you are excited about?

MOTTI: Everyone seems to have discovered the online community in 2020? Chabad has been doing this all along. Chabad.org was operating in the late 1980s and has about fifty-four million unique visitors annually. Yet, we've always encouraged people visiting us on the website to build real-world—in-person—community. I know a lot of Jewish funders and institutions are very excited about online right now, but that's virtual, and it can be a very nice alternative to make do with now; it's not a substitute. I think COVID created a lot of opportunities for communities to grow. The barrier for engagement was lowered. You could attend your rabbi's class from your kitchen with your coffee. People attended these classes, enjoyed them, and made them part of their life, part of their routine. Those people can flood synagogues when they reopen fully. But for that to work, you can't just Zoom everything—you must engage!

We published a Haggadah on Chabad.org during COVID. We didn't send it to a printer. We put it on Amazon; it became Amazon's top Haggadah. It broke into Amazon's top 100 selling books across all categories. It was downloaded hundreds of thousands of times from Chabad.org, where we made it available for free. So, I think there are a lot of opportunities with doing things online, but don't try to substitute community building.

RON: I have a question. What was the Rebbe's thinking in terms of sending a couple to one community for life?

MOTTI: Well, we all have our corner of the world that is waiting for each of us to uplift and bring light to—that doesn't just mean geographic. It's our *avodah*, our work, our purpose. And by divine providence, we end up where we end up, and we serve where we serve. You're there to serve this community. It's not a career. In a career, you advance yourself. A *shlichut* is a mission, a life's mission. It's not about you, but your calling and the people you're serving and the community you're serving, and you become part of the community. It becomes your family. You don't move from family to family.

RON: I can't help myself, but you know, the opening line of Rick Warren's famous book *The Purpose Driven Life*, which is the second most published book in the English language next to the Bible, is "It's not about you," which is what you just said.

MOTTI: If we're able to put ourselves aside, put our own needs and egos aside, it's incredible what we're able to achieve.

BRETT: It's funny you said that Ron, because I just wrote down a note about the connection between Chabad and Saddleback Church.

RON: Well, the bottom line is that those guys are evangelical, which etymologically means bringing people to their guy, and Chabad is the one group and certainly the best and I think the most effective group in reaching every single person they want to reach. I mean, that's what we've just heard for an hour: it's about the individual and that's what counts. And you can't call it evangelical etymologically. But that's one of the many things that's very admirable about what Chabad is able to do.

BRETT: My other observation comparing what you're saying and what we heard from Saddleback is that there's a real sense of a divine purpose behind the work. When Ron asked the question, like, honestly, why would a couple from New York move to Mumbai or Alberta, where there aren't many Jews or just a tiny Jewish population, why even do that? And if they truly believe that that region is their *chelek b'olam*, their place in this world, and that's where God wants them to be, that's where they're going. I think that's such a beautiful way to live your life. And Rick Warren's story began the same way. He really felt like God was sending him on this mission to Saddleback Valley. So, when God is a part of it and infuses everything you do, I think that's where so much of the success of both these movements is coming from.

MOTTI: We each have our *chelek b'olam*, our place in the world that is waiting for us. It's important to remember that we need to plug into something higher and godly and more effective than any self-help book or business plan at Bain & Company. If our business plan is God's business plan, we're set! And on the recipient's side, they are seeking Jewish authenticity. What's Jewish authenticity? People want the real thing, and they want a godly spiritual connection. They don't want what they get everywhere else repackaged as something Jewish. They can get all that at Starbucks, and there are like five billion, with a *b*, ways that they could have their coffee at Starbucks. When they come to shul, they want to connect with something bigger. They want to hear something divine. To Ron's question about being in a place and sticking with it, there's an element of that as well—it's not about what you want, but about your responsibility, and through that we grow.

BRETT: I'm going to take that advice, that people don't want the rabbi to say, "Okay, so what do you guys want to learn today?" I've definitely said that to students before. Now I'm thinking it's better to say, "I have the greatest thing to show you," and then just go for it.

MOTTI: Right, that's absolutely true. Push back at what congregations want their rabbis to say. The Rebbe felt that rabbis should not talk about politics, certainly during the High Holy Days in their sermons, because it doesn't relate to the individual's *avodah*, the work of all these people. You absolutely should cast your vote and be a part of the democratic process. But, when you're a rabbi, you have this opportunity, you have your whole congregation there in a sacred space, and what are you going to talk about: politics, sports?

RON: My beloved students here could be on the cutting edge of pushing forward the Conservative movement or some movement, to engage and teach and inspire the next generations of Jews. What can we learn from you about the role of the national group? You're in a position to answer this question. What is Chabad's goal as an international organization to support your local *shluchim*? What are the key points that we could take away? Are there efforts to create the next movement?

MOTTI: There are a few points here. The first one is, you have the same responsibilities, and you're the same person as you would be in a local congregation. The rules are the same. You may have a bigger budget that you're responsible for, but you have the same responsibility to the individual. The buildings are just buildings; they're the platforms. They're just like Zoom, and they get very old and expensive and leaky and drafty. But Judaism and Jewish life doesn't. So, Judaism could be in your living room. It could be in your kitchen. When you're sitting at your desk, you should never feel that you're in an ivory tower no matter how good the view. When you're in a central position in an organization or a movement, it's critical that you never lose sight of what you're doing and what your purpose is, as an individual and as a group. And that never stops meaning helping another person and being able to drop everything just to help someone else. I think that is the path to success on a personal level and much more broadly.

RON: Well, that's what Motti did for me when I got lost in Brooklyn.

MOTTI: You're not going to let that one go, are you?

RON: No. But in all seriousness, Motti illustrates exactly the theme of this session: it's all about relationships and our ability to treat each other as *b'tzelem Elohim* and to understand that.

MOTTI: That's the fundamental message of the Rebbe for the world. Everything else, as you said, is details.

RON: Yeah. But as the head of PR, this is what we've been learning from you today. And I can't thank you enough for spending this time with us. Really.

MOTTI: It's my pleasure. Sara and Brett, I wish you all the success in the world in finding your *chelek b'olam*, your place in the world. If you're ever lost in Brooklyn, or have any other questions, or want to come by 770, feel free to reach out. As Pesach is around the corner may we all experience real liberation, and *g'ulah* (redemption), in a general sense and also in a personal sense.

> **Questions for Creating Your Sacred Community**
>
> 1. A Chabad community is based on three goals: reaching every individual, encouraging observance of mitzvot, and taking responsibility one for the other. What are the top three goals of your sacred community?
>
> 2. Chabad's first goal is relational—reaching every person, regardless of their membership status. How would your sacred community look if you embraced this goal?
>
> 3. How do you balance the major categories of communal activity—worship, learning, social justice, acts of loving-kindness?
>
> 4. Interestingly, both Pastor Rick and Rabbi Motti, who represent "evangelical/outreach" organizations, emphasized principles and ideology rather than "tactics." How do the principles and ideology of your sacred community animate your strategies and practices?

CHAPTER 11

Crafting Culture in Schools and Synagogues

Dr. Bruce Powell

Dr. Bruce Powell is the Distinguished Lecturer of Jewish Education at American Jewish University in Los Angeles and director of the Institute for Day School Excellence and Sustainability. He helped found three Jewish day high schools and has consulted on the founding of twenty-three more throughout North America. Honored with the Covenant Award and the Milken Jewish Educator Award, Bruce is president of Jewish School Management and co-author of Raising A+ Human Beings: Crafting a Jewish School Culture of Academic Excellence and AP Kindness.

BRUCE: It is always an honor to be in class with the future of the Jewish people sitting in the room, so to speak. And I believe that very, very strongly.

My mentor, a man by the name of Shlomo Bardin, was speaking to the faculty club at Columbia University in 1930 and said, "American education is too much about measuring and not enough about meaning." I probably heard that when I was fifteen years old. So, fifty-seven years ago, it created an explosion in my mind and in my life. It became the guiding piece of my educational philosophy as I grew up, and it also became the underpinnings of this notion of creating a culture in a place, whether it's a synagogue or a camp, or a company, or a school—it doesn't matter. All the principles are the same: we have to be more about meaning than we are about measuring. I wish the people who run big companies would have that more in their minds, then it would be less about profit and more about meaning. And if they had more meaning in their businesses, they'd make more money. Do well by doing good.

I was in school leadership positions for over forty years. And so, in education, my philosophy always was to present the information and let the kids debate. Don't tell kids what you believe. Let them tell you what they believe. Let them think it through. I personally have strong political opinions, but I don't use my bully pulpit to influence kids. They have to come to their own conclusions. They need to know the facts, and having facts is a vital skill set for today's students.

There was a sort of pivotal moment for me when I was running an all-girls school called the Yeshiva University of Los Angeles High School. It was right after Passover, finals were around the corner, and during morning announcements one day, I could feel the tension in the room. This was 1980. There were about two hundred girls in the room, and the seniors had already gotten into college, so they were okay. The eleventh graders were stressed out of their minds because these finals counted for colleges. The ninth graders were going nuts because this was their first time around, and the tenth graders were like in a fog. And so, I got up after the announcements and said, "You know, I'm feeling the tension in the room here. Did anybody do a mitzvah today?" And one girl raised her hand and said, "Yeah, I did, I visited my grandmother." And I said, "Great, then you're an A+ human being, and it doesn't matter what you get on Mr. Cohen's chemistry exam." And all of a sudden, the notion popped into my head: we're way too much about measuring and not enough about meaning. You can be an A+ human being, even if you're not an A student in every subject. And this took on a life of its own, and the kids were saying, "Oh, okay, I can be an A+ human being by doing mitzvot every day," and I could use that language since it was a yeshiva girls high school, and they got it immediately. What I discovered is that language, words, actually change people's physiology, actually changes people's brains—it rewires things.

I would sit and talk to the ninth graders, and I would say, "Look, there are five things you need to focus on here. First, you need to focus on no cliques." Now remember, I'm talking to ninth graders, and you all are young enough to remember being in ninth grade. I would say that a clique is an insecure group of people who won't let anybody in. Well, then what do we do? Well, you make a circle of friends. A circle of friends is a secure group of people who will let anybody in and always have a place at the lunch table for them. Now remember, I'm talking to fourteen-year-olds. There is not a secure fourteen-year-old on the planet Earth, and certainly not in the ninth grade coming into high school. So that was the cultural point—number one. Number two: it is as important to be an A+ human being as it is to be an A+ student. The relief in the room was like, "Oh, you know what? I'm great at English. I'm not so good at math. That's okay." Number three is academic excellence, and I redefined "excellence." Excellence is not an absolute, but a function of that which is related to where you are. I might never play in the NBA, but I can excel in basketball and make five out of ten free throws, instead of one out of ten free throws. You have to excel based on where your baseline is, and so all of a sudden, the kids are saying, "I can do that!" The notion that every human being is created *b'tzelem Elohim* [in God's image] now is for real. What is your gift? *Our job as educators, your job as rabbis, in running a culture is to help each person to find his or her gift.*

So, I tell the kids, "You can be an A+ human being, you can have circles of friends—no cliques—academic excellence," and then we said to them, "And we want to get rid of all the *lashon hara* [gossip]." Now remember, we're talking to teenagers, so I explained what that meant. In our school, nobody is allowed to say anything negative about anybody behind their back. If you have a complaint, if you have a problem with somebody, go directly to that person, and talk to them on the side, and either work it out or don't work it out, or get a teacher to help you work it out, but do not trash them. We have to stop that because it completely destroys a community. Words are very important, and the kids start to integrate that into their thinking and into their souls.

And then the key to the whole thing is redundancy. You have to say it over and over and over again in twenty different forms. So, the basketball coach says to the players, "There will be no *lashon hara* on this court. You cannot trash-talk the other players, and if she falls down or he falls down on the other team, you're going to be the first one there to help him or her up. You're going to be there to help them up before their own teammate helps them up." The school won five sportsmanship awards in a row. And in those five we also won championships. So, you can have kindness and excel at the same time. All right, I'll stop here for a minute. Brett, question?

BRETT: How do you continuously reinforce that lesson other than just saying it? How did you go about changing the culture?

BRUCE: Well, first of all, the beauty was that I was the school founder; the first head of school. I didn't have to change the culture. The key is that if you start your own institution, you have *tabula rasa*, and you do what you want, right? The second key here is to have everybody on the same page all the time. So, for example, when we opened de Toledo High School, I bought Rabbi Joseph Telushkin's book *Words That Hurt, Words That Heal*. It's a book about *lashon hara*, and I did what Ron Wolfson would have told me to do if I'd known him then: we did a community read with Telushkin's book, and now the concept in the minds of the teachers was that they understood *lashon hara* and could apply that concept in their classrooms. The notion of intentionality and redundancy is so important.

We had a speaker come to the school named Bryan Palbaum, who is the president of Trader Joe's. He said that there is a big banner at the corporate headquarters in Los Angeles where they are all wearing Hawaiian shirts, even when meeting with bankers. The banner says, "Everything matters every time." So, you have to develop this culture starting with the security guards who welcome you into the school, where the offices are placed so that students have access to the head of school or to the college counselor or to whomever. When you walk into de Toledo High School, the college counseling offices are right off the main hall—just make a right and it's right there. For the head of school offices, you just walk a few more feet and go into the main lobby and it's right there. It's the front office, not the back office. Visibility, transparency, welcoming, embrace—it's all there, and that helps to build culture. So, there's a structural piece to this and a redundancy piece to this.

Another great example of this is from a colleague named Michael Brooks, who was the very long serving Hillel director at the University of Michigan. Michael had a fabulous receptionist. People would walk in and they just loved coming to Hillel because this woman would welcome them and embrace them. And so, he called her into his office one day and he said, "I'm changing your title. You're now the director of first impressions." Bam, culture. Now words literally lifted and changed that woman's entire persona. She was good at what she was doing. She was making first impressions. Now she's the director of first impressions. Who ever heard of a title like that? So, this is what we're talking about. It's the redundancy from the teachers, and the maintenance staff, and the security staff, and the office staff. Everybody needs to be on board with this. It's a community read, so to speak. Everybody's on board; nobody is left out, especially the board.

So, another cultural thing is that there are six expected schoolwide learning results, and they come right out of Talmud in *Shabbat* 31. There are six questions God asks of us when we pass from the world: Were you honest in business? Did you make a set time to study? Did you raise up children or a community? Did you have hope? Did you act with wisdom? And did you understand a big thing from a small thing or one matter from another? And so, I use those as our expected schoolwide learning results. They're posted on every wall, not specifically in the same language. I gave the language more educational overtones and so on. But you know you've achieved that kind of culture, top to bottom, board to teachers, when the board sits down and the president says when they're setting tuition for the following year, "Ladies and gentlemen, are we going to be honest in our business today? Are we going to act with wisdom? Should we spend last year's surplus on the teachers or not charge as much tuition so that more families can come, or increase the budget for tuition assistance?" That's being honest in business. Because we're a nonprofit organization, our goal is not to have a surplus. Our goal is ultimately to break even. A little surplus is always good, by the way, and certainly not to have a shortfall. So how are we going to do that? Because that's being honest in business.

School is about the kids, synagogue is about the members, camp is about the campers, right? Your business is about your clients. We try to get inside their heads. Get inside the head of the other; don't ever, ever, be inside of your own head. Always a big mistake. I need to get inside the head of the other to know what he or she or they are thinking and then respond to that. We teach that over and over to teachers, and it all comes out of *b'tzelem Elohim*. It's all there; nothing new here. I didn't make it up. If I'm dealing with you as a parent, and you're all stressed about your child, because the child isn't achieving or whatever, and you start the conversation by yelling and screaming at me, am I going to get defensive? No. What I'm going to do is get into your head and say, thinking to myself, "This person is not really mad at me. This person is frustrated and worried sick about her kid. She doesn't know what's going to become of this child." Parents worry about those things, so get inside their heads, and don't get defensive.

Change the metaphor, change the language. Another practical thing: when you get into a position of power, don't ever do *evaluations*. I hate the word "evaluation." Change the word. Sit down with your employee and say, "We're going to have a conversation about value-added." Let's take the root of the word "evaluation," which is "value," and simply make it new. How can you "add value"? What do you think? The stress goes away. I'm not being evaluated. It's not a threatening conversation. Now it's a collegial conversation. Why? Because I'm in your head. I know if I say I'm going to evaluate you, I'm going to cause you stress. What's the point if you shut down?

SARA: Dr. Powell, I love everything that you're saying. One thing that I always noticed is that we talk about the value of community, but we don't always talk about what type of community we want to be. It's almost like by being together, it checks a box. My question is: What propelled you into this? Do you trace your interest in creating kind and values driven communities to a particular experience, or a set of experiences?

BRUCE: Great question. First of all, let me just say, what kind of community do we want to be? Rabbi Sharon Brous is a genius, right? She created a community around *Tzedek tzedek tirdof* ["Justice, justice you shall pursue"; Deuteronomy 16:20], and now she can't find enough seats in her synagogue. So, what propelled me to this happened over time and life experience. I've never read in an obituary what a person's SAT score was. I read the *New York Times* and *LA Times* obituaries every day. What do they say? The person was a great mother, or father, or uncle. The person was a leader in the community or was honest in business. At the end of the day, what do we want to really be known for, and what do we want our meaning to be? It's that Shlomo Bardin piece: not measuring, but meaning, and that just guided everything I did.

So, then kindness had to be part of that, and welcoming had to be part of that. Relationships, as Ron talks about, had to be part of that. Embrace, not accommodate. Let me give an example of this. If you come to my house on Passover, and you're a vegetarian or have celiac disease, my wife has four pots on the stove. I call this the Parable of the Four Pots. She has chicken soup with real chicken and matzah balls, chicken soup with no matzah balls for the people who are always on a diet, which is everybody in my family. You've got the vegetarian soup, and then you've got the soup that the celiac disease people can eat. And when the soup comes out, it all looks the same, and it's personally delivered to each person so that nobody knows which soup they have, but they know they have the right soup. That's embrace.

All right, how do we embrace our children? We were all on that call with Rick Warren. One of the most powerful things he said is, "If God didn't want diversity in the world, then why did God create six thousand different kinds of beetles?" And then he topped it off with, "and racism is idolatry, because you're saying to God, 'You made a mistake.'" We have a level of idolatry in the Jewish community where Harvard,

Yale, and Princeton are our idols. That's where everybody needs to go. We have three thousand colleges in America. The bottom line is that we have to stop measuring people and start embracing people and say, "This human being was created *b'tzelem Elohim*. Now how do we embrace that person, rather than how do we accommodate that person?

RON: What I learned about Bruce is that in his school, he has a required Shabbaton. Everyone in the school goes away to camp for three or four days: faculty, staff, kids, families of the faculty. So, talk about getting everybody on the same page. As we know, camp is the most powerful form of Jewish education. It's the most powerful form of shaping a sacred community.

BRUCE: Ron just reminded me, I didn't finish answering your question, Sara. Where did this whole notion come from? It comes from camp, because I realized that at camp there are no grades and no tests. Yet, kids come out learning over time a hundred dances, a hundred songs, but there are no tests. No tests, but everybody's up in the dining hall singing on Friday night. Everybody's out on the dance pavilion on Friday night dancing: ten-year-old boys dancing—that's unheard of. No judgment. From zero to five years old in a child's life, there are no tests, no grades, no school, yet they learn a whole language. They learn all their colors and shapes and massive amounts of information. You can talk to a five-year-old and actually conceptualize with them because they're brilliant. But we spend so much time and wasted energy measuring all these kids. *Stop measuring them, and just start embracing them and teaching them and you know what, they'll learn!*

BRETT: You said earlier that you had a community read for Telushkin's book to steer school culture away from *lashon hara*. The idea of having a common text, almost like a theme for the culture, is really compelling as a way to break the spell of these negative cultural forces.

BRUCE: Look, we have a community read, if I recall, three times a week on Monday, Thursday, and Shabbat. I didn't make up any of this. All I did was apply Jewish values with American metaphors, putting it into our modern context. It's Torah. That's all it is. We have a community read every week. The problem is we don't have enough people doing it. So, our job as leaders, as rabbis, as educators, is to make sure people are reading [and understanding] the community's book.

I used to give an open house talk where I would start out by saying, "Now, who remembers Wannsee?" There are five hundred people in the room, and people look at me going, I don't know what you're talking about. "You know that suburb of Berlin, winter of 1942? There was a conference there at a big mansion, and we call it the Wannsee Conference today. And it was there that they planned the 'Final Solution' for the Jews of Europe. You may know something about this. Twenty-five percent of the people who went to the conference had MDs and PhDs from great German universities. So, what do we learn? You can be a PhD and an SOB." People laugh, and they go, "Uh-huh." And now by the way, I haven't said a word about the school yet.

Then I would pull out a slide rule and say to the room, "Anyone know what this is?" The old people in the room raise their hands. This is how we used to do math when I was in high school. Then I pull out my iPhone and say, "Who knows what this is?" Everybody laughs and I say, "Well, you're all laughing now. But this fourteen-year-old sitting in the front row over here, when she is head of school and stands here and holds this up thirty years from now, no one will know what it is. These exact kids will have invented the future."

Then I hold up a Yale T-shirt, and in the middle, there is Hebrew that says *urim v'tumim*. Everyone goes, "What?" That's Hebrew in 1701. Now I've got their attention. Now I've got the kids creating the future. I've got them looking at Hebrew on the Yale T-shirt. I explain to them that at Harvard, the graduation speech was given in Hebrew for two hundred years. "Now come to de Toledo High School, where knowledge without wisdom and Jewish values is dangerous, Jewish values and wisdom without knowledge is weak, but the combination of the two form a de Toledo education. Welcome to de Toledo High School."

Now you have a bigger vision. I never said anything about our STEM program, our math program, our AP program, all that kind of thing. What I gave them is a different way of thinking about education. By the way, I would not use the Holocaust today. I would use Jennifer Doudna and gene editing. "We can edit you. We can edit you, we can clone you, and we can make you as big and strong or as blue-eyed or brown-eyed as you want. We have the power of God. We better have the Jewish values to manage that power. Otherwise, we will destroy ourselves. Knowledge and wisdom. Welcome to de Toledo High School."

SARA: One thing that I took away from Rick Warren's visit, in addition to the racism and idolatry comment, was about grace, the notion of giving someone grace as a form of kindness, because you are allowing for someone to be imperfect. That's so kind. My question is, what can we do to create communities where kindness is a central focus?

BRUCE: I agree in part. I think by the way, your configuration of making a community whose central focus is kindness is a brilliant concept. First of all, the notion of grace is true. I mean, we have it. Rick didn't make this up, right? He got it from Christianity. The Jews are, you know, stiff-necked people—we're very critical. I lived in New York for six summers. It's brutal, just brutal. Our judgmentalism has almost become part of the religion. And I think it's passed down. I mean, it's part of our gene pool on one level, but I think it's taught by example. You know, especially today when kids come home and say, "Oh, my teacher gave me a D," and the parent says, "What do you mean the teacher gave you a D? How dare they!" Let me tell you what my Marine Corps father said to me: "The teacher didn't give you anything. You earned a D. You want to get a better grade? Go to work." Teachers aren't giving you anything, you're earning it. So there has to be a whole attitudinal and dogmatic change among adults in how we speak and how we criticize. There's a way to critique that is value-added and not necessarily hurtful. Why don't we teach a community how to do that? They have to learn how to do that. Again, some of this stuff for me is obvious. Ron always yells at me that nothing is obvious. It's not obvious. This one is definitely not obvious.

BRETT: When you say, "Give a critique that is value-added and not necessarily hurtful," what's an example of that?

BRUCE: So, this actually happened to me. There was a student in one of my high schools who was very bright, very capable, but simply was not doing well. His mother came in and she brought with her a salad bowl, and she started to put ingredients in the salad bowl, and she said, "Bruce, we're going to make the salad here. There are all these different kinds of ingredients. Each ingredient in the salad bowl has a special flavor and a special purpose in the salad. My son is somewhere in the salad bowl. Let's see if we can find my son in the salad. Let's see if we can pick out his flavor." That was a critique that we were not reaching her son. She didn't come in yelling and screaming. She came in with a metaphor. And I go, "You're right."

Another example of this is when a parent came in and was very upset that we weren't reaching his daughter. He happened to be on the board actually. And the art teacher got the teachers together with the parents and said, "This child is a great artist. Let me show you how this child thinks." And he holds up his arm like this. He says, "What do you all see?" We say, "We see your arm." And he says, "Well, what she sees is the negative space around the arm." And the teachers nod and say, "Wow, I never understood that before." And no one was yelling at the teachers. No one was telling them they were doing something wrong. They were giving a positive critique. And it completely changed the way the English teacher taught poetry. This girl saw the space around the words, she wasn't focused on the words themselves, and that changed everything.

RON: One of things that I want to reflect from my perspective for my colleagues here is that what we've been talking about is not only about schools. It's about any culture that you find yourself in. Every place you find yourself as a rabbi, you're going to be looked at to establish the norms of the culture, to be redundant about it, to shape the kind of relationships that you want to have with the people you're trying to lead. So, it's one of the reasons that I think all this work that Bruce has done in schools is so applicable. The principles are so applicable to all the work we do in shaping our spiritual communities.

BRUCE: I have a graduate class that I'm teaching in an hour and a half, and I have to give them grades. These are all adults twenty-five to fifty years old, and I'm giving grades. Really? All right, do the reading, do the assignments, do the final, and everyone's going to get an A. It's an absurd notion that we're giving grades to people who are mature adults who've chosen to go back to school. Listen, I definitely want the guy who's flying my plane in June when I go visit my daughter who's having her first child—I definitely want him or her to pass the landing exam at 100 percent. But the ultimate test was for a guy named Captain Chesley Sullenberger, wasn't it? He landed the jet on the Hudson River and saved 151 lives. There was no test for that. Both engines cut out because birds fouled the engines, and he landed the plane on the Hudson River. He said, "I put a lot of experience into a bank, and at that moment I took out a really large deposit."

SARA: Now we need a book called *Making A+ Rabbis*!

BRUCE: There's a great story about this, so I'll end with this sort of humorous tale. A rabbi gets up one Shabbat and talks about how he loves children, and how we should always be kind to children. One day, he's paving a new driveway in his front yard and a kid comes by on a bike and goes right through the wet cement, leaving a great big gash. He starts screaming at the child, "You little brat, blah blah blah!" and somebody comes up and says, "Rabbi, I thought you loved children?" The rabbi says, "I love children in the abstract, but not in concrete!"

RON: Thanks for an A+ seminar, Bruce!

Questions for Creating Your Sacred Community

1. How is language used as a tool for positive change in your community?

2. Bruce shares five areas he encourages his school communities to prioritize: no cliques, being an A+ human being, excellence, no *lashon hara*, and redundancy. What values are you prioritizing as a community to build a stronger culture?

3. How are you using empathy to "get inside the heads" of your fellow community members to better meet their needs?

4. In what ways does your community value meaning over measuring? Where do you find the balance?

5. Consider Bruce's Parable of the Four Pots. What role does "embrace" play over "accommodation" in your community?

CHAPTER 12

A Synagogue President's View

Norman Levine, Esq.

Norman Levine is an attorney, specializing in all matters of real estate law. He was the managing partner of a major Los Angeles firm, Greenburg Glusker from 1998 to 2011. He has served the Jewish community as president of Valley Beth Shalom in Encino, California, and chair of the Ziegler School of Rabbinic Studies board of directors.

RON: Norm Levine is the best attorney in all of Los Angeles, let's get that straight. That's his day job. In his spare time, he's a past president of Valley Beth Shalom, a large Conservative shul in the San Fernando Valley north of Los Angeles. Every year, I ask Norm to come and talk with the Ziegler students about the relationship between clergy and laity. Of all the people I've met in my career, Norm really has this right. So, Norm, it's all yours. Sara and Brett are very smart and will ask lots of good questions.

NORM: That's very kind. I knew Ron a little bit before I became president of VBS, but one Shabbat morning, I was talking with Ron and Bill Goodglick. And Bill asked me, "You are about to become the president. Do you know what you're supposed to be doing?" And I said, "Sure, I know everything I need to be doing. I just read Ron's book!" After that, you were kind enough to have breakfast with me, and that was the start of our relationship, which has been very lovely.

I went on the board at Valley Beth Shalom perhaps fifteen years ago. I'd been asked to come on years before and didn't for complicated reasons. And then I did, but back then I didn't really understand the role of the board. My father was on the board of directors of our synagogue in Cleveland, Ohio. It was a very short tenure. He came back from the first meeting and announced, "They're all really stupid." And he came back from the second meeting and he announced, "They're all really stupid . . . and I quit." That was my exposure as a child to synagogue boards of directors. But, when I joined the board at VBS, I didn't find it to be that way. I found it to be a group of very bright people who cared about the synagogue and saw an opportunity to do something worthwhile. I was the president from the middle of 2012 until the middle of 2014. And I loved it. Because I love being part of the conversation about where we're going with the Conservative movement and the shul . . . and the future of what the two of you will be spending your life doing. I love that conversation.

Being the president was a personal opportunity that I had never really understood. Nobody really ever wanted to talk to Norman Levine. But *everybody* always wanted to talk to the president of the synagogue. And that's what you will have as the rabbi—everybody will want to talk to you. They may or may not want to talk to Sara or Brett, but they all want to talk to the rabbi. My view is that the most important day in the membership of any person in a synagogue is the first day the rabbi calls them by their first name. That's the day it becomes *their* synagogue. When Ron Wolfson teaches you about Relational Judaism, that's what it is. Everybody wants to be in relationship with the rabbi. It may be that the relationship doesn't work out in all instances, that's just natural.

Maybe some people are more cynical even than I am, but I think every board member wants to like the rabbi. You start with that advantage. I'm not sure that you wanted to like all of your professors at the Ziegler School; I don't know if you did or didn't. But in synagogues, everybody starts with the premise that they want to be in relationship with the rabbi, they want to like their rabbi. And they want the rabbi to like them . . . to know them and to appreciate them and to call them by name.

I concluded for myself that I had three roles as a member of the board and then as the president of the congregation. I don't want to sound Pollyannaish and say that everybody thinks the same way I do, or that everybody looks at it the way I do. But I had three things I wanted to do as president.

Number one: my role was not to take the position of the rabbi, it was not to take the responsibilities of the rabbi, to be the spiritual leader, or the orator, or any of those things. My job was to try to provide the resources—human and economic and emotional—to enable the clergy to do their job. Sometimes that puts you at odds with the clergy. Sometimes the rabbi comes to you with an idea . . . and you say, "Rabbi, that's a great idea, but you can't do it—we can't afford it." Or sometimes you say, "That's a great idea, but you can't do it *now*. We've got to find a way to afford it." My number one job was to do what I could to make sure the resources were there so that the clergy could do *their* job, which is different from *my* job.

Number two: the second thing that I thought was my job was, as much as possible, to take a bullet for the rabbi. Being a pulpit rabbi today is a tougher job than it used to be because we're so divided politically. It's so difficult to not offend somebody at every moment in time. I attended Rabbi Wexler's class on Monday, just as an observer, and the subject came around to what can a rabbi say and what can't a rabbi say. I don't think when Ron and I were growing up that was such an issue. Jews thought more alike about Israel and about American politics. But now, we're very much divided. But I really thought it was my role to protect the rabbis in any way I could, so that they could do what they wanted to do. I had a two-year job. So, if you don't like me, don't worry, there'll be somebody after me, and you can deal with them. But in a stable congregation, the rabbi will be there long after I'm president.

Number three: then the third role came as a surprise to me, but it's one I've already referred to—nobody cares about talking to Norm, but everybody wants to talk to the president of the shul. If forming a relationship between the synagogue and the members is important, which of course it is, then I found I had a role to play. I didn't understand that before I took the job. I never knew the presidents of the synagogue as a kid. I never knew presidents of a synagogue my first twenty years as a member of Valley Beth Shalom. I quickly learned that people like to be acknowledged by the leadership of the shul, especially if the leadership is human, not arrogant, and does a good job.

So, I did something I'd never seen synagogue presidents do ... and I'll tell you who I learned it from. If you go to a lecture given by a certain speaker you might know, he will be standing in the hallway and greeting you as you arrive. He says, "Hi, I'm Ron!"

I tried to be the third or fourth person to arrive at the synagogue every Shabbat morning. I'd stand outside the back door of the sanctuary for the first hour of the service and just greet people, just shake their hands, welcome then, and talk to them. Then, I would just walk around the sanctuary, shake people's hands. And people seemed to like that. It *connected* them to the leadership and to the synagogue. Because it was an acknowledgment of something, of relationship. I enjoyed it; it was fun. And I think it made a difference for people. I used to sometimes come to the shul at night when there was a program. I live and work on the Westside of Los Angeles, and it is a schlep to get to the San Fernando Valley with all the traffic. But when there was a program in the evening, I sometimes would arrive just before it was scheduled to start, walk in the main door, walk around and greet as many people as I could. Then I would sneak out a different door and go home and have dinner. I thought that there was value to this. For me, it was enjoyable to greet people and acknowledge them, but it was more than just fun. It was valuable. It says to a members that the leadership of the synagogue cares about them, that they have value. So those were my three roles as president as I saw it.

RON: Great, Norm. What is the role of the clergy vis-à-vis the lay leadership?

NORM: I think the first thing a rabbi should acknowledge is that these laypeople are doing things they aren't obligated to do, they aren't getting paid to do, and they do in addition to all of their other obligations to their families and to their careers and to everything else. Just acknowledge that they have a role. Listen, and then just be respectful and appreciative. The roles are different. I was always very concerned about budget and membership numbers—quantity. The rabbi has a different role to play—quality. When somebody dies and the rabbi has to go to the home and the cemetery, that has nothing to do with numbers, or membership dollars. They shouldn't be distracted by numbers all the time. But somebody's gotta mind the store. So, my advice to you is: don't resent it too much, because you really need someone doing that. Say you have something you want to do, and the leadership is pushing back: "You can't do that because we don't have the money." They're only saying that out of love for the institution, preserving the institution. Recognize the difference in the roles, treat the lay leaders with respect, and recognize that even when they don't agree with you, the leaders really want to like you, they really, really want to like you, and they really want you to succeed. And just let that inform how you relate to them.

Let me talk about institutional structures. I'm a lawyer, so I look at things a particular way, a formal way. I know how things are set up, management, decision-making and reporting structures, things like that. I was the managing partner of my law firm for a number of years, and I know how law firms operate. But synagogues are unusual structures, very different from organizations in the for-profit world, where there's a relatively simple organizational chart. There is the leadership—a managing partner, or a chairman of the board, or a chief executive officer. The structure is vertical; things start at the top and work their way down. That's the easiest structure to understand. The second kind of structure is your basic nonprofit—there's a CEO or an executive director and people under that person. And you have a second, parallel structure—the board led by a chairman or a president, with committees and the like. There is always a push and pull between the professional staff and the lay leaders over who makes decisions, over who answers to whom, over how things get done, and that's more complicated. When you look at the synagogue structure, it's even more complicated! You've got three lanes. You have the executive director and the professional staff, which in a large congregation includes the controller and accounting staff, and directors of communications and development and membership and facilities and security, the office, maintenance and security staff, etc. Then, you've got the board of directors and the executive committee of the synagogue. And then, you've got the third line of command—the rabbis and cantors. It's a three-legged stool: the executive director, the senior rabbi, and the president. And then you might have departments like the schools, which don't fit obviously in one place or another. If you're lucky, all of the leaders—the president and the executive director and the rabbi—respect and like each other and work together and don't get on each other very often. But if you're not lucky, you've got a big problem there as to who makes decisions and how those decisions are made. Looking at it as a lawyer—reading the bylaws and the Corporations Code, I know the answer. All power runs vertically from the president and the board. But that's a legal answer, not a practical one. And if you're fortunate, as we are at Valley Beth Shalom, to have a long-serving and very much beloved and respected senior rabbi, that might be another complication. My predecessor as president said to me one day, "Do you know what is the hardest part about being the president?" I knew the answer before he finished: "Saying 'no' to the rabbi."

RON: Norm, I have a question. Both Sara and Brett are likely not to be working in the synagogue congregational setting at this point in their careers, although maybe down the road somewhere. Do you think these principles that you're outlining apply to any relationship they might have with the organization that hires them—a media organization, a Hillel, or day school?

NORM: So, does this apply everywhere? Absolutely. I think most of the jobs that you might take, whether it's a Hillel position, or a camp position, or a high school position, you're going to have the potential for conflict between the executive director and the chairman of the board of directors and you as the rabbi. It's going to be difficult to maneuver sometimes. All of us who have made our way through various levels of education, who have had our successes, we all think that we're in the best position to make all the decisions. It's more complicated in these structures. If you're lucky, you'll have good relationships with those people. You're going to have to work on those relationships. You're going to have to learn how to maneuver those relationships in a respectful and nonconfrontational way. You need to recognize that the president of a congregation or the chair of a board is likely to have skills that you don't have, and you're going to have to learn to accommodate them.

BRETT: I imagine that the transition at VBS from Rabbi [Harold] Schulweis to Rabbi [Ed] Feinstein was made easier because they were co-rabbis for such a long time. But I also imagine when there is that shift of seniority, the dynamics maybe have to shift. Is part of the board's job to ensure that that transition is as easy as possible? And how did you go about navigating that?

NORM: I was not involved in that transition. It happened before I joined the board. But the key to any transition is that everyone needs to accept the fact that things are changing. And in a synagogue transition, the lay leadership needs to make sure everyone—not only the rabbis but also the staff and the board and the membership generally—understands and accepts (even begrudgingly) that things are changing.

In the case of Rabbis Schulweis and Feinstein, there was an excellent relationship between those two rabbis. And we were exceptionally fortunate to have them as back-to-back senior rabbis. Rabbi Schulweis was very heavily invested in making it work, and that helped a lot. The board set up a "transition committee." It was a group of people who had been involved for a very long time, who were overseeing and very carefully watching the transition.

Transitions are difficult, because, as you know, it's hard to give up power. George Washington was probably the first person in history who ever voluntarily gave up power. A lot of people aren't very good at it. Let me give you an example of what makes a transition work. All great analogies are, in my experience, derived from only three sources of wisdom. One of course is the Torah. One is the operation of law firms. And the third is baseball. My law firm was founded in 1959. We are managed by a managing partner and a five-member management committee. One of the two founding partners was the managing partner for many, many years, and then there was a second person, and then I took over the job in 1998. The senior partner remained on the management committee for a while, but then he resigned from the committee. Sometimes on a Friday, I would see him walk by, and he would just stop and look in through the glass walls of the conference room, and you could see it on his face: "Oh, my God, what's going on? What are they doing with me not in there?" But he would keep walking.

He has a really nice habit that I learned from: When something was on his mind, he would come into my office and he'd sit down across from me, and he'd say, "I hear you're thinking of doing such and such." And I would say, "Yes, we're thinking of doing just that." He would say, "Have you thought about X?" And I would give him one of two answers: Either, "Yes, I've thought about it." And he'd say, "Good." And he'd get up and leave. Or I'd say, "No, we haven't thought about that." Then, he would say, "Well, think about it." And he'd get up and leave. I thought that was a great way of handling it. He never told me, "You must do this." There were things on his mind . . . and he wanted to make sure I knew them. But he accepted the fact that there was a transition and that things had changed. He never told me I was wrong. He's just told me I should think about something.

I think the past presidents of Valley Beth Shalom do a very good job of stepping aside on July 1. Under the bylaws, we remain in the role of immediate past president and stay on the executive committee for two more years. But that role is to support the next president, not to usurp the role or to expect the successor to do it your way. Oh, I get questions asked of me once in a while—I'll get an email or a phone call asking, "What's your opinion on this?" I try—or at least usually try—not to express an opinion unless asked.

I think Rabbi Schulweis understood that. I think that he was available to help. I'm sure he would drop a hint from time to time, but it's really important for the person leaving to step aside a little bit. Rabbi Schulweis didn't leave; he just switched offices. He came on Shabbos. He was around. I'm sure a lot of people would tell him when they were unhappy with this change or that change. But when you step aside from a position, it's important to actually step aside.

The president and the lay leadership are critical to the transition. They need to accept change, too. The new rabbi needs the freedom to make changes, to impose her or his vision, and not to be encumbered by the past. The transition won't work if the lay leadership is constantly saying, "That's not how the last rabbi did it."

BRETT: I want to ask about COVID-19, which has obviously changed Jewish life and synagogue life significantly. I recall that VBS was in the process of renovating a new building. I'm wondering what the status of those plans are now and what your predictions are in terms of synagogue life as we approach the end of the pandemic.

NORM: I'm going to do much better answering your question about the building than I am with predicting the post-pandemic future, but I'll try to answer both questions. We are not buying a new building. We are adding to and renovating our existing campus. We have a four-phase construction plan. Phase one was to build a new community center consisting of a gymnasium and a library; that was completed about two years ago. Phase two is to redo the entryway and the access from the parking lot to the building; that began two weeks ago. Phase three is to redo the chapel, where we have daily minyan, Torah study, and other events; that started yesterday. Phase four is the main sanctuary. I'm guessing that is still a year or two off; we still need to raise some more money, and fundraising was not enhanced by COVID-19.

The sanctuary of Valley Beth Shalom reflects the Conservative Judaism of the 1950s and 1960s. There are seven steps from the floor to the bimah—that's three or four too many. It reflects the model of the old days when the rabbi stood high on the bimah and talked down to the congregation in a deep voice and his (then, it was always his) arms held high in the air. That's not Conservative Judaism for 2021, where the rabbi should be in conversation with the congregation. In the renovated sanctuary, the bimah will not be so high. The seating will not be in rows like a movie theater; they will be in a horseshoe so people can be in conversation with others and the rabbi can stand among the congregation. I think it's going to be wonderful because we've evolved over the years from what I grew up with in Cleveland, Ohio, to what I aspire to in Encino, California. So that's the process. We've got to raise more money, but we're going to do it.

RON: Norm, have you seen the renovated sanctuary at Temple Beth Am [a Conservative congregation in West Los Angeles]?

NORM: I have not. I've not been in it. Have you guys seen it?

BRETT: Yes. It's beautiful.

RON: Good thing they renovated it. I thought the old sanctuary was really problematic. The seats were movie theater type, but they were sloped on a forty-five-degree angle. You felt like you were taking off in an airplane. When everyone got up, the seats flipped up and made this horrible sound, so every time people got up to pray, it felt like an earthquake. The bimah was way, way up high; it was like three layers of a wedding cake. The new sanctuary is gorgeous—in the round, intimate, relational. They did a beautiful job . . . and it's important that the meeting space of your sacred community is itself sacred and accessible.

NORM: That's wonderful. I wish we were moving faster, but we'll get there. What else have we learned during COVID? The most important thing is that synagogues are all about relationships and community. During this pandemic, we're all just starving for relationships and community. There is a real opportunity for the synagogues to play a very important role as we come out of this thing. But doing stuff virtually is not going away. One thing that will not go away is doing synagogue business online. To get from my office in Century City to Valley Beth Shalom at six o'clock at night in normal times is between a fifty- and seventy-minute drive. Just to give you an idea: When there was a board meeting at 7:00, I would have to leave my office by 5:45. If I wanted to have dinner before 10:00 that night, I'd have to leave at five o'clock. So, typically I'd get there by 6:15 and grab a salad across the street at my Valley office, the Corner Bakery. That's worth doing for a two-hour meeting—certainly, for a large board meeting. But for a half-hour meeting, I'm not schlepping out there anymore. There are going to be a lot of committee meetings that we'll be doing virtually.

Look, would I rather be with you in person today, sitting in a room with the three of you? Sure. But this is working okay. Normally, for a 1:00 class, I would have left my office at noon; I didn't have to stop for lunch, there was always food in Ron Wolfson's classroom. I'd meet with you students and get back to the office by 3:30. Except, of course, the year I got sick while teaching the class and Ron insisted on driving me to the emergency room at UCLA hospital. I thank God that when I got sick, Ron Wolfson was there.

From now on, things are going be part virtual and part live. Like all non-Orthodox synagogues, we've done all of our services for a year on Zoom, Facebook, and YouTube, and many people have loved it. We're not going to give that up, I'm sure. But I sure am looking forward to coming and sitting in the sanctuary with my friends and having Shabbos lunch afterwards. I hope people will come back in person, but I do worry about whether people will want to pay dues for a synagogue that they don't really have to go to.

We have put all this money into a building, but at the same time, we've proven to the world that we can function without a building. It feels very scary. I assume there are a lot of people thinking about this. My sister, who went to Ron's alma mater, Washington University in St. Louis, is an architect. She had one of her busiest best years ever because everybody's been stuck at home, so instead of spending their discretionary money on a trip somewhere, they are renovating their houses. People may not want to go out. They might be just as happy to watch services on their big-screen TV in their newly renovated den. I don't know. As I said, it's unknown . . . and scary for synagogues.

RON: I'd like you to honestly address the question, How do you build this relationship between a lay leader and a rabbi? What do you do, Norm? Do you want the rabbi to hang out with you? Do you want the rabbi to have you over for Shabbat dinner? God willing, when this pandemic subsides, what are the things these two young rabbis can do—wherever they end up working? Look, let's be honest. I don't like to use the language of "boss" and "employee," but in a way the rabbi has a contract with the congregation; you've been employed. Is that the level of relationship? How can it be deeper?

NORM: I'm not sure I'm the best person to answer because I'm not sure that my views on this are typical. I very much enjoy spending time with my rabbi. But I don't need to be invited to dinner at his house. I don't want to impose on his time. The amount of time he puts in as a congregational rabbi is extraordinary. And the last thing I want to do is make anybody feel that because of my involvement with the synagogue, he owes me time. There are other people who need the rabbi's time more than I do. What I want from the rabbi as a lay leader is this: if I need him or her, I need him or her to get back to me, to send a text or leave a message. And I won't ask unless I really need the rabbi's time and attention. I just want to hear back. I don't want to be agreed with all the time, but I want to be listened to. So, I want access when I need it. And I want there to be mutual respect between the lay leaders and clergy.

We all get into routines. My routine was to attend the daily minyan on Thursday morning at VBS, followed by the sit-down breakfast we serve to the people coming to daven. It was a highlight of the week just to sit with the group of folks and have breakfast together. Then, on I would go down the hall and sit with the executive director, and that would be our one-on-one in-person meeting of the week. We would talk on the phone and email constantly, but on Thursday mornings we would sit for thirty or forty-five minutes, with or without an agenda. Then, I'd walk upstairs to see the rabbi. If he was there, we would have a similar meeting. If he wasn't there, or if he was in a meeting with a congregant, or if he had something else to do, that was okay. We'd talk on the phone or email later, and we'd meet the following Thursday morning. I just wanted to have some time to talk, again sometimes with and sometimes without an agenda. Again, I never wanted to impose an additional time obligation. Frankly, I am plenty busy myself. I have a full-time law practice; I have a wife and family. Look, you may have a leader who is retired or is not working full-time, who may hang around a lot more than I did. There probably are advantages and disadvantages to that. My time at the synagogue was Thursday morning, Saturday morning, and every other Tuesday evening for the board and executive committee meetings. Then there would often be another meeting or two during the week and some event I would attend, even if only to walk in one door, greet people, and walk out the other door. That was plenty for me.

RON: I have another question, Norm. Do you think rabbis need legal representation when they make their contracts with whatever organization they're going to work for?

NORM: Absolutely, positively! Oh, you might ruffle some feathers; there will be people saying, "Why are you doing that?" The answer is, "Because this negotiation is important to me, this is my job, this is my career." You can be sure there will be lawyers and businesspeople on the board of directors, and you don't want to be at their mercy. The answer is, "Yes, positively." Our clergy don't take a vow of poverty; they have the same right to negotiate their employment contract as any member of the congregation. And when somebody yells at you about it, you can call me and I'll write you a note. It'll say, "Please, please excuse Sara and Brett. They hired lawyers and they were right to do it!" If I can help, you can call me anytime.

RON: One last thing, Norm, that you did when you were president that I never heard another president of the synagogue ever do. Please share that with us.

NORM: I think I know what you're asking, Ron. I always say that the second most important thing on Shabbos morning is the *Kiddush*. That's where community is formed and maintained. Everybody always, of course, asks, "What's the most important thing?" And I would say, "Everybody knows that the most important thing Shabbos morning is the president's announcements!" Here's how I ended my announcements: "If you're a new member or you're a visitor, or if you're an old member and you just haven't been here for a while, please come by during the *Kiddush* and say hello. I'd love to have a chance to greet you personally."

Now, let me tell you why I said that every week. For years, I was the guy who didn't know anybody in the sanctuary and didn't feel comfortable at the *Kiddush*, so I would just leave after services. I never really understood how important it was. When I became president of the shul, I didn't want anybody ever to walk out of the synagogue because they had nobody to talk to at the *Kiddush*. With all due respect to all of the important things you will do on the bimah as a rabbi, the time the members of the congregation spend with each other might be the most important part of Shabbat morning. The connections they form there are what makes people want to come back, to care about the place and connect to the synagogue.

When Barbara and I moved to Santa Monica after I lived in the hills closer to Valley Beth Shalom of the Valley for more than thirty years, we knew we weren't going to leave VBS. But it's so difficult to get to Encino on Friday night with the traffic, so we thought it would be nice if there was some place nearby that we could go from time to time. We literally visited every synagogue west of the 405 freeway in West Los Angeles—some of them once and some of them more than once. Walking into a small synagogue as a stranger on Shabbos morning is an amazing experience. Everyone notices you and everyone knows you are new. The question is, will they offer you an *aliyah* when you sit down? Or will they offer you an *aliyah* before you even get to your seat? Small synagogues can be very welcoming. Often, when strangers walk in, they will immediately be visited by three people: the rabbi, the president, and the chair of the membership committee. And then they'll be invited to the *Kiddush*. If the rabbi is on the ball, the rabbi will literally walk you into *Kiddush* and sit you down next to someone that she or he thinks you might like. But if it's a large congregation, no one will notice you coming in, you will sit by yourself, and no one will say a word to you. In fact, people will be afraid to walk up and welcome you, for fear you will respond, "What do you mean welcome? I have been a member here for twenty years." And when no one talks to you, you will walk out after the services, because it's no fun or too intimidating to walk into *Kiddush* by yourself and because the place doesn't seem very friendly anyhow. So, my goal was to do what I could to encourage people to walk into *Kiddush* and have one person that they could walk over to and talk with. It's the same reason I greeted people at the beginning of services. I once had a couple come up to me and say, "We're not members here. And you invited us to come talk to you. And we just want you to know that at our synagogue, we don't let the president make announcements. But we're glad you made yours!" I got all kinds of reactions. People came up and talked to me. When I was a new member of a congregation, I would never have had the nerve to walk up to the president of the synagogue.

RON: Norm, you're the original relational president of a congregation!

NORM: I just read your book.

RON: Well, lots of people read books, but then there are others that implement the ideas in books. You did an amazing job as president of Valley Beth Shalom.

NORM: Well, that hour I spent from noon until 1:00 in our social hall was a highlight of my week.

RON: Thank you so much, Norm, for spending this time with us.

NORM: My pleasure, my friend. Nice to see you Sara and Brett ... and mazel tov on your upcoming ordination. I'll be there!

> **Questions for Creating Your Sacred Community**
>
> 1. What is the organizational structure in your sacred community?
>
> 2. Norm outlines three major tasks of being president of the synagogue. Do you agree? Are there others?
>
> 3. What do you think about the relationship between the rabbi and the president?
>
> 4. In what ways does your president support the clergy and staff of your sacred community?

CHAPTER 13

Engaging the Next Generation

Rabbi Mike Uram

Rabbi Mike Uram is the chief vision and education officer for Pardes North America. For sixteen years, he was executive director and campus rabbi at Penn Hillel. Author of Next Generation Judaism: How College Students and Hillel Can Help Reinvent Jewish Organizations, *a National Jewish Book Award winner, Mike is a sought-after consultant and speaker on the changing nature of the American Jewish community.*

RON: Welcome, Mike! I'd like you to meet these two beautiful people who we have here. Sara, you know Mike, yes?

SARA: Yes. Rabbi Mike and I know each other from Penn. Rabbi Mike is amazing!

RON: And, Brett, tell Mike a bit about yourself.

BRETT: I'm an alum of Washington University in St. Louis, just like you and Ron. So, three Wash U alums on this call! I am also a screenwriter. I wrote a film a couple years ago called *The Tattooed Torah*, a twenty-minute animated film based on a book that my grandmother wrote. So far, we've gotten into forty film festivals.

RON: I met Mike when I was working on *Relational Judaism*. I had heard about his fantastic work at Penn Hillel. So I interviewed him. Then he went ahead and wrote a book about his work, *Next Generation Judaism*, a terrific book, which actually won the National Jewish Book Award in 2016. I watched him teach a couple of times and thought, "This guy gets it." He's now taken a big job building a new Pardes North America, but how long were you at Penn Hillel?

MIKE: Sixteen years.

RON: That's a long run. Mike, we've been talking about how to shape sacred communities. You've been at this awhile. What have you learned?

MIKE: First, I want to say something about the impact that Ron had on my life. When I first reached out to Ron for help on my book, he didn't really know me and yet he was incredibly generous in offering help. He was so encouraging of my work and agreed to write the foreword for the book. That generosity has stayed with me. No matter how busy I am, I always try to pay that kindness forward. What an amazing profession you've chosen, Sara and Brett. To have senior colleagues, very well-established famous colleagues who are willing to take time out of their day to talk to you and help you create something is very special. I thank Ron from the bottom of my heart for setting that example.

Okay, now on to our topic. The first thing to say about creating sacred communities is that we have to blow up this notion of "*the* Jewish community." I hear this all the time from people in the organized Jewish world. This language is actually really dangerous. The truth is that there is not really one Jewish community. That language makes it seem like we're all one. It misses the nuance. It creates a false binary choice: you're either in the community or outside of the community. But Jewish identity is more nuanced than that. We cannot underestimate the way language affects the way we think, the way we act, and ultimately how we strategize. To build community, we need the right language. Jewish life is more complicated than imagining one centralized structure, and more than that, if we function like there is just one Jewish community, it forces our strategic positioning out of alignment with the emerging trends of how Americans today think of identity. A friend of mine once said to a bunch of Conservative rabbis, "From where I sit, there's no such thing as *the* Jewish community, there's no such thing as *a* Jewish leader, there's no such thing as *a* Jewish institution, and there's no such thing as *a* Jew." You could hear a pin drop. What he meant is the boundaries for all those things are much more fluid than they used to be. The trends are shifting from macro to micro, from "one size fits all" to "customization." What are some examples in the larger world that show that we are moving away from macro community to micro community and from a one-size-fits-all model to customization?

BRETT: Think of the polarization trends in our politics. Yes, Obama ran on "there are no red states and blue states—there are just the United States," but that seems farther and farther from reality. We each have our own political groups in silos, we speak a specific language, we talk about certain issues and values. There are multiple political communities, not just one.

MIKE: Yes, we have our own media, our own news feeds, and our own news outlets. What are other metaphors in American life where we see this?

SARA: I think the way that we use technology now. Back in the day, if you wanted entertainment, you had to go to a public venue and be around others. Now, everything's on our phones or on streaming services and tailored to specific preferences.

MIKE: That's a great example. In 1952, approximately 70 percent of Americans watched *I Love Lucy*. So, when 70 percent of people are watching the same show, they go to the office the next day and they're talking around the water cooler, and there is so much commonality, it's synchronous, right? Today, everyone is watching something else. Even big shows like *Breaking Bad* or *Game of Thrones* only reach about 3 percent of Americans. Even the Super Bowl is losing market share. You see it in Starbucks, right? Not that long ago, a cup of coffee was a cup of coffee; there was no customization.

RON: My Spotify list is different from yours. And my Amazon list is different from yours. Even during Rosh Hashanah last year, I customized my own davening experience by dipping into maybe six different prayer experiences that morning.

MIKE: How about the famous daily meeting at the *New York Times* where the editorial team would debate what goes on the front page. Now, all that is nearly irrelevant because the editors of the *New York Times* are no longer the gatekeepers. It's all being customized by what you see on your newsfeed and what your friends are recommending.

There's another layer. There's been a radical shift in joiners to anti-affiliation across the board. There is massive distrust of institutions, whether political affiliations, community organizations, synagogues, or churches. Pew's generation research going back to the World War II generation, asking, "Can you trust people?" The Greatest Generation answered 42 percent "yes," while millennials answered "yes" 18 percent. Brands used to be trusted; not so much anymore. The one-size-fits-all approach also doesn't work. Just think about the operating system for American Jewish life. Eighty percent or more of the Jews served in North America are served through an operating system that is totally perpendicular to all of the trends. Yes, synagogues say they have a softball group, and yoga, and a men's club and sisterhood, right? But it is actually still a one-size-fits-all model because it uses the same organizing methodology in which leaders who love the organization and are on the *inside* are trying to figure out ways to get the people *outside* of the organization to get excited and show up. And they just do the same thing over and over again.

Imagine you're a Blockbuster Video. You're sitting around wondering why no one is coming to your store. Maybe we should offer free popcorn? What if we get rid of late fees? What if we have a special section for family videos? But you are missing the transformative shift. Now, you can stream everything you want on Hulu, Netflix, Disney+, right? Innovations like offering free popcorn are not going to solve the problem, because at the end of the day, the model is still to get people to show up in your brick-and-mortar store to rent a videocassette. Most rabbis are trained to only think and care about the Jewish life that happens in the seats. It's only a class if you're teaching it in the building.

The mission of the synagogue isn't "Jews in the pews." The is growing Jewish life. Of course, there are so many good organizations that are doing amazing work and they are trying to change, but often the change is too incremental and too slow to really make a difference. New greeters, an updated program calendar, adding a staff person is not going to be enough. We need a new way of thinking.

BRETT: This has me thinking about how people get their news now. It used to be everyone watched Walter Cronkite. Now, there are all sorts of channels and ways to get the news.

MIKE: Right. The leaders of organized Jewish community are like executives at NBC trying to figure out how to get more people to tune in to Lester Holt at five thirty. Another great example is what happened with record labels. They thought streaming music would be the end of their business. They thought their job was to sell records, then compact discs. Instead of thinking, "Our job is to distribute music to enrich lives," they thought, "Our job is to sell these discs." They could have seen streaming and MP3 as tools as opposed to threats. The truth is the music industry is doing fine. They just needed to figure out a different way to monetize the beauty of music . . . and we're going to have to figure out different ways to monetize the beauty of organized Jewish life. Our mission is not the survival of organizations. Our mission is to create a more vibrant Jewish future.

SARA: So, why are synagogues so resistant to changing their model?

MIKE: Part of the problem is the work of simply sustaining the existing operating systems consumes so much energy and money, there are limited resources left for new thinking. I see this all the time. Organizational leaders think, "Well, if people get Jewish stuff for free, if they get it on their own, without the rabbi's help, that's going to hurt us." That kind of thinking is missing the point. How can getting more people inspired by Judaism ever end up hurting the organization in the long run? I understand the fear. A rabbi worries about keeping the lights on. Membership declines. It's been tough and you've laid people off. You took a pay cut. I am deeply empathetic to these challenges, and yet on a strategy level, the only way to make real change and to get around these challenges is to think bigger and be more mission-driven.

RON: Mike, we saw this again during the pandemic High Holy Days of 2020. Some synagogues put locks on their livestreamed services, a password only available to members. One rabbi who did this told me his job was to meet the needs of his members . . . period. Other synagogues made their livestreamed services open to anyone for free . . . and some attracted thousands of screens from all over the world, becoming the first national, even international congregations. IKAR in Los Angeles gained two hundred "IKAR from AFAR" members.

MIKE: Right. Look, in my book I adapted language from Richard Joel, the former head of Hillel International, describing two kinds of Jews: "Empowerment Jews" and "Engagement Jews." These are two different generalizations about how identity is formed in American Jewish life. It's not one's good and one's bad. Empowerment Jews are people who spend a lot of time with other Jews. They live in Jewish neighborhoods. They are more likely to work in Jewish businesses and firms. They have a high degree of Jewish self-direction. They look to organizations to find community. Empowerment Jews have long résumés of institutional experiences: synagogue, youth group, Israel trip, camp, etc. Engagement Jews are different. Most feel just as Jewish as Empowerment Jews (94 percent say they have positive feelings about being Jewish). But they don't have the résumé. Engagement Jews tend to live in neighborhoods that are less Jewishly dense. In other words, it's not just about the affiliated and the unaffiliated, or the involved and uninvolved. Engagement and Empowerment Jews are different in ways that have nothing to do with how often they show up. They have different Jewish stories, Jewish needs, and social networks. If we don't understand these differences, it's very hard to develop a good strategy for connecting them to Jewish life.

And what do Empowerment Jews who lead synagogues do to recruit Engagement Jews? They put up flyers in coffee shops in predominantly Jewish neighborhoods, but the Engagement Jews don't live there. We post it on synagogue websites, but Engagement Jews don't see it. These people don't wake up every morning and say, "I want to be an Empowerment Jew." They say, "I feel like a Jew. I wish I could have a richer Jewish life on my own terms. I want to know more, to feel more confident and find Jewish wisdom and rituals to make my life better." But what they really don't want to do is join our clubs. They don't want softball leagues, dance parties, and barbecues. Research shows they want intimate, safe spaces that offer deep, unique, and challenging content. If organizations could expand their thinking, have a mindset of being responsible for every Jew, there's an incredible growth opportunity for the work we're doing. If the organized Jewish community has 15 percent Empowerment Jews, there are 85 percent Engagement Jews out there who can be reached.

BRETT: So, what you're saying is that the brick-and-mortar institutions currently work in the 15 percent bubble, and that there's this 85 percent that is untapped.

MIKE: Right. Less than a third of American Jews are currently affiliated with synagogues. Only about a third of American Jews have ever been to Israel before. Only 15 percent of American kids are going to Jewish summer camp, according to the Foundation for Jewish Camp. So, Empowerment Jews like us, we are living in a bubble in ways we often don't realize. That's the first big wake-up call.

The second wake-up call is that the approach to Engagement Jews starts in the wrong place. Empowerment Jews see Engagement Jews as potential clients. So, they greet newcomers, "We're so happy you are here!" "We want families with young children, so you'll get 50 percent off membership dues." What we're communicating implicitly is, "We're on the inside; you're on the outside. We hold the keys to the kingdom; you don't yet." The offer is a transactional relationship. "Join our club." Engagement Jews want to feel more, they want to do more, but they don't want the kind of extracurricular clubby stuff most Jewish organizations offer. They want the "I want to deepen myself" stuff.

SARA: I think people feel intimidated entering the Empowerment bubble. It's just so interesting; there's this paradox. You're saying that the Engagement Jew seeks real content and real learning—that's what they truly crave. And yet, at the same time, some are feeling intimidated by institutions that could teach them this. So, there is potential learning that's not happening between these two bubbles.

MIKE: Right. So, part of the answer is not trying to be all things to all people all of the time. And another key to reaching Engagement Jews is to read Ron Wolfson's amazing book *Relational Judaism*. He teaches us that we can't reach Engagement Jews with programming. The way to reach them is through relationships. It's Community Organizing 101. If you ask an Engagement Jew what they want, they'll say, "No, I'm good. I'm really proud to be Jewish. I still go home for Seder with my *bubbie*." You'll do a focus group and they're going to generate a whole bunch of BS. And they'll tell you all the programs that they think they'd want . . . and then they'll never show up. The only way that you can really activate someone Jewishly is through a relationship.

BRETT: How are we supposed to build these relationships?

MIKE: That's a really good question. One key is to shift the first question we ask from "What should we do?" to "Who should we talk to? Who do we know?" This is putting relationships over task. So, then we have a list of people to invite for a coffee conversation. The question at the one-on-one is not "What could the synagogue do that would be of interest to you?" The questions are "Who are you? What's your Jewish story? What inspires you, and what turns you off?" When we did this work at Penn Hillel, we would try to get down people's anger, insecurity, and curiosity. We would hear stories about a bad rabbi experience, parents who forced them to go to the Hebrew school, and showing up somewhere Jewish and feeling out of place. Then, the offer is not "We're going to give you something." The offer is "We can connect you with others who feel just like you do." We can offer you relationships with others who can go on the journey with you. When people feel the exact same way, we've got home-court advantage.

The next step is to push people to action. Rabbi Joel Nickerson coined this formulation while working at Penn Hillel: investigation, validation, provocation. Organizers begin with investigations: get to know the people you wish to engage, and get them to tell their story. Then, validation: tell them it's okay to feel that way, that many others feel like this, too. And provocation is: what are we going to do about this?

RON: This is exactly the origin story of IKAR we heard from Sharon Brous and Melissa Balaban. They got a group of people together, they shared their Jewish stories, and they couldn't believe there were so many people "like us" that want something different. They started with a handful of people ... and now there are one thousand in the sacred community.

MIKE: If Jewish organizations are spending 85 percent of their time thinking about how to sustain the organization, not about how to make Judaism come alive, it means we're stuck in the thinking that we've got to recruit more people, more young families into synagogues, more freshmen into Hillels. The theory of change is that if we get people to show up, they're going to feel something, they're going to learn something, and eventually it will help the individual. I'm saying: Let's invert the values pyramid. Start with how you make a difference for the individual, then get the individuals together into community to do things of meaning together. It's the difference between a "receiving" model, where we try to get people to show up in our spaces to live Jewish lives, versus a "seeking" model, which begins with us seeking people out to build relationships and hearing people's stories, their passions, their concerns, and then lead them into community with others.

SARA: Can you give examples of the seeking model?

MIKE: This may surprise you, but I think Federation fundraising is one. If they just they took what they know on the fundraising side and started applying it to the program side, they would be golden. If you sell your company for $200 million and there's an article in the *LA Times* about it, Federation will seek you out. They will be relational. They will have a customized concierge approach to engaging you.

RON: All fundraising is friend-raising.

MIKE: Yes. Beautiful. There you go. And by the way, another truism around fundraising is "Ask people for money, you get advice. Ask people for advice, you get money." This fits into the community organizing model, getting them to tell their Jewish story. That's getting them to the "investigation." Then asking for advice is the "validation," right? It's like dating. You don't go on a first date with someone and say, "Listen, I'd love to talk to you about how we can live together, grow old together, help each other through moments of great pain and suffering." You hold that commitment piece back. When you put recruitment before relationship, it doesn't work. First, you share your stories; then later, you talk about commitment.

RON: Noah Farkas talks about "connection comes before commitment."

MIKE: Right! Who else is doing this model? I hear BBYO, B'nai B'rith Youth Organization. Each chapter takes their high school yearbooks and maps out every Jew who's in their school. Who are they friends with? Then, the high school leaders divvy up this list and invite kids to meet relationally. Six months down the road they ask, "Hey, do you want to join our chapter?" Hillel also has a successful engagement model. We recruited student leaders to build relationships, not plan programs. Rather than jumping right into planning activities, the first thing on their job description was to build relationships with 180 college students who were not already connected to Jewish life.

Think of how to apply this principle to Jewish organizations. You've got a board. Good governance says board members have job descriptions that stipulates that board members have to attend meetings, engage in committee work, and make a minimum gift. What if in addition to these institutional responsibilities, we also added relational engagement responsibilities? We could ask each board member to build relationships with sixty other Jews who are not already active in organized Jewish life and work with those new friends to create one meaningful Jewish event per month. That would be a relational seeking model. Where do you find these sixty Jews? You build a map: Who do you know in your neighborhood? At work? Who do you know through your country club, or your kids' soccer league? So, take them out for lunch, get a beer, grab a coffee; do whatever it is you do to socialize. Then, you're off to the races. A great example of this theory in action is jBaby Chicago. The Federation hires ambassadors who have young children to be on the lookout for other people their age with young kids. If they see someone in the grocery store, the park, the pharmacy, they introduce themselves and, in a disarming and appropriate way, begin to build a relationship. Once the relationship is established, the jBaby ambassadors work one-on-one to introduce them to other young Jews and invite them to customized opportunities for Jewish life that are a perfect fit.

Rule number two: We need to add something I call the "Passover paradigm" to what already exists on the "Yom Kippur paradigm." So in thinking about the Yom Kippur paradigm, what gets someone into that service?

BRETT: A ticket.

MIKE: What else?

SARA: Guilt.

MIKE: Guilt! A huge issue, right? You go because you'd feel guilty telling your *bubbie* you didn't go to services. Same thing with a program. Your friend is on the host committee for a speaker event, and she makes you come.

But the key to the Yom Kippur paradigm is that it's an institutional relationship that gets you in the door. The people who control the service sit up front and have special titles. The goal is to design an experience that can work for a group of people who have different backgrounds, different needs, and different preferences. Therefore, by default, a Yom Kippur service has to be general enough to work for a large group of people. While it may not be designed perfectly to your needs, there is real power in being part of a mass gathering with common rituals.

The Seder paradigm works differently. What gets you into a Seder? A personal invitation. Not an email. Not a Facebook post. Not a flyer. It's Brett saying, "We're doing a friends-only Seder for second night. Why don't you come? We're asking everyone to look up some stuff on the Internet to share about the Haggadah and Passover ... oh, and bring a bottle of wine." So, this is a model of organizing that is totally decentralized, totally relational rather than institutional. The gap between leader and participant is shrunk. And the power of it is that even though you're in your own little micro community, you feel like you're part of something much larger. No one has ever been accused of destroying the Jewish community by having their own Seder. But there's so much fear about breaking from the Yom Kippur paradigm.

BRETT: One of the tensions that I'm seeing here is between tradition and innovation. This past Seder, I was sitting next to my fiancée and I was just saying, "We really need to rewrite this Haggadah for next year, because it's just so unengaging." It's based on the traditional Maxwell House Haggadah that we've used for thirty years. But the idea of my family using anything else is ridiculous. "That's the Haggadah that we know," the 85 percent group says, while the 15 percent group desperately wants to do something more engaging. We are so bogged down by the idea of custom and tradition, that it's hard to break from that mold in order to get to the other group to say, "There's actually a better way to do this that's fresh, that's still a Seder, but it might be a little different from what the tradition is."

MIKE: If you could really think deeply about the relational piece and you built into your Seder opportunities for people to share their stories, their own take on the Haggadah, you'd have something special.

RON: Every single time you gather people, there needs to be a relational moment, a relational strategy. If people leave an event, a worship experience, a program and they haven't met anybody, if no one has asked them their story, even if there has been good learning, as far as I'm concerned, it's been a wasted opportunity.

MIKE: I'll give you a couple of concrete examples of this. This year, our COVID High Holy Days were stuck in the Yom Kippur paradigm; it was Zoom services from the sanctuary. Some people wanted to host services in their backyards outdoors. They called a rabbi to borrow High Holy Day prayerbooks, maybe even a Torah. A lot of that happened, but it was not the seeking model I'm talking about. An engagement version of this would be to get as many people on Zoom as you can. Then you find one hundred ambassadors who are going to organize Zoom watch parties in their backyard. Then you find thirty ambassadors who have the capacity to lead an independent service. It's all one-on-one mapping. At Penn Hillel, we would have eight hundred people in the building for Seder on first night of Passover if it was midweek. But we also would tap another fifty students to lead Seders for another eight hundred people in different fraternities and sororities and in the student newspaper office. That's an example of one organization using both methodologies on the same holiday—Empowerment Jews gathering in the building, Engagement Jews finding Jewish experiences that come to them, to meet them where they are at.

One more thing: there is a big difference between the receiving/Yom Kippur/program paradigm and the engagement/Passover/relational paradigm. The first measures butts in seats, but that's a very shallow way of measuring success. To truly reach the vast Engagement Jews out there, the organization needs to build circles of relationships, of people who know one another, to unlock the power of their social network. Each circle can multiply. And it's the job of the central organization to get rich Jewish content out there into these clusters and to weave them together so they feel a sense of being part of something bigger than their own thing.

BRETT: It's almost become cliché at this point to say that COVID accelerated these trends already. It seems to me that the engagement/

relational/seeking/Passover paradigm is even more important. Now that COVID has happened and Jewish life is moving away from buildings, synagogues and institutions that have typically been perceived as a center of Jewish life, how has COVID impacted your thinking about all of this?

MIKE: I think COVID accelerated the trend toward relational engagement. There's an amazing Conservative synagogue in Newton. They organized a massive army of people to check in with people one-on-one, asking "How are you?" and then inviting them for an outdoor Shabbat dinner. I heard about innovative Jewish organizations that went out and brought Shabbat in a box or Lag b'Omer kits to people's homes rather than trying to get people to show up at the synagogue to participate in the activity. Once the synagogue ambassadors are already dropping off some kind of DIY Jewish experience, there is also room for more relationship building and more engagement all running on the seeking model.

RON: Once again, "a synagogue is not a building" is my big takeaway from the COVID experience. A synagogue is a community of relationships. Mike, how are we going to come back from COVID? If you had all the resources in the world, and all the influence in the world, and you were to reinvent our organizations on these models you've described, what would we do?

MIKE: I would love to see a hybrid model with two parallel operating systems: one for Empowerment Jews and one for Engagement Jews. That's what we did at Penn Hillel. We created an autonomous, separately branded engagement effort to reach hundreds of Jewish college students who would never consider coming to the Hillel building. Some synagogues are doing this.

RON: Yes, in the last years of our Synagogue 3000 initiative, we had four synagogues experiment with creating a parallel effort to engage young Jews, funded with a grant from the Marcus Foundation. We branded it "Next *Dor*," and the four synagogues came up with their own brands:

"The Tribe," "The Kitchen." And, what's wonderful is that all four synagogues have continued their groups after our funding ended. And, again, it's going to sound repetitive because you heard the whole presentation.

MIKE: Yes. What else would I love to see? I'd love to see organizations try to be disciplined about their language, to be disciplined about what takes up time at board meetings, planning meetings, program meetings. I'd like them to shift from "How do we get them to come to programs" to "How do we make a difference in people's lives?"

So, let's focus on impact over affiliation. I would love to break the addiction to affiliation.

I want to share with you one other fantasy I have. One of the things I write about in the book is the theory of multiple Jewish intelligences. We're still stuck with "You're a good Jew because you go to services" and "You're a bad Jew because you don't." What if there are really different intelligences that inform those preferences? "I enjoy big groups"; "I like intimacy." "I love ritual"; "I hate ritual—I want to be spontaneous." "I'm super ethnocentric"; "I'm universalist." What if synagogues could write a strategic plan to increase the number of people coming for formal organized prayer in the building by 20 percent while also developing a plan dramatically expanding home-based rituals, whether it be lighting Shabbat candles, reciting blessing upon waking, or developing a spiritual practice of giving tzedakah each morning to cultivate a sense of gratitude? The same could apply to Federations. I would love to see them develop a plan to grow their annual campaign while also creating thirty new small giving circles. It's not all about giving to the mothership.

RON: I love what you're saying, Mike. This guy gets it! And he's brave enough to put it out there. And my only frustration for Mike is that he goes out and does all this consulting, tells this truth to power, and then the people say, "We should do a huge barbecue?" You see all the scars here [*pointing to his forehead*] from banging my head against the wall? Mike's got the same scars. Sara and Brett, it's going to take you guys and your generation to change this paradigm.

SARA: I just have one burning question. A rabbi came to speak to Brett and me recently in our other class. One of the things he said was the future of Jewish life is "community," not "content." As a writer working with a Jewish media company, who believes in the power of media and content to create remarkable learning experiences, I did not love that comment. I was wondering what your reaction to that kind of statement would be?

MIKE: I get that. I want to go back to the idea that there is no such thing as "the Jewish community." A better way of saying this is to talk about the network of communities that make up Jewish life. I was really proud of the mission statement of Penn Hillel: "Create the relationships, the experiences, and the communities for college students"—not programs but experiences, and not community but communities. So, if the other presenter is talking about fostering a real sense of community in a way that means more than affiliation but is really talking about the deep sense of belonging and support that real communities create, then I am all for it. I often say, "Nothing meaningful happens without community," meaning that content will make a bigger difference in people's lives if they encounter that content in a trusted community. I reject the binary choice between community and content. It needs to be both. But I do agree that if we focus on programs and affiliation rather than really creating community, the content won't make much of a difference.

RON: I would agree 100 percent. You could have community, but what's the content? I'll tell you the pushback I get about Relational Judaism. People say, "I've got lots of friends. I don't need the synagogue to find my friends." But they're missing my point. The point is that in a synagogue, in a *sacred* community, you have *sacred* relationships. These questions Mike listed get asked and answered . . . from the bottom up. And then you learn some Torah and realize that here, you can discover a path to figuring out the meaning and purpose of your life.

BRETT: Yes, I feel like we have an idealization of community. I've said this before in our class: we don't spend as much time thinking about what *kind* of community we want to shape—what's the Torah of that community, what's the content of that community, what is unifying that community?

RON: Mike, thank you so much for doing this.

> ### Questions for Creating Your Sacred Community
>
> 1. Does your sacred community consist of "Empowerment Jews" or "Engagement Jews"?
>
> 2. What would be your steps to create a parallel effort to reach Engagement Jews?
>
> 3. If "a synagogue is not a building," how do you bring Jewish ideas and practice to people outside the physical campus?
>
> 4. What could change if you thought of your organization as a "community of communities"?

CHAPTER 14

The Relational Rabbi

Rabbi Dan Moskovitz

Rabbi Dan Moskovitz is the senior rabbi of Temple Sholom in Vancouver, Canada. Prior to joining the congregation, he was associate rabbi at Temple Judea in Los Angeles. Ordained at Hebrew Union College–Jewish Institute of Religion, Dan is the chair of the Reform Rabbis of Canada and an active leader of social justice causes.

RON: Dan, thank you for joining us. I told Brett and Sara that of all the rabbis I know, you are the most relational rabbi that I'm aware of. Dan and I first met when he was an undergraduate student at Lee College at the University of Judaism back in the early 1990s, then again when he returned to LA after ordination from HUC-JIR as assistant rabbi at Temple Judea, a Reform congregation in the San Fernando Valley. I watched him transform that synagogue. Dan did so many great things. Just one example: he would take a group to Whole Foods in the middle of the day, like a Wednesday, and teach Torah to whoever walked in. I mean, come on, who does that?

DAN: Our temple was under construction. So, I moved our Torah study class to Whole Foods. They just opened a new store with a salad bar, and so I said, "Well, there's no place for us to meet at the synagogue. Let's go to Whole Foods and we'll have lunch." You do first and then you ask permission later. So, as we were doing it, the manager came by asking, "What's going on here?" I said, "It's a Bible study class." He said, "Oh, great. We love that you're here." They brought us bottles of water and cookies from the bakers, and then they started to put out table tents to save it for "Temple Judea." We would get all sorts of people drop by: congregants, Jews, non-Jews, some Christians coming by for Bible study too. It was a lot of fun. When people used to ask where they could find us, I would say with a smile, "We are in the back by the nuts."

RON: Then Dan took on the senior position at Temple Sholom up in Vancouver, BC, Canada, and he has transformed the place. I mean, it's just incredible what he's been able to achieve. So, when people say to me that synagogues are dying, and you know, nobody wants to join a synagogue, I just say, "Look at Dan's example."

DAN: Thanks, Ron. I'll start with just a little bit of my philosophy and approach to all this. And it's certainly changed since COVID. COVID is a totally different world. I think that much of what we've experienced in COVID, what we've learned in COVID, we're going to keep with us. I think we're just going to have to expand the bookshelf; we're not going to be replacing things. A long time ago, I was in the Synagogue Transformation and Renewal (STAR) Fellowship run by the Schusterman Foundation, and I remember one of the people who came and presented to us—this was before Ron had coined the phrase "Relational Judaism"—began his seminar with the phrase "Connection before Content." That has always been sort of a refrain in my mind. And so, in everything that I do, whether it's teaching an introduction to Judaism course, or beginning services, or even for that matter, a funeral or a funeral intake, I try to start with that: "Connection before Content" in a real relational kind of way.

I have no musical ability whatsoever, but I start any adult education class with a niggun, the one I used to put my kids to sleep with when they were little, and it might put classes to sleep now. I do that because it just kind of breaks everybody down from whatever they brought into the room and the person they're trying to present themselves as. So, we sing poorly, or hum along poorly, and then dive into some kind of connected moment, whether it's a question or it's a sharing of something. It's not rocket science, but I think that the first place that we start in any interaction, in any organization, is connection before content.

And as I've learned, the real superpower of any rabbi is the relationships that they make. Part of my role is to have a relationship with the people I teach or pastor to, and the other is to try to help them have relationships with each other. That's not rocket science either, but that is as basic and as important as it gets.

The mantra that we have in our synagogue office is if you can say it on the phone, don't use email. If I were to give a rule for Jewish professionals in the twenty-first century, especially in the midst of post-COVID, it's not to rely on email, but to let email be the invitation for a phone call or personal conversation. When I first came to my synagogue, a fifty-plus-year-old congregation, we had a weekly *yahrzeit* list of fifty to seventy-five people on a Shabbat, and I didn't know any of them. The rabbi had been here for thirty-three years. So, using that Connection before Content rule, realizing that I didn't know any of these people whose names I was reading and hadn't buried any of them, I called the entire list every week and asked them to tell me about their family member who had died. "Tell me about your mom, and then tell me about you; what do you remember about her? If she died thirty years ago, how is she still present in your life?" So many would tell a memory that they hadn't thought about in thirty years, or didn't even remember it was the *yahrzeit* perhaps, never saw the note from the synagogue. Then that led into another conversation. I did that for an entire year. It took four hours or so of my week, and I had to block it out on my calendar. I was fortunate I was new to the synagogue, so I didn't have a huge amount of meetings yet. But I am still withdrawing on the interest of those relationships that I created in those phone calls. Just that one moment of connection was so critical for all the other relational pieces that I've tried to do, rabbi to congregant. So anytime there's an opportunity to make that connection, I think that's more important than whatever else it is I'm working on.

As another example, we are doing our membership renewal campaign right now, and we really try to have a culture of philanthropy in the congregation and not see these as transactional things. But you have to, at some point, send out a notice that says, "This is what you gave last year, and we are hoping you can contribute this in the coming year." Transparency is the key to building trust and ultimately philanthropy.

So, in a very intentional way we sent a letter to every household, detailing all the things we did and making our case for why this year we are asking for an increase. But knowing that we had about 30 percent of our congregation who were already giving above our sustaining level, I wrote a personal note to those 240+ families, thanking them for already giving above and beyond. I added to that personal note a sentence or two about them; it wasn't just a form letter.

Two hundred and forty notes is a lot, so I actually had a font made of my handwriting to speed this along. I used a mail merge system, and I could easily personalize notes that I sent out to people that were hand-signed. That took three days. It was like writing my bar mitzvah thank-you notes. Not only has our revenue come in significantly from that, but we're also currently realizing a 22 percent increase from those who have contributed or renewed their dues, and we are 100 percent ahead on annual renewals from where we were at this time last year. It's that relational thing. Many have written notes back to me just to say I'm increasing because you sent me a note, you acknowledged the gift we already made. Again, it just needs to be one touch point. When I run an Israel trip, I try to make sure that every day on that trip, if there are thirty-five people on the bus, that I've sat or I've had a conversation as we walk to or from a thing with every one of those people. I try to make sure that throughout the year, I or my colleagues have at least had a moment of connection with every single family in the congregation. It's a team effort, from our receptionist through the *k'lei kodesh* [clergy].

Brett: I know a rabbi in Thousand Oaks who says he has every congregant's birthday on his calendar, and when it comes up, he'll call, and that way he ensures that he talks to everybody. Have you ever done something like that?

Dan: I did that for a little bit, but I didn't like it. Partly, everybody's hearing from somebody on their birthday, so I get lost in the noise. It's not the day they need to hear from the rabbi. There are certain things we have, like my assistant sends me a list of all the "big events" for the month, like a sixtieth wedding anniversary or milestone birthday, and I call for those. But that's fifteen people in a month, maybe. In our staff meetings, we're constantly going through the people we haven't heard from. We used to have a hundred people sign up for Shabbat dinner—this is the hard thing about COVID. Where I could get to a hundred people at an *Oneg*, now I have to get to those people one at a time, and I'm not getting to all of them. High Holy Day honors, pre-COVID, we had about 250 opportunities to participate in the service, between ark openings and readings and other things like that. We created a tag in our system that noted if we had invited someone to have an honor, until everybody had been. We looked for those who hadn't had an honor yet and tried to make sure they are recognized. I'm pretty confident that after five years, everybody in the synagogue, every family, every household in the synagogue has at least been invited to participate in the service. Maybe a quarter of them accepted, but we invited every single one of them. That's a big deal.

When we did our Torah project campaign where we wrote a new Torah, the way we designed that program, where normally you would have a list like, the *Sh'ma* costs you this, and Book of Exodus costs you that, we didn't do that. Instead, we designed this emotional experience where congregants were greeted, they had a little introduction with one of our laypeople about the Torah, they went up to the scribe and wrote their letter in the Torah. Then I met them in the sanctuary and we went back to my study, we sat down, and I have an associate colleague, so we each took whatever family was next. And they sat down in one of our studies for twenty minutes, and we began with "What was that like? What did that feel like with the kids there?" And then at the end of it we would say, "You know, look, this is a tzedakah project to help us continue to make meaningful moments like this for generations to come. There's no specific number, but can we ask you to think about making a gift of tzedakah for how this felt?" We raised a half a million dollars. Some said, "You know, I knew this was coming, and here's the already written check." One person who had written a $360 check said,

"You know, Rabbi, this was so special. I'm going to add a zero." Wow. Those are great moments.

SARA: How do you approach connecting with people who you don't have a natural connection with?

DAN: When we moved to Vancouver (Vancouver is known for actually being hard to make friends) we had a built-in mechanism, which is that we have three young children and through them and their schools and playdates we got to know people. As the rabbi in a community, you have a built-in opening. You know, I haven't dated in a long time, but I guess it would be like your opening line kind of thing, right? Around here often? or whatever. If you're new to the community, my simple line is, "I'm brand-new to the synagogue. You've been here for five years. Tell me why. What do I need to know about the synagogue? Why are you still here? What should I know about you?" I just put it right out there. People love to tell you about themselves. And then, you know, this is sort of Community Organizing 101, just shut up and listen. Just listen, don't take notes. Just listen. If I'm not able to reconstruct the entire conversation, that doesn't matter, I just take it in and have it. I tell my kids all the time: when you're talking, you're not learning.

The greatest thing a rabbi can do is help somebody find a job through your connections in the congregation; it's a *shidduch*—that's the magic of community. And we don't have enough of that anymore. So, *my role is to be that conduit for connection*, knowing this person should talk to that person. And when you're doing that, the people you connect are going to see the blessing in what you're trying to do, and they're going to try to do the same thing for others. It's one thing for me to know their story, but the best thing is for them to know each other's stories. That's what I'm trying to get to. But I might need to know their story in order to get somebody else to hear their story.

BRETT: Can you talk a little bit about how you work the room during *Kiddush*? What's your philosophy? Do you spend a lot of time with a couple of people, or do you try to connect with everybody?

DAN: My wife's name is Sharon. She thinks this is an art for me, and she also can tell that I'm working the room. I start at a corner, and I get to every table. We've had tremendous growth in our synagogue. We've grown three hundred-plus families since I arrived. So right now, nine hundred families. Pre-COVID, over one hundred people would come for Shabbat lunch—at a Reform synagogue! It's bigger than our Friday night services, and that's without a bar mitzvah. That's just our regulars. So, I sit down and I have my lunch, and then I go and I work the tables like it's a wedding. I'll stand at one table, and I'll say hi and try to have a brief connection with everybody. There might be two people at the table who I don't know, and I'll have a bit of a conversation with them. Or maybe there are people at a table who I do know really well, and I might only have a conversation with one of them, but it's an open enough conversation that everybody's sort of a part of it. They know I'm working the room, and so they know that I'm going to move to the next table. They saw me come from another table, and they know I'm going to go to the other tables after and are cool with that. But at the same time, they see me coming, so I need to make sure I don't miss a table. Now if they weren't at the table, like they were at the buffet or something, I might miss them, but I make sure I get to the whole room. And often when I go home, I'm worn out. Because in truth, I am actually an introvert. Talking does not recharge me, and that's fine. One thing I've learned is when you meet somebody and you're not sure you've ever met them before: "Nice to see you." Not "Nice to meet you." "Nice to see you." And don't be afraid to use your kids or your partner who is with you to introduce them so you can get their name.

RON: Could you say a word about how you engage the young professionals in Vancouver?

DAN: We actually have a couple of different programs we use for young professionals and for young families also. My take on things is that your generation and those younger don't want to join anything, barely want to sign up for Netflix. And certainly, associating with this big institutional thing is not their thing, but they love the experiences, and they want to sit and connect with each other. So, you know, food is the social lubricant, and so we do Shabbat dinners, and we always serve craft beer. And we have an engagement person, going out to coffee shops, or lunch in the afternoon, meeting people getting off of work, and that's their job. If we see a lot of charges on the expense line for Starbucks, then we are doing it right.

We have a separate program called East Side Jews that's not branded for the synagogue but takes place in community centers. And it's a once-a-month Shabbat dinner or an activity in the park. You don't have to be a member of the synagogue. They have a board that plans things, so it's not all planned by us. But our rabbi and our outreach worker are there, so when they are ready to matriculate into Hebrew school or they need a rabbi for something, we are their obvious choice, and we give them a first year's membership to the synagogue, as an East Side Jews family, for $360. We probably get, I think, close to 70 percent of them joining our synagogue. There are 120 families in that program at any given time, and they can stay in the East Side Jews and be members of the synagogue. So, we do a lot of this sort of going out into the neighborhood and bring Judaism to where they are kind of stuff. And I've learned more and more about that since COVID. You know, even though we're not doing anything physically, that threshold is so high for people to cross over that the building is really just a base for operations. So certainly, your rabbinate is going to be your cell phone and whatever mode of transportation you have, and then your study is going to be the Starbucks or the gym, and your pulpit might be the gazebo in the park.

RON: You're also one of the most transparent rabbis I've ever met. Synagogues are notorious for not being transparent about numbers of families, units, budgets, and stuff like that. But Dan's reports to the community are outstanding, because everything is transparent. What's your philosophy on that?

DAN: I think part of it is what we already know. If people are invested in something and they've paid dues, they want to know how their money is being spent, and they also want to try to solve the problems. So, when we put our annual membership renewal before them, we say we need an average of $2,000 per family, and we also say in that same letter, if you pay $1,700 a year and that's all you can afford, that's perfectly fine, because other people are paying more in order to make that happen. They can do the math. So, we share an annual report every year that has our budget and has some bar graphs and pie charts in it. So, the budget is not only the purview of the board, but people see the numbers. I just wrote an entire letter to our congregation because we hired an interim cantor just out of HUC. It's our first full-time cantor. We're nine hundred households, two clergy, and it's getting a little much. So, after I sent out the letter introducing her, people wanted to know why she was an interim cantor, and I said it's because we don't know if we can pay her for more than a year. But you know, if we can, we need to raise about $100,000 in order to afford this. And we're going to take the next year to figure out how to do that. I got a number of phone calls from people saying, "Well, Rabbi, I'll give $20,000 for this." I was happy about the $20,000, but actually we need it to come from the annual commitments, because one-off gifts are not a way that we can ensure the future of the synagogue. So, thank you for your $20,000 pledge, we'll certainly put it to good use, but for this we need to sort of "raise taxes," so to speak. So, we're very transparent about that; our major donors appreciate it, and our membership remains invested in the project.

The other thing we do is town halls three times a year. We give a little presentation on where we're at and how our membership came in, and we answer questions. We do one after the High Holy Days, then we do another one in January, and then another one at our annual general meeting in June. Everybody gets a financial statement before that of wherever we're at—a snapshot—and we talk about the challenges and the opportunities. Those are great moments, and again, it's another moment for connection and transparency.

BRETT: How do you handle the boundaries between your relational work with your now growing congregation and your own personal life?

DAN: Poorly! We're just kind of all in it. I will say that I get one day off a week. What I've learned after twenty-plus years of doing this is to really try to protect that day off, because I get really cranky if I don't get it. Honestly, COVID has been great. I mean, I'm home. I've never been home this much in my entire career. I had lunch with my wife during the day, and the kids have been in school in Vancouver pretty much the whole time during COVID; but when they get home, I am home, which is something they have never experienced before in their lives. Usually I am at the shul till dinnertime or later. I try to have some semblance of boundaries, but I'm really actually pretty bad at it.

RON: I'm looking at our wonderful students here. Brett's going into the school system. Do you have any advice for him on handling this new job he's coming into?

DAN: All I can bring is how I would approach it in a congregational setting, which is that you're still a rabbi. You might be the only rabbi in their life. Someone gave me advice once, which was never to forget that when you're meeting with board members, to be their rabbi in a moment. So, I would find a rabbinic moment in every interaction as a pastoral care opportunity. But you know, when you are pastoral, they'll see you differently. You hear somebody is sick, make a phone call, be their rabbi. Let that classroom of students and their parents be your congregation. That would be my suggestion: not because it's going make your job any better, but because it's going to make their lives better, because they need a rabbi.

RON: Sara, you should know that Dan is a very good writer. He writes all the time to his people. Any advice for her?

DAN: I'm not sure that I'd have much to add. But I will say that with some of the rabbinical students I work with, they come into the pulpit for the first time, and they have this rabbinic voice. And it's not only an auditory voice, but it's in their writing. And they think they have to use big words, and they have to constantly quote the Talmud, but I'm sure you're not doing this. I will spend the better part of whatever time

I have with them trying to find their voice and lose the rabbinic voice and speak authentically. *When you have an opportunity to speak, trust yourselves to know your Torah.* When I do a funeral intake, I record it and I take my notes afterwards. Now there are these great services where you can just upload your audio file and it'll transcribe it in fifteen seconds, and I can extract my notes from there. The more you can be present, the more you can *Sh'ma*, right?—the more you can listen without a barrier between you—and I just think it makes it better for everybody.

SARA: I have a question from a fellow introvert. Did you have to get over a fear of public speaking to become the rabbi that you are?

DAN: That's a really good question. I've been doing public speaking since I was a teenager. I was very involved in youth groups also growing up. I was the international president of AZA [BBYO]. So, when I was eighteen years old, I was traveling all over the world, and every three days I was in a different city giving speeches. So I've been doing it for a long time. I don't remember when I was scared of doing it. If I have a role to play, then the introvert stuff doesn't come up, because I have something to do. It's when I don't have a role to play and I'm wondering, Why am I in this room?—that's when I revert into myself. So, I don't know if that's true for others, but that's how it worked out for me.

RON: The other thing I would add about public speaking is the use of story, especially personal story. I mean, it's true in writing as well, Sara. You know, people will comment about my books all the time, that they love the personal stories, they love the stories that I relate to make a point. I think that's true in public speaking, as well. And in sermon making, I think when you start—you know, Harold Schulweis was my rabbi, and he always started his Rosh Hashanah sermon, which was his big moment of the year, with a story from his study. It was like, "Here is a peek into my study. This is what people are worried about." You know, it's about raising kids, or it's personal relationships between spouses, or it's health, or whatever it is. And you felt you were sitting there in a congregation of a thousand people and you thought, Oh my God, he's opening the door and letting us peek in; it's a peek behind the curtains. But that illustrates the principle, which is to use personal stories to engage your readers or your listeners. I think that's the key to the whole thing, really.

DAN: If I can add to that, Ron, two thoughts came to mind as you were sharing that. I'm always very conscious when sharing personal stories as to why I am sharing them. Is it my need to share? Is it really illustrating the point that I want to make? Because I often find with young rabbis, or new rabbis, that they're telling a long story about their *bubbie*'s brisket, and it's a great story, but it has very little to do with the point they're trying to make. About ten years ago, I started using a wonderful editor, Frank Levy (*z"l*), because I wanted my writing to be better, and I wanted to start getting published. He taught me that a sermon begins with one of three things: a question, a story, or a "wow" statement. That's the only way to start, and that's your hook. Then there are all sorts of techniques of signposting, telling people what you're going to tell them and reminding them of what you told them. You know, there's the old joke: I'm sorry my sermon is so long—I didn't have time to make it shorter. So constantly cut things down, and then the other thing is just admitting that we all need coaches. I will always ask for people to help me with my stuff, unabashedly. It only makes me better.

There was a period of my life when I was going through my own stuff. I had been married before, but was not married at the time, and kind of wondering what happened and what was expected of me. I let that vulnerability lead me toward some 12-step groups, which had nothing to do with why I wasn't married anymore, but the honesty that was in those 12-step groups led me to create a men's group at our synagogue that was unlike the beer and softball groups. We sat around and talked about real stuff. Work and personal life balances, how we raise our children, that kind of thing, and they were all text based. Anytime you can take a group and spend time together, and then give them the safe space to do that, that's where the magic happens. And so that's another thing we try to do as rabbis or educators: just create spaces for the sacred conversations that don't happen hardly ever anymore, because of the online stuff and because people are just not congregating in other meaningful places.

RON: Dan, thanks for a great seminar. You are the relational rabbi!

> **Questions for Creating Your Sacred Community**
>
> 1. In what ways does your community practice "connection before content"? Is there at least one connection point with each community member every year?
>
> 2. As a community, have you considered tying philanthropy opportunities to powerful Jewish experiences like writing a letter in a Torah scroll? What might some of those opportunities be?
>
> 3. Are the people in your community given opportunities to share personal stories as a means of connection? When is time given for that?
>
> 4. How can your community continue working toward "creating spaces for sacred conversations"?

Afterword

Rabbi Sara Himeles

Rabbi Sara Himeles is an editor at Unpacked for Educators and OpenDor Media, a Jewish media and education company. Before entering the Ziegler School of Rabbinic Studies, she handled communications for former secretary of homeland security Janet Napolitano and presidential candidate Barack Obama. She earned her BA from the University of Pennsylvania and rabbinical ordination from the Ziegler School of Rabbinic Studies.

One of the many takeaways I'll remember from our incredible class and speakers was Pastor Rick Warren's comments about grace. "Treat people with grace, and treat yourself with grace," Warren said, adding that his "location" on his Twitter profile is listed as "the State of Grace."

"Grace" is not a term that is in our typical lexicon as Jews. As Rabbi Shai Held said, we tend to think that "Christianity owns love, Christianity owns grace. The problem with that is that love and grace are really fundamental Jewish theology, and we abandon those terms at a tremendous spiritual loss to ourselves."

How could "grace" be a Jewish idea? While the biblical term *chein* means "grace," Judaism has another close equivalent for this in the concept of *teshuvah*. In his brilliant remarks to our class, Rabbi Ed Feinstein underscored that *teshuvah* is a critical component of any sacred community: "In community, there has to be a process of *teshuvah*."

Translated as "repentance" or "return," *teshuvah* is based on the notion that no one is perfect and that we all do things sometimes for which we need to repent. Jewish tradition affirms that everyone is capable of *teshuvah*—of growing, improving ourselves, and being forgiven.

When someone who has committed a wrongdoing completes the steps of *teshuvah* (including recognizing their wrongdoing, resolving not to repeat it, and feeling remorse) and asks for forgiveness, Jewish law directs the person who was wronged, in the vast majority of cases, to forgive the offense.

Rambam explains Judaism's basic attitude toward forgiveness this way: "It is forbidden for a person to be ill-natured and unforgiving.... When a sinner implores him for pardon, he should grant him pardon wholeheartedly and soulfully. Even if one persecuted him and sinned against him exceedingly, he should not be vengeful and grudge-bearing, for such is the path of the seed of Israel."

I believe Rambam is also describing a Jewish posture of "grace" here. Imagine how our communities could be transformed if each person truly committed to implementing this vision and were more forgiving of ourselves and one another. This would not be an excuse to commit more acts of wrongdoing, knowing that we would immediately be forgiven; rather, it would be shaping cultures in which kindness, respect, and grace are central values.

Reflecting on my own answer to the central question of our class—how to create *sacred* communities—I think that reclaiming the idea of "grace" is a key part of this. As rabbis, Jewish educators, and leaders, we can model this and set the tone for our communities and classrooms by openly sharing the ways we forgive ourselves and others. We can publicize and celebrate acts of compassion and kindness, an important way to encourage and guide our sacred communities.

I am so grateful to my teacher Dr. Ron Wolfson, to my friend and colleague Rabbi Brett Kopin, to all of the incredible speakers who joined us, and to the Ziegler School of Rabbinic Studies for everything I learned from this seminar.

Acknowledgments

Ron Wolfson

I have often said that publishing a book is an extension of my classroom teaching. I, however, never imagined that it would be possible to literally invite thousands of people to sit in on one of my very favorite seminars, "Creating Sacred Communities."

I am grateful to my coauthor and collaborator, Rabbi Brett Kopin, who enthusiastically embraced the concept of this volume and worked diligently to edit and shape it. Brett is a talented screenwriter and educator, and I foresee only great accomplishments during his rabbinate.

My thanks to Rabbi Sara Himeles for her insightful questions of our guests and her summary thoughts about the experience of the seminar in the afterword. Sara is much more than an accomplished journalist; she, too, is an educator through her writings.

Rabbi Angela Warnick Buchdahl accepted our invitation to "write" the foreword, eagerly agreeing to the interview format to mirror the class sessions in this book. Her leadership of Central Synagogue in New York City has elevated the congregation and extended its reach around the world. Thank you, Angela!

My deepest gratitude to each of our Master Class Contributors for bringing their "A+ game" to each session. Your willingness to share your experience, your innovative brilliance, and your honest insights into the task of creating sacred community shines brightly from the pages of this book. *Todah rabbah* to my good friends and colleagues: Rabbi Josh Warshawsky, Rabbi Jonathan Bernhard, Janice Kamenir-Reznik, Rabbi Nicole Auerbach, Rabbi Lydia Medwin, Pastor Rick Warren, Rabbi Sharon Brous, Melissa Balaban, Rabbi Ed Feinstein, Rabbi Motti Seligson, Dr. Bruce Powell, Norman Levine, Rabbi Mike Uram, and Rabbi Dan Moskovitz.

I am forever grateful to Rabbi Bradley Shavit Artson, dean of the Ziegler School of Rabbinic Studies, and Rabbi Cheryl Peretz, associate dean, for inviting me to teach the "Creating Sacred Communities" seminar.

You entrusted your precious students to me, and I am honored with this privilege. Thanks to the president of the American Jewish University, Dr. Jeffrey Herbst, for his support.

The publishing team of LongHill Partners, formerly the home of Jewish Lights Publishing, once again has blessed the Kripke Institute by producing an important contribution to the literature of Jewish education. Thanks to my mentor and guide, the indefatigable Stuart Matlins, Amy Wilson, Tim Holtz, Robert Weinberg, and Debra Corman for their expertise and care.

As always, my extraordinary family has encouraged and enabled me to continue my teaching, even in the midst of the COVID-19 pandemic. My love to each and every one of you: Havi, Dave, Ellie, Gabe, Michael, Regina, and, most of all, the resilient Susie Kukawka Wolfson, who while recovering from a successful kidney transplant during the semester nevertheless lovingly supported my work. You are my inspiration. I love you.

Brett Kopin

I would first like to thank my family: my siblings, Samantha and Yoni, Gabe and Brie, for your love and support, and for my nieces and nephew; my grandparents, who continue to be a source of love and pride; my parents, Jeff and Beth, who walk the talk as the greatest role models I have ever known in demonstrating exactly what it means to build and sustain sacred communities; and my wife, Sofia, who waited patiently for hours, day after day, as I worked on editing transcripts and whose love, support, and belief in me are my greatest blessing.

Thanks to all of my teachers: first, Dale Griffith, who has encouraged my writing and my voice since I sat in the back of his high school English class and who remains a dear friend, mentor, and *chavruta*; Marc Bennett, my creative partner and friend, who always encourages me to "do more"; my dear friends and professors at the Ziegler School of Rabbinic Studies, in particular Rabbi Cheryl Peretz and Rabbi Bradley Shavit Artson, who grounded me in Torah and sacred community for five years; and my colleagues at Milken Community School, who teach me every single day what it means to nurture community both inside and outside the classroom.

Thanks to all of our guests from the spring 2021 "Creating Sacred Communities" seminar, whose wisdom continues to guide me every day; to Rabbi Sara Himeles, for being a great classmate, friend, and collaborator; and to Dr. Ron Wolfson: thank you for graciously inviting me to undertake this project with you. Your wisdom has provided an invaluable foundation for my rabbinate.

About the Authors

Dr. Ron Wolfson

Dr. Ron Wolfson is the Fingerhut Professor of Education at American Jewish University, where he has been on the faculty for forty-six years. He has had a profound influence on the Jewish community through his books *Relational Judaism: Using the Power of Relationships to Transform the Jewish Community* and *The Relational Judaism Handbook*, coauthored with Rabbi Nicole Auerbach and Rabbi Lydia Medwin.

In addition to training clergy and educators, Ron is the author of eighteen books bringing the values and rituals of Jewish life to a popular audience, including *God's To-Do List, The Seven Questions You're Asked in Heaven, The Spirituality of Welcoming*, the Art of Jewish Living series, and a memoir, *The Best Boy in the United States of America* (all Jewish Lights Publishing). He serves as president of the Kripke Institute.

Ron is a living kidney donor on behalf of his wife of fifty-one years, Susie Kukawka Wolfson. They are blessed with two children, Havi, married to Dave Hall, and Michael, engaged to Regina Pruss; and two delicious grandchildren, Ellie and Gabe Hall.

Rabbi Brett Kopin

Rabbi Brett Kopin was born and raised in Chicago, Illinois, graduated with a BA from Washington University in St. Louis in 2013, and received rabbinic ordination from the Ziegler School of Rabbinic Studies in 2021. He is the co-screenwriter of the award-winning animated film *The Tattooed Torah*. He lives in Los Angeles with his wife, Sofia.

A Word about the Kripke Institute

Established to honor the memory of Dorothy K. and Myer S. Kripke, the Kripke Institute endowed the National Jewish Book Award in Education, sponsors the PJ Library project in Omaha, Nebraska, and funds the Center for Relational Judaism. The institute has published *The Relational Judaism Handbook: How to Create a Relational Engagement Campaign to Build and Deepen Relationships in Your Community* (2018) and *Raising A+ Human Beings: Crafting a Jewish School Culture of Academic Excellence and AP Kindness* (2021). *Creating Sacred Communities: Lessons Learned from Leading Practitioners* is the third publication of the Kripke Institute.

Resources for Building Dynamic Jewish Communities from The Kripke Institute

Raising A+ Human Beings: Crafting a Jewish School Culture of Academic Excellence and AP Kindness ($19.99) by Dr. Bruce Powell and Dr. Ron Wolfson, preface by Rabbi Elaine Zecher, foreword by Rabbi Ed Feinstein, is designed for all those responsible for shaping the culture of day schools, synagogue schools, youth groups and camps—heads of schools, principals, teachers, administrative staff, boards and parents/grandparents.

The book details the "what," "who" and "how" of culture creation, focusing on the best principles and practices to guide you in the sacred task of raising children in an environment steeped in Jewish values.

Designed to be read together as an educational community, each chapter includes discussion questions and a "culture audit" to facilitate assessment, discussion and plans for crafting the culture of your setting.

TO ORDER: aplushumanbeings.com

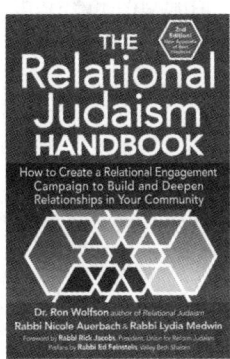

The Relational Judaism Handbook: How to Create a Relational Engagement Campaign to Build and Deepen Relationships in Your Community ($19.99), by Dr. Ron Wolfson, Rabbi Lydia Medwin and Rabbi Nicole Auerbach, foreword by Rabbi Rick Jacobs, preface by Rabbi Ed Feinstein, is designed for Jewish leadership—both professional and lay—to create and implement a Relational Engagement Campaign, a comprehensive strategy for building and deepening relationships throughout the synagogue, JCC, Hillel, or other organization.

The book presents a step-by-step guide to help boards and staff plan and implement an effective strategy for strengthening connections between the leadership of the organization and its members, between members and each other, and between each person and the Jewish experience itself.

Filled with many successful Spotlights on Best Practice and Case Studies from leading practitioners, this interactive guide will help you improve the welcoming ambience and high quality experience offered to members and guests, as well as give you detailed instructions on how to build a robust small-groups initiative to engage your people.
TO ORDER: relationaljudaismhandbook.com

Creating Sacred Communities: Leading Practitioners Share Lessons Learned, by Dr. Ron Wolfson and Rabbi Brett Kopin, preface by Rabbi Angela Warnick Buchdahl, afterword by Rabbi Sara Himeless ($24.99). Creating a sacred community is one of the most important tasks facing congregational leaders—rabbis, cantors, educators, executive directors, and lay leaders—in the twenty-first century. This unique book presents a master class by frontline practitioners who share cutting-edge lessons learned from their success in shaping sacred communities.

Each chapter features actual transcripts of the conversations between the outstanding Master Class Contributors and the students.
TO ORDER: creatingsacredcommunities.com